MW01635440

Sugar FREE

THE COMPLETE COLLECTION

THE AUSTRALIAN
Women's Weekly

Contents

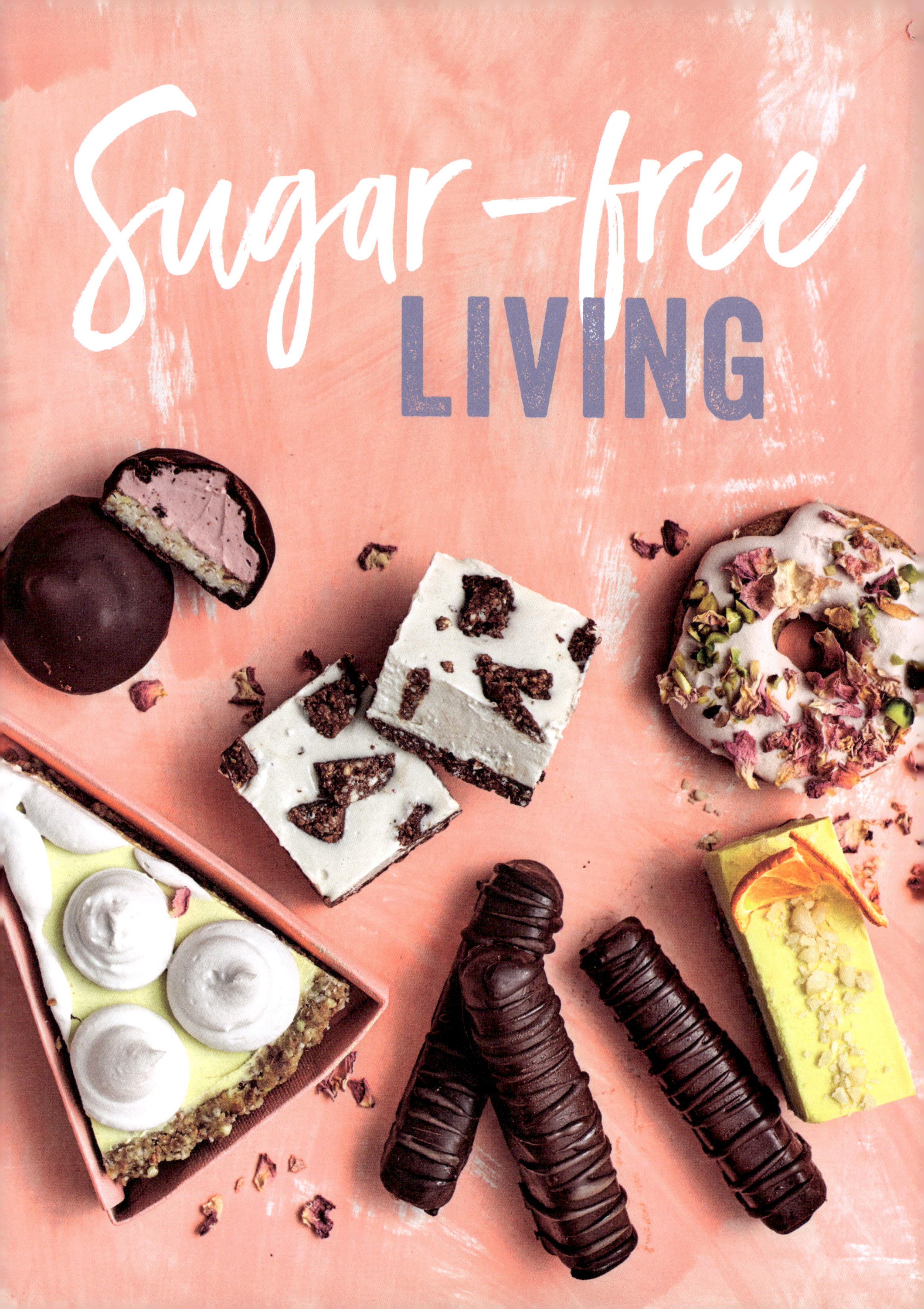
Sugar-free
LIVING

THE RECIPES IN THIS BOOK ARE FREE FROM ADDED REFINED SUGARS, INCLUDING SUCROSE (TABLE SUGAR). HOWEVER, UNREFINED SUGARS AND SUGARS NATURALLY PRESENT IN WHOLEFOODS ARE INCLUDED.

A quick read of the ingredient list on the back of many food products these days reveals the variety of forms and unexpected places sugar crops up. You will see syrups, including rice malt syrup (brown rice syrup), molasses, agave syrup, treacle, cane juice, rapadura, coconut sugar; then perhaps less well known forms of sugar — dextrose, glucose, sucrose, maltodextrin and maltose.

Natural sweeteners

Of all the sweeteners, honey, if chosen wisely, is one of the most natural. It can be from a single source or a blend from multiple sources. Honey has been a part of human diets since hunter-gatherer days. Maple syrup is also a sugar, and like honey is not as refined as most others. From a cooking perspective both maple syrup and honey add a delicious flavour to recipes. Nevertheless be aware, they are still sugars, and if you have chosen to follow a truly sugar-free diet you'll need to give them a miss. Natural alternatives to sucrose include sorbitol (commonly used in sugar-free gums and mints), xylitol, stevia or monk fruit (sold as norbu). These are all naturally sweet, provide fewer kilojoules, do not raise blood sugar levels and are tooth friendly. For more information on these and other alternatives, see page 8.

Sugars in fruit & vegetables

In the quest for better health via improved eating patterns it is important to understand the difference between naturally occurring sugars and those that are added to food. Fruits and vegetables are rich in fibre and contain a host of antioxidants, vitamins, minerals and phytonutrients that are beneficial to our health. They have an essential place in our diet. It is also important to eat from a wide array of plant sources rather than making restricted choices to guarantee better nutrition.

Take a big picture look

A word of caution however, is that you don't become so fixated on sugar that you forget to step back and look at your whole diet. There are many aspects of diet that are important, and blaming just one thing is dangerous as it blinds us to other, just as important, aspects. Instead, focus on reducing or, if you like, completely cutting out foods with added refined sugars — starting with the obvious no-nos such as lollies, biscuits, cakes and sugar-sweetened soft drinks, as they contain little or no nutritional value.

Wholesome food

The recipes in this book take a more holistic approach to food. The focus is on eating whole foods from all food groups and choosing wisely within them. We've covered all manner of every day dishes where refined sugars are often unnecessarily present — from the obvious baked goodies to the not-so-obvious marinades, salad dressings and savoury sauces. Using unrefined alternatives and wholefoods we've developed scrumptious breakfasts, main meals, make and save items, 3pm pick-me-ups and sweet treats the entire family will love — they won't even notice what's missing.

SWAP THIS	FOR THAT
toasted granola	rolled oats
diet mayonnaise	full-fat mayonnaise
orange juice	whole oranges
fruit yoghurts	natural yoghurt
white bread	wholegrain bread
muesli bars	a handful of nuts
tomato sauce (ketchup)	mustard
bought dressings	olive oil & lemon juice
commercial chai latte	regular teas
energy drinks	mineral water
drinking chocolate	dutch cocoa
milk chocolate	85% dark chocolate
pasta sauce	tomato passata

Sugar ALTERNATIVES

COCONUT SUGAR

Coconut sugar (coconut palm sugar) is not made from coconuts, but from the sap of the blossoms of the coconut palm tree. The sap is collected and then boiled to evaporate the water content, leaving a sugar that looks a little like raw or light brown sugar with a similar caramel flavour. It has the same amount of kilojoules as regular white sugar, but on the plus side it does contain some trace minerals.

Rice malt syrup

RICE MALT SYRUP (BROWN RICE SYRUP) IS MADE BY COOKING BROWN RICE FLOUR WITH ENZYMES TO BREAK DOWN THE STARCH INTO SUGARS. THE MIXTURE IS THEN FILTERED AND THE WATER REMOVED TO GIVE A THICK, SWEET SYRUP WITH A MILD TASTE. IT IS AVAILABLE FROM MOST MAJOR SUPERMARKETS AND HEALTH FOOD STORES. RICE MALT SYRUP IS FRUCTOSE-FREE AND IS A POPULAR VEGAN ALTERNATIVE TO HONEY.

Agave Syrup

Agave syrup (agave nectar) is a sweetener produced from the agave plant (a succulent with thick fleshy leaves) native to South Africa and Mexico. It has a low GI due to the high percentage of fructose present, which may be harmful if consumed in high quantities. Sweeter and slightly thinner than honey, it is a suitable vegan substitute for honey. It is available from most supermarkets.

YACON SYRUP

FROM THE ROOTS OF THE YACON PLANT, CONTAINS A HIGH PERCENTAGE OF FRUCTOOLIGOSACCHARIDES WHICH AREN'T DIGESTED SO IT HAS ONLY A THIRD OF THE CALORIES OF SUGAR. IT IS NOT SUITABLE FOR COOKING.

Barley malt syrup

A dark brown, thick unrefined syrup made from sprouted (malted) barley, with a "malty" flavour. It is less sweet than honey or regular sugar and is low in glucose, fructose and sucrose.

STEVIA

MADE FROM THE LEAVES OF THE STEVIA PLANT; HIGHLY REFINED TO PRODUCE A SUGAR-LIKE MIXTURE THAT HAS A MINIMAL EFFECT ON BLOOD GLUCOSE LEVELS AND HAS NO KILOJOULES.

Raw honey

Honey is one of the most natural sweeteners. Pure floral honeys have a low GI, but cheaper, blended honeys tend to be high. For a low GI honey look for Yellow Box, Stringy Bark, Red Gum, Iron Bark or Eucalypt.

PURE MAPLE SYRUP

Pure maple syrup is the concentrated sap of the maple tree, whereas maple-flavoured syrups are usually just processed glucose syrup with added flavourings. Real maple syrup is much tastier and contains significant amounts of nutrients and antioxidant compounds. It has a low GI, making it a good choice for blood glucose control.

RICE MALT SYRUP
Coconut sugar
Agave syrup
YACON SYRUP
Barley malt syrup
Raw honey
STEVIA
PURE MAPLE SYRUP

Power Starts
BEGIN THE DAY RIGHT

Bone broth SMOOTHIES

THE CONCEPT OF INCLUDING BROTH (STOCK) IN A SMOOTHIE MIGHT AT FIRST SEEM ODD, OR EVEN UNPLEASANT. FREEZING NEUTRALISES THE TASTE OF THE BROTH, ADDING NO DISCERNIBLE MEAT TASTE TO THE SMOOTHIE. BONE BROTH ADVOCATES BELIEVE THE NATURALLY OCCURRING GELATINE (COLLAGEN), AMINO ACIDS AND MINERALS IN HOMEMADE BROTHS CONTRIBUTE TO GOOD GUT HEALTH. WHILE THERE ARE NO RELIABLE STUDIES TO BACK THIS UP, DRINKING BROTHS IS AN AGE-OLD PRACTICE IN MANY CULTURES. IF YOU DECIDE TO SKIP THE BONE BROTH, THESE RECIEPS STILL MAKE DELICIOUS FRUIT SMOOTHIES.

prep time 5 minutes serves 2

RASPBERRY & CACAO SMOOTHIE

» 270ml (8½ ounces) canned coconut milk
» 1 cup (150g) frozen raspberries
» 2 frozen beef bone broth ice cubes (see page 121)
» 1 tablespoon pure maple syrup
» 1 teaspoon cacao powder
» frozen raspberries, extra, to serve

1 Blend ingredients in a blender until smooth.
2 Pour between two small glasses; top with extra raspberries to serve.

prep time 5 minutes serves 2

MANGO, MAPLE & MESQUITE SMOOTHIE

» 1 cup (250ml) almond milk
» 1 large mango (430g), peeled, chopped, frozen
» 2 frozen beef bone broth ice cubes (see page 121)
» 1 tablespoon pure maple syrup
» 1 teaspoon mesquite powder (see page 295)
» sliced mango, extra, to serve

1 Blend ingredients in a blender until smooth.
2 Pour between two small glasses; top with sliced mango to serve.

prep + cook time 20 minutes serves 4

Banana & cinnamon PIKELETS WITH PAN-FRIED GRANOLA

Get a head start on this breakfast by making the pan-fried granola a couple of days ahead; store in an airtight jar for up to 2 weeks.

- 2 medium overripe bananas (400g), mashed
- 4 eggs
- ¼ cup (60ml) almond milk
- ½ teaspoon ground cinnamon
- ½ cup (75g) self-raising flour
- ½ teaspoon bicarbonate of soda (baking soda)
- 2 tablespoons coconut oil
- 2 medium bananas (400g), sliced lengthways
- ⅓ cup (95g) unsweetened coconut yoghurt
- 2 tablespoons fresh passionfruit pulp

PAN-FRIED GRANOLA

- ½ teaspoon coconut oil
- 2 tablespoons coconut flakes
- 2 tablespoons pecans, chopped coarsely
- 2 tablespoons pepitas (pumpkin seed kernels)
- ¼ teaspoon ground cinnamon
- 1 teaspoon pure maple syrup

1 Make pan-fried granola.

2 Whisk mashed banana, eggs and milk in a medium bowl until well combined. Sift over cinnamon, flour and soda; fold to combine.

3 Heat 2 teaspoons of the coconut oil in a large frying pan over medium heat. Working in batches, add four 2-tablespoon quantities of the batter; cook for 1 minute or until edge of each pikelet has set and bubbles appear on the surface. Turn pikelets using a spatula; cook for a further 30 seconds or until cooked through. Transfer to a plate; cover to keep warm. Repeat three more times with remaining coconut oil and batter to make a total of 16 pikelets.

4 Top pikelets with sliced banana, yoghurt and passionfruit. Serve sprinkled with pan-fried granola.

pan-fried granola Heat coconut oil in a small frying pan over medium-high heat. Cook coconut flakes, pecans, pepitas and cinnamon, stirring, for 2 minutes or until lightly toasted. Add maple syrup; cook, stirring for 1 minute or until granola is golden. Remove from pan; cool.

prep + cook time 35 minutes serves 4

Big beautiful BREAKFAST BOWL

'EAT BREAKFAST LIKE A KING, LUNCH LIKE A PRINCE AND DINNER LIKE A PAUPER'. THIS CLASSIC SAYING HAS A LOT TO COMMEND IT. A HEARTY BREAKFAST HAS BEEN PROVEN TO MAINTAIN BLOOD SUGAR LEVELS ACROSS THE DAY.

- 1 cup (200g) white quinoa, rinsed
- 1¾ cups (430ml) water
- 4 eggs, shells rinsed well
- 170g (5½ ounces) asparagus, trimmed, halved crossways
- 1 tablespoon extra virgin olive oil
- 2 tablespoons pistachio dukkah (see tips)
- 300g (9½ ounces) baby spinach, washed well
- 1 avocado (250g), sliced thinly

TAHINI DRESSING

- ¼ cup (70g) unhulled tahini
- 1 tablespoon extra virgin olive oil
- ¼ cup (60ml) lemon juice
- 2 tablespoons water

1 Place quinoa and the water in a saucepan; bring to the boil. Reduce heat to low; simmer, covered, for 12 minutes or until water is absorbed and quinoa is tender. Remove from heat; stand, covered for 5 minutes.
2 Meanwhile, cook eggs in a saucepan of boiling salted water for 6 minutes for soft-boiled or until cooked to your liking. Remove with a slotted spoon; cool under running water. Return water to the boil. Cook asparagus for 3 minutes; drain. Cut asparagus in half diagonally.
3 Meanwhile, make tahini dressing.
4 Peel eggs, place in a bowl; drizzle with oil. Place dukkah in a small bowl; roll eggs in dukkah to coat.
5 Serve quinoa with asparagus, spinach, avocado and eggs; drizzle with tahini dressing and season to taste.
tahini dressing Whisk all the ingredients in a small bowl until combined and emulsified; season to taste.

tips Dukkah is available in different forms from supermarkets and delis; any variety is suitable for this recipe. Alternatively, you can roll the eggs in toasted sesame seeds mixed with a little ground cumin. Mornings can be a rush, so have all your ingredients weighed out and ready to go. If you want to speed things up further, make the tahini dressing and cook the eggs the night before; store, separately in the refrigerator.

prep + cook time 40 minutes (+ cooling) serves 8

GREENOLA

THIS COMBINATION OF SEEDS AND NUTS, PLUS A HEALTHY DOSE OF KALE, OFFERS A WIDE RANGE OF NUTRIENTS.

- ⅓ bunch green kale (100g)
- ½ teaspoon melted coconut oil
- 2 teaspoons ground cinnamon
- 1 cup (140g) sunflower seeds
- ⅓ cup (55g) white chia seeds
- 1½ cups (300g) pepitas (pumpkin seed kernels)
- 1 cup (140g) slivered almonds
- 1 cup (170g) raw buckwheat
- 3 teaspoons spirulina powder (see page 250)
- 1 teaspoon pure vanilla extract
- ¼ cup (60ml) melted coconut oil, extra
- ¼ cup (60ml) pure maple syrup

1 Preheat oven to 180°C/350°F. Line three large oven trays with baking paper.
2 Tear kale leaves from stems; discard stems. Place kale on one oven tray, drizzle with coconut oil and sprinkle with 1 teaspoon of the cinnamon; massage oil and cinnamon into kale. Bake kale for 15 minutes, stirring halfway through, or until crisp. When cool enough to handle, using your hands, crush kale finely.
3 Meanwhile, place seeds, almonds and buckwheat in a large bowl; sprinkle with spirulina and remaining cinnamon. Stir vanilla into extra coconut oil, drizzle over seed mixture with maple syrup; toss to coat. Spread mixture evenly over remaining oven trays.
4 Roast for 20 minutes, stirring halfway, or until nuts are golden. Cool. Combine crushed kale with seed mixture.

tip You can melt the coconut oil in a microwave; alternatively, sit a bowl of coconut oil in a bowl filled with a little boiling water, then stir until melted.

try this for breakfast with ⅓ cup almond milk, half a thinly sliced pear and half a kiwifruit. Alternatively, keep a jar handy on your desk at work to ward off the 3pm slump.

keeps Store greenola in an airtight container in the pantry for up to 1 month.

prep + cook time 1 hour 15 minutes (+ refrigeration) serves 4

Beetroot & cacao pancakes
WITH RASPBERRY CHIA JAM

CHIA SEED JAM IS A GREAT ALTERNATIVE TO CANE SUGAR JAMS, AS THE NATURAL THICKENING PROPERTIES OF CHIA SEEDS MEAN THAT THE TRADITIONAL JAM RATIO OF EQUAL SUGAR TO FRUIT NEED NOT BE ADHERED TO. INSTEAD ONLY A MINIMUM AMOUNT OF NATVIA IS REQUIRED AS A SWEETENER.

» 2 small beetroots (200g), peeled
» 1 cup (250ml) coconut and brown rice milk blend (see tips)
» 2 eggs, beaten lightly
» 2 tablespoons Natvia
» 1½ cups (225g) self-raising flour
» ¼ cup (25g) cacao powder
» 2 tablespoons cacao nibs
» 1 tablespoon coconut oil, at room temperature
» ⅔ cup (190g) unsweetened coconut or Greek-style yoghurt
» 1 tablespoon cacao nibs, extra
» 125g (4 ounces) fresh raspberries

RASPBERRY CHIA JAM

» 1 tablespoon Natvia
» 1 cup (150g) frozen raspberries, thawed
» 2 tablespoons water
» 2 tablespoons white chia seeds

1 Preheat oven to 200°C/400°F.
2 Make raspberry chia jam.
3 Wrap beetroot individually in foil, place on an oven tray; roast for 40 minutes or until tender. Cool; chop coarsely.
4 Blend beetroot to a smooth puree; transfer to a bowl. Measure ½ cup of puree, return measured puree to blender with milk; blend until smooth. Add egg, Natvia, sifted flour and cacao; process until a smooth batter just forms. Transfer to a jug; stir in cacao nibs.
5 Working in batches, heat 1 teaspoon of the coconut oil in a medium frying pan over low heat. Add ⅓ cup batter, repeat with another ⅓ cup batter; cook pancakes for 3 minutes or until bubbles appear. Turn pancakes; cook for a further minute or until cooked through. Repeat with remaining coconut oil and batter to make a total of 8 pancakes.
6 Serve pancakes topped with yoghurt, raspberry chia jam, extra cacao nibs and raspberries.
raspberry chia jam Process Natvia in a spice grinder until consistency of icing sugar. Blend or process raspberries and the water until pureed. Pour into a small bowl; stir through chia seeds and powdered Natvia. Cover; refrigerate for at least 1 hour or until thickened to a jam-like consistency.

tips You may need to add 1-2 tablespoons of water to help the beetroot blend to a smooth puree. We used Coco Quench, a blend of coconut milk and brown rice milk, available from selected supermarkets and health food stores. Substitute with your favourite non-dairy milk or, if preferred, regular milk. The jam can be made a day ahead; store in an airtight container in the fridge, for up to 1 week. If your jam thickens in the fridge, add 1 tablespoon of water.

prep + cook time 35 minutes serves 4

KITCHARI

KITCHARI IS A NOURISHING TRADITIONAL INDIAN MIX OF RICE, LENTILS AND VEGETABLES. WHILE THESE INGREDIENTS MAY NOT SEEM LIKE TYPICAL BREAKFAST FARE, THEY HAVE MANY BENEFITS, SUCH AS PHYTOCHEMICALS, DIETARY FIBRE AND PROTEIN, WHICH HELP KEEP BLOOD SUGAR LEVELS STABLE. YOU'LL LAST THE DISTANCE UNTIL LUNCH TIME.

- 1 tablespoon ghee (see tips) or olive oil
- 1 small brown onion (80g), chopped finely
- 1 medium carrot (70g), diced finely
- 2 small tomatoes (180g), diced
- 1 teaspoon yellow mustard seeds
- 1 teaspoon cumin seeds
- ½ teaspoon ground turmeric
- 1 cup (200g) brown basmati rice
- ½ cup (100g) dried red lentils
- 3 cups (750ml) water
- Greek-style yoghurt, coriander (cilantro) and lime wedges, to serve

1 Heat ghee in a medium saucepan over medium-high heat. Cook onion, carrot and tomato, stirring, for 3 minutes or until softened. Add spices; cook, stirring, for 1 minute or until fragrant. Add rice and lentils; stir to coat in spices. Add the water; bring to the boil. Reduce heat to low; cook, covered, stirring occasionally, for 20 minutes or until rice is tender and lentils are soft. Season to taste.

2 Serve kitchari with yoghurt, coriander and lime wedges, seasoned with freshly ground black pepper, if you like.

tips Make a batch of kitchari and store it in an airtight container in the fridge for up to 3 days for quick breakfasts throughout the week. Reheat on the stove or in the microwave. Ghee is clarified butter and can be found in tubs alongside butter in the refrigerator section or in jars in the Indian section of supermarkets.

prep time 20 minutes (+ freezing) serves 2

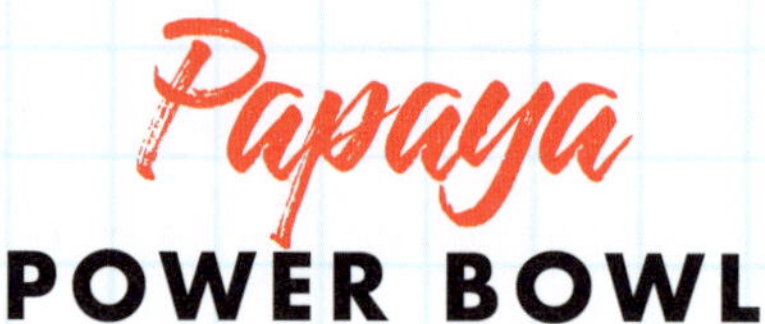

POWER BOWL

DRAGON FRUIT, ALSO KNOWN AS PITAYA, IS AN EXOTIC PINK-SKINNED FRUIT OF THE CACTUS FAMILY. INDIGENOUS TO MEXICO, IT HAS BEEN TRANSPORTED AROUND THE WORLD, AND IS PARTICULARLY POPULAR IN SOUTH EAST ASIA. IN AUSTRALIA THE FRUIT IS GROWN IN THE TROPICAL NORTH. THE FLESH CAN BE EITHER YELLOW, RED OR WHITE, WITH A MILD TASTE LIKE KIWIFRUIT, AND WITH SIMILAR SMALL TEXTURAL BLACK SEEDS.

You will need to start this recipe a day ahead.

» 1 pink dragon fruit (pitaya) (425g) (see tips)
» 1 small orange papaya (650g), halved lengthways, seeded
» 2 tablespoons Natvia
» ¼ cup (60ml) lime juice
» 1 small banana (130g), sliced
» 1 kiwifruit (85g), halved crossways
» 2 purple figs (120g), halved lengthways
» 125g (4 ounces) fresh or frozen raspberries
» cherries and lime wedges, to serve

1 Wearing food handling gloves, peel and coarsely chop dragon fruit. Transfer to a freezer-proof container. Freeze overnight or until firm.
2 Chill papaya halves in freezer, for 30 minutes.
3 Process frozen dragon fruit with Natvia and lime juice until smooth.
4 Divide dragon fruit mixture between chilled papaya halves or two wide bowls. Top with banana, kiwifruit, fig and raspberries. Serve with cherries and lime wedges. Serve immediately.

tips If all you can find are white dragon fruit (pitaya), use those instead and add 1 small beetroot (100g) when blending all the ingredients for a similar vivid pink colour, if you like. Dragon fruit is generally not found at major supermarkets, but is available from independent greengrocers and Asian grocers.

health facts Fruit contains sugar in an unrefined form, along with beneficial fibre and antioxidants. Dragon fruit (pitaya) are a very low-kilojoule fruit, rich in vitamins C, B1, B2 and B3, plus, one small fruit is said to contain eight percent of our daily iron needs.

prep + cook time 45 minutes (+ standing) serves 2

AMARANTH PORRIDGE

AYURVEDA IS AN ANCIENT INDIAN HEALTH PRACTICE INCORPORATING MEDICINE, YOGA AND DIET. AN AYURVEDIC DIET ENCOURAGES EATING FROM A WIDE RANGE OF FOOD SOURCES, INCORPORATING SIX PRINCIPLE TASTES: SOUR, SALTY, PUNGENT, SWEET, BITTER AND ASTRINGENT.

You will need to start this recipe a day ahead.

- 1 cup (200g) amaranth (see tips)
- 1 cup (250ml) coconut milk
- 1 cup (250ml) water
- ½ teaspoon ground cardamom
- ½ teaspoon ground cinnamon
- 2 fresh dates, pitted, chopped
- 1 vanilla bean, split lengthways, seeds scraped
- 2 teaspoons pepitas (pumpkin seed kernels)
- 2 teaspoons sunflower seeds
- 2 teaspoons black sesame seeds
- 2 tablespoons coconut milk, extra
- 1 tablespoon pure maple syrup
- frozen raspberries, to serve, optional

1 Place amaranth in a medium bowl with enough water to cover; stand overnight. Drain amaranth, rinse under cold water; drain well.

2 Place amaranth, coconut milk, the water, spices, dates, vanilla seeds and bean in a saucepan; bring to the boil. Reduce heat to low; simmer gently, stirring frequently, for 25 minutes or until amaranth is no longer gritty. If the porridge dries out, add a little extra water. Discard vanilla bean.

3 Meanwhile, heat a small frying pan over medium heat; cook seeds, stirring for 2 minutes or until toasted. Remove from pan; cool.

4 Divide amaranth porridge between bowls; drizzle with extra coconut milk and the maple syrup. Serve topped with toasted seeds and raspberries.

tips While sometimes referred to as a grain, strictly speaking amaranth is a nutritious gluten-free seed with a nutty taste. It can be found at large supermarkets and health food stores. It is important to soak the amaranth overnight in cold water, otherwise the mixture will be gritty and the cooking time will double.

prep + cook time 20 minutes (+ refrigeration) makes 6

Turmeric chia BREAKFAST PUDDINGS

- 3 cups (750ml) coconut milk
- 1 cinnamon stick
- 1½ teaspoons grated fresh turmeric
- 1½ teaspoons grated fresh ginger
- ¼ cup (90g) honey
- ⅓ cup (55g) white chia seeds
- 500g (1 pound) unsweetened coconut yoghurt
- 2 medium bananas (300g), sliced thinly
- ½ cup (40g) coconut flakes, toasted

TURMERIC & PASSIONFRUIT HONEY

- ⅓ cup (115g) honey
- 1 teaspoon grated fresh turmeric
- 1 passionfruit, pulp removed

1 Place coconut milk, cinnamon, turmeric and ginger in a small saucepan, bring to a simmer over medium heat; cook for 5 minutes to infuse milk with spices.

2 Strain milk mixture through a fine sieve over a small heatproof bowl; discard solids. Stir honey and chia seeds into hot infused milk; cover bowl with a clean tea towel. Refrigerate for 30 minutes or until thickened.

3 Meanwhile, make turmeric and passionfruit honey.

4 Divide one-quarter of the chia pudding among six 300ml jars or 1-cup (250ml) glasses. Top with one-quarter of the coconut yoghurt. Press half the banana slices in a ring around the inside of the jar. Repeat layering with remaining chia pudding and yoghurt to create four layers of each. Top puddings with remaining banana and coconut flakes; drizzle with turmeric and passionfruit honey.

turmeric & passionfruit honey Place all ingredients in a small saucepan; bring to the boil. Reduce heat to medium; simmer for 1 minute to infuse. Cool to room temperature.

swap out the fresh grated spices with ground spices; use 2 teaspoons ground cinnamon, 1½ teaspoons ground turmeric and 1 teaspoon ground ginger. You could also use dairy milk and yoghurt instead of coconut, if preferred. If you are not a fan of spices, stir in 1 teaspoon pure vanilla extract and 1 teaspoon finely grated orange or lemon rind into the milk instead.

keeps Store layered puddings in the fridge for up to 2 days, or the unlayered chia mixture in the fridge for up to 1 week.

tip Make the chia base mixture on the weekend, then layer the mixture each morning in jars, either with the banana and yoghurt in our recipe, or with the fruit of your choice, for a quick and easy breakfast to almost see you through the week.

prep + cook time 35 minutes serves 4

Pea & kale fritters WITH SMOKED SALMON

- 1 cup (150g) buckwheat flour
- 1 cup (280g) Greek-style yoghurt
- 4 eggs
- 3 cups (360g) frozen peas, thawed
- 6 cups (170g) loosely packed shredded kale leaves (see tip)
- ¼ cup (60ml) extra virgin olive oil
- 1 lemon (140g), rind finely grated, cut into wedges
- 2 x 150g (4½-ounce) hot-smoked salmon fillets, flaked into large pieces
- ¼ cup finely chopped fresh chives
- ¼ cup finely chopped fresh flat-leaf parsley

1 Preheat oven to 150°C/300°F.

2 Whisk buckwheat flour, ½ cup of the yoghurt and the eggs in a large bowl; season well. Add peas and kale; stir until well combined.

3 Heat 1 tablespoon of the oil in a large frying pan over medium-high heat. Add four heaped ⅓ cupfuls of fritter mixture to pan; cook for 3 minutes each side or until golden and cooked through. Transfer to an oven tray, cover loosely with foil; keep warm on the lowest oven shelf. Repeat twice more with remaining oil and fritter mixture to make 12 fritters.

4 Whisk remaining yoghurt with lemon rind; season.

5 Top fritters with yoghurt mixture, salmon and herbs. Serve with lemon wedges.

tip To prepare kale, tear the leaves from the stalks; discard stalks. Coarsely shred the kale leaves.

Hunger Busters

prep + cook time 5 minutes serves 1

FIVE-MINUTE HUNGER BUSTER

Lightly grease a 1½ cup microwave-safe mug. Combine ¼ cup wholemeal spelt flour, 2 tablespoons LSA, ½ teaspoon baking powder and ¼ teaspoon ground cinnamon in a bowl. Whisk 2 tablespoons melted coconut butter, 1 egg, 2 tablespoons milk of choice, ½ teaspoon pure vanilla extract and 2 teaspoons pure maple syrup in the mug. Stir in dry ingredients. Place in the centre of the microwave tray. Microwave on HIGH (100%) for 2 minutes or until just cooked. Top with a slice of butter, extra pure maple syrup and a pinch of ground cinnamon and serve immediately.

tips Coconut butter is the ground flesh of the coconut; you can find it in health food stores. Or substitute coconut oil or regular butter. LSA is a ground mixture of linseeds, sunflower seeds and almonds available from supermarkets.

prep + cook time 5 minutes serves 1

BLUEBERRY, ORANGE & OAT HUNGER BUSTER

Lightly grease a 1½ cup microwave-safe mug. Combine ¼ cup wholemeal spelt flour, 2 tablespoons quick oats, ½ teaspoon baking powder and ¼ teaspoon ground cinnamon in a small bowl. Whisk 2 tablespoons melted coconut butter, 1 egg, 2 tablespoons milk of choice, 1 teaspoon finely grated orange rind, ½ teaspoon pure vanilla extract and 2 teaspoons pure maple syrup in the mug. Stir in dry ingredients and 2 tablespoons frozen blueberries; top with an extra 1 tablespoon frozen blueberries. Place in the centre of the microwave tray. Microwave on HIGH (100%) for 2 minutes or until just cooked. Serve immediately, topped with unsweetened coconut yoghurt and extra orange rind.

prep + cook time 5 minutes serves 1

COFFEE, DATE & COCONUT HUNGER BUSTER

Lightly grease a 1½ cup microwave-safe mug. Pit 2 fresh dates; chop coarsely. Combine ¼ cup wholemeal spelt flour, 2 tablespoons desiccated coconut, 2½ tablespoons melted coconut butter, 1 egg, 2 tablespoons milk of choice, 1 teaspoon instant coffee granules, ½ teaspoon pure vanilla extract and 2 teaspoons pure maple syrup in the mug. Stir in the dry ingredients and three-quarters of the dates. Top with remaining dates. Place in the centre of the microwave tray. Microwave on HIGH (100%) for 2 minutes or until just cooked. Serve immediately topped with extra pure maple syrup.

tip You can melt the coconut butter in the mug in the microwave for 30 seconds.

prep + cook time 5 minutes serves 1

BANANA & TAHINI HUNGER BUSTER

Lightly grease a 1½ cup microwave-safe mug. Chop ½ small ripe banana finely. Combine ¼ cup wholemeal spelt flour, 2 tablespoons LSA, ½ teaspoon baking powder and ¼ teaspoon ground cinnamon in a bowl. Whisk 2 tablespoons tahini, 1 egg, 2 tablespoons milk of choice, ½ teaspoon pure vanilla extract and 2 teaspoons pure maple syrup in the mug. Stir in the dry ingredients and three-quarters of the banana. Place in the centre of the microwave tray. Microwave on HIGH (100%) for 2 minutes or until just cooked. Serve immediately topped with unsweetened coconut yoghurt, remaining banana, sliced thinly, and extra cinnamon.

prep + cook time 35 minutes (+ standing & refrigeration) serves 4

Strawberry, ricotta & basil BRUSCHETTA WITH BITTER HONEY

You will need to start this recipe a day ahead.

- » 3 cups (750ml) full-cream milk
- » 300ml pouring cream
- » ½ teaspoon salt flakes
- » ¼ cup (60ml) lemon juice
- » 500g (1 pound) small strawberries, trimmed, halved
- » ¼ cup (60ml) sugar-free balsamic vinegar or red wine vinegar
- » 8 thick slices (600g) wholegrain sourdough
- » 1 cup small fresh basil leaves

BITTER HONEY

- » 1½ tablespoons roasted dandelion and chicory root blend (see tips)
- » 2 teaspoons instant coffee granules
- » 1 cup (350g) honey
- » ¼ cup (60ml) water

1 To make ricotta, combine milk, cream and salt in a 2 litre (8 cup) heavy-based saucepan over medium heat. Cook, stirring occasionally using a wooden spoon, for 10 minutes or until just below simmering point, or a digital thermometer reads 85°C (185°F).

2 Remove from heat and stir through lemon juice. Stand for 30 minutes or until solid curds form. Strain mixture through a muslin-lined sieve over a bowl. Refrigerate for 2 hours or until curds and liquid whey are separated. Reserve whey (see tips). (Makes 2 cups (475g) ricotta)

3 Meanwhile, make bitter honey.

4 Transfer drained curds to a large bowl, whisk until smooth; season to taste. Transfer to an airtight container; refrigerate overnight to set.

5 Place strawberries and vinegar in a large glass bowl, season with pepper; stir to combine. Cover tightly with plastic wrap; leave in a warm place for 1 hour. Stir again before serving; drain.

6 Heat a chargrill plate on high. Grill sourdough for 2 minutes each side or until grill marks appear.

7 Serve ricotta spread on toast, topped with strawberries and basil; drizzle with bitter honey.

bitter honey Using a mortar and pestle or a spice grinder, grind dandelion and chicory blend and coffee granules to form a coarse powder. Place honey and the water in a saucepan. Sift over dandelion and chicory mixture; bring to the boil, whisking occasionally. Simmer for 3 minutes. Leave to cool for 15 minutes before skimming surface; transfer to a sterilised jar (see page 485). Cool to room temperature.

keeps Store bitter honey in the pantry for up to 1 month. Store ricotta in an airtight container in the fridge for up to 1 week.

tips When making ricotta, use the drained liquid (whey) in your next batch of bread or pizza dough instead of water or use a few spoonfuls to jump-start the lacto-fermentation process when making pickles. Roasted dandelion and chicory root blend is a caffeine-free coffee substitute available from health food stores.

prep + cook time 15 minutes serves 4

Warming QUINOA PORRIDGE

- 1 litre (4 cups) soy milk or nut milk
- 3 granny smith apples (450g), grated coarsely
- 1 vanilla bean, split lengthways, seeds scraped (see tips)
- 125g (4 ounces) blueberries
- ¾ cup (70g) quinoa flakes
- ¼ cup (50g) black chia seeds
- ⅓ cup (140g) unsweetened coconut or other vegan yoghurt
- ⅓ cup (45g) skinless roasted hazelnuts, chopped coarsely
- ⅓ cup (80ml) pure maple syrup or honey

1 Place milk, apple, vanilla bean and seeds in a medium saucepan over low heat; cook for 5 minutes or until milk is almost boiling and apple is softened.
2 Lightly crush half the blueberries, add to the pan with quinoa flakes and chia seeds; cook, stirring, for 5 minutes or until thickened. Remove vanilla bean, rinse well; reserve for another use (see tips).
3 Serve porridge topped with yoghurt, hazelnuts and remaining blueberries. Drizzle with maple syrup.

swap out apples for pears, blueberries for strawberries and hazelnuts for almonds, for a different take on this porridge.

tips Take your pick as to how you want to introduce the vanilla flavour to this porridge. Vanilla beans provide the purest flavour and the bean itself can be reused if it is rinsed and dried. Alternatively, you can use 1 teaspoon pure vanilla extract. However, it does contain a trace amount of sugar, but really nothing one should be too bothered about. Another option is vanilla bean powder from health food stores, which is both the ground bean and seeds; though vanilla in this form tends to be less potent.

prep + cook time 45 minutes serves 6

Muesli with poached pears & SHEEP'S MILK YOGHURT

EATING A HEALTHY BREAKFAST WITH A GOOD MIX OF SLOW-RELEASE CARBS AND PROTEIN WILL HELP TO KEEP YOUR BLOOD SUGAR LEVELS IN CHECK FOR THE REST OF THE DAY. YOU CAN SKIP THE POACHED PEAR PART OF THIS RECIPE IF YOU LIKE, AND TOP WITH A MIX OF FRESH OR FROZEN BERRIES INSTEAD.

- ⅓ cup (95g) almond spread
- ⅓ cup (80ml) pure maple syrup
- 2 cups (180g) rolled oats
- 1 cup (50g) flaked coconut
- ½ cup (80g) flaked almonds
- ¼ cup (50g) pepitas (pumpkin seed kernels)
- ¼ cup (35g) sunflower seeds
- ¼ cup (20g) quinoa flakes
- ¼ cup (35g) rolled amaranth or rolled rye
- 2 tablespoons black or white chia seeds
- 1 cup (160g) dried sweetened cranberries
- 6 small corella pears (600g)
- 2 cups (500ml) apple juice
- 2 cups (500ml) water
- 1½ cups (420g) sheep's milk yoghurt
- 2 tablespoons raw honey or pure maple syrup

1 Preheat oven to 160°C/325°F. Line a large roasting pan with baking paper.
2 Stir almond spread and maple syrup in a small saucepan over low heat just until combined.
3 Combine oats, coconut, almonds, pepitas, sunflower seeds, quinoa and amaranth in a bowl. Pour syrup mixture over dry ingredients; working quickly, stir to coat ingredients in syrup mixture.
4 Spread muesli, in an even layer, in pan. Bake 15 minutes. Remove from oven; stir well. Bake for a further 5 minutes or until oats are golden. Cool for 10 minutes; stir in chia seeds and cranberries.
5 Meanwhile, peel, halve and core pears, leaving stalks intact. Place pears in a medium saucepan with juice and the water; bring to the boil. Reduce heat to low; cover pears with a round of baking paper, simmer for 8 minutes or until tender.
6 Place yoghurt and honey in a small bowl; stir gently to swirl through.
7 Serve muesli topped with poached pears and honey yoghurt. If you like, sprinkle with a little ground nutmeg or cinnamon.

tips Similarly to quinoa, amaranth is a seed treated as a grain. You will be able to find the ingredients for this muesli either in the health food aisle at most supermarkets or health food stores.

keeps Store muesli in an airtight container in the fridge for up to 1 month.

prep + cook time 20 minutes (+ cooling) serves 4 (makes 2 cups)

Chia & almond
TOASTED MUESLI

- » 1 cup (90g) rolled oats
- » 2 tablespoons black chia seeds
- » ⅓ cup (55g) coarsely chopped almonds
- » 1 tablespoon Natvia
- » ½ teaspoon mixed spice
- » 2 tablespoons almond spread (see tips)
- » 3 teaspoons coconut oil, melted
- » 2 tablespoons sunflower seeds
- » 2 tablespoons LSA (see tips)

1 Preheat oven to 180°C/350°F. Grease an oven tray; line with baking paper.
2 Combine oats, chia seeds, almonds, Natvia and mixed spice in a medium mixing bowl. Add almond spread and oil; using fingertips, rub mixture together until it resembles coarse breadcrumbs. Spread mixture evenly over oven tray.
3 Bake muesli for 10 minutes or until mixture is browned lightly. Cool on tray.
4 Transfer cooled muesli to a medium bowl, add sunflower seeds and LSA; stir to combine.

tips Almond spread or almond butter is available at health food stores and most supermarkets. To make your own, blend or process whole roasted almonds to a fine paste. LSA is a ground mixture of linseeds, sunflower seeds and almonds. It is available from major supermarkets and health food stores.

keeps You can make double or triple the recipe. Store it in an airtight container in the fridge for up to 1 month.

serving suggestion Serve topped with kiwifruit, banana, strawberries and yoghurt.

prep + cook time 45 minutes makes 6

Za'atar-roasted tomato, BACON & EGG CUPS

- 6 cherry tomatoes (120g), halved
- 1½ tablespoons olive oil
- 1 teaspoon za'atar (see tip)
- 4 slices shortcut bacon rashers (140g), chopped finely
- 1 medium onion (150g), chopped finely
- 10 eggs
- ¼ cup finely chopped fresh flat-leaf parsley
- ¼ cup (60ml) pouring cream
- ¼ cup (60g) fresh ricotta, crumbled

1 Preheat oven to 180°C/350°F. Grease a 6-hole (¾ cup/180ml) texas muffin pan; line each hole with two 15cm (6-inch) squares of baking paper. Line a small oven tray with baking paper.
2 Place tomatoes on lined tray; drizzle with 2 teaspoons of the oil, sprinkle with za'atar. Bake for 20 minutes or until tender.
3 Meanwhile, heat remaining oil in a large frying pan over medium heat. Cook bacon and onion for 5 minutes or until soft and browned. Spoon mixture into lined muffin holes. Whisk eggs, parsley and cream in a large bowl; season. Pour into muffin cases.
4 Bake for 20 minutes. Top with ricotta and tomatoes; bake cups for a further 5 minutes or until set. Season; serve warm or at room temperature.

tip Za'atar is a Middle-Eastern spice blend that generally includes thyme, sesame seeds, sumac and cumin in equal proportions, with a little salt. You could also use dukkah or ½ teaspoon smoked paprika instead.

swap out bacon and replace with tofu bacon (see page 184) to make the recipe vegetarian. Serve with a salad of radish wedges, snow pea sprouts and halved sugar snap peas or pea pods, if you like.

7
9

prep time 5 minutes serves 2

Strawberry & passionfruit BREAKFAST TRIFLE

- » 2 Weet-Bix (50g), broken into chunks
- » ½ cup (40g) All-Bran cereal
- » 1 cup (280g) low-fat plain yoghurt or soy yoghurt
- » ⅓ cup (80ml) fresh passionfruit pulp
- » 140g (4½ ounces) strawberries, sliced

1 Layer half each of the Weet-Bix and All-Bran in two 1¼-cup (310ml) glasses. Divide half each of the yoghurt, passionfruit and strawberries between glasses.
2 Repeat layering with remaining Weet-Bix, All-Bran and yoghurt. Top breakfast trifles with remaining strawberries and passionfruit.

tips Assemble the trifle just before you're ready to eat so the cereals keep their crunch. You will need about 4 passionfruit. You can make the breakfast trifle with any seasonal fruit combination or even with canned fruit in natural juices. Canned pears and frozen raspberries go well together.

prep + cook time 20 minutes serves 2

Quinoa PORRIDGE

- » ½ cup (100g) white quinoa, rinsed
- » 1½ cups (375ml) water
- » ½ cup (125ml) skim milk or almond milk
- » 1 medium red apple (150g), grated coarsely
- » ⅓ cup (95g) plain yoghurt
- » 1 tablespoon raw honey or pure maple syrup
- » 1 medium mango (430g), sliced
- » 1 tablespoon goji berries
- » 2 tablespoons pistachios, roasted, chopped coarsely

1 Combine quinoa and the water in a small saucepan; bring to the boil. Reduce heat; simmer, covered, for 10 minutes. Add milk; cook, covered, for a further 5 minutes or until quinoa is tender. Stir in apple until combined.
2 Place yoghurt and honey in a small bowl; stir gently to swirl through.
3 Serve porridge topped with mango slices, goji berries, pistachios and honey yoghurt.

tips Although most quinoa comes rinsed, it's a good idea to rinse it yourself under cold water until the water runs clear. This removes any remaining outer coating, which has a bitter taste and can make it difficult to digest. Quinoa absorbs a lot of liquid, so depending on how you like your porridge, add a little boiling water at the end of step 1 to thin it out. We used a pink lady apple in this recipe.

prep time 20 minutes (+ refrigeration) serves 4 (makes 5 cups)

Cherry, ginger & CHIA BIRCHER

- 2 tablespoons Natvia
- 2 cups (300g) frozen pitted cherries
- 5cm (2-inch) piece fresh ginger, chopped coarsely
- 1¼ cups (310ml) water
- ½ cup (140g) unsweetened coconut yoghurt
- 1 cup (90g) rolled oats
- ½ cup (80g) white chia seeds
- ¼ cup (50g) pepitas (pumpkin seed kernels)
- 1 small green apple (130g)
- ¼ cup (40g) natural almonds, roasted, chopped
- fresh cherries and bee pollen (see tip), to serve, optional

1 Blend Natvia in a high-speed blender until consistency of icing sugar.
2 Process cherries, powdered Natvia, ginger and the water until smooth. Pour into a large bowl.
3 Stir in coconut yoghurt, oats, chia seeds and pepitas until combined. Cover with plastic wrap; refrigerate for 2 hours or until thickened, or overnight.
4 Coarsely grate apple and stir through soaked bircher mixture. Divide bircher among four bowls, serve sprinkled with almonds. Top with fresh cherries and bee pollen, if you like.

tip If you don't have a honey allergy, serve with bee pollen, if you like. Alternatively, serve with fennel pollen, which are the flower tips and pollen from fennel flowers, available from health food or spice stores.

keeps You can make the bircher mixture a day ahead; store covered, in the fridge. Stir through grated apple just before serving.

prep + cook time 50 minutes serves 8

Spelt & oat scones
WITH BERRY CHIA SEED JAM

THIS JAM TAKES ONLY 10 MINUTES TO MAKE. IT WON'T STORE AS LONG AS REGULAR JAM, HOWEVER IT CAN BE FROZEN IN PORTIONS TO EXTEND THE SHELF LIFE.

- 1 tablespoon Natvia
- 1 cup (160g) wholemeal plain (all-purpose) flour
- 1 cup (150g) white spelt flour
- 2 teaspoons baking powder
- 1 teaspoon fine sea salt flakes
- 100g (3oz) cold butter, chopped coarsely
- ¾ cup (180ml) buttermilk
- 1 tablespoon buttermilk, extra
- 2 tablespoons rolled oats
- 50g (1½oz) butter, extra

BERRY CHIA SEED JAM

- 400g (12½ ounces) frozen mixed berries
- ¼ cup (35g) white chia seeds
- 1 tablespoon Natvia
- 1 teaspoon finely grated lemon rind
- 1 teaspoon lemon juice
- 1 vanilla bean, split lengthways, seeds scraped

1 Make berry chia seed jam.
2 Process Natvia in a spice grinder until consistency of icing sugar.
3 Preheat oven to 220°C/425°F fan-forced (see tip). Line an oven tray with baking paper.
4 Sift flours, powdered Natvia, baking powder and salt into a large bowl; rub in butter until mixture resembles coarse breadcrumbs. Add buttermilk; using a dinner knife, cut liquid through mixture until it starts to clump. Turn out onto a floured surface; knead gently for 45 seconds or until dough just comes together. (Don't over work the dough or it will be tough.)
5 Shape dough into a 16cm (6½-inch) round on tray with floured hands. Mark the round into 8 wedges, using the back of a floured knife. Brush top with extra buttermilk; sprinkle with oats.
6 Bake scones for 20 minutes or until top is golden. Serve warm with extra butter and jam.
berry chia seed jam Cook berries in a medium saucepan over medium heat, stirring occasionally, for 5 minutes or until berries release their juices. Reduce heat to low, add chia seeds and Natvia; cook, stirring occasionally, for 6 minutes or until thickened slightly. Stir in rind, juice and vanilla seeds.

tip The even heat provided by the fan function of the oven will help give these scones an extra boost. For conventional ovens, increase the temperature by 10-20 degrees.

keeps Scones are best made on the day of serving. The jam can be made up to 3 days ahead; store in an airtight container in the fridge for up to 1 week or freeze for up to 1 month.

prep time 15 minutes (+ standing) serves 4

Cherry & walnut SMOOTHIE

You need to start this recipe a day ahead.

- » ½ cup (60g) walnuts
- » ⅓ cup (55g) natural almonds
- » 1¾ cups (430ml) filtered water
- » 750g (1½ pounds) frozen pitted cherries
- » 1 tablespoon Natvia
- » ¼ cup (30g) walnuts, extra, chopped coarsely
- » 1 teaspoon black chia seeds

1 Combine walnuts, almonds and the water in a medium bowl. Cover; stand overnight.
2 Blend nut mixture for 2 minutes or until as smooth as possible. Strain mixture through a muslin-lined sieve over a medium jug; twist and squeeze the cloth to extract as much liquid as possible. Discard solids in cloth.
3 Blend or process nut milk, cherries and Natvia in a high-powered blender, if available; this type of blender will produce a very smooth consistency. Pour into 1-cup (250ml) glasses, top with extra walnuts and chia seeds. Serve immediately.

tips For a thicker smoothie, blend the chia seeds with the other smoothie ingredients. You can make other flavoured nut milks using 105g (3½ ounces) total of your favourite nuts and 1¾ cups (430ml) filtered water. Use pecans instead of walnuts, if you like.

Fruit Compotes

prep + cook time 45 minutes serves 4

PEAR, CARDAMOM & GINGER COMPOTE

Place 4 (1kg) cored and thickly sliced packham pears in a medium saucepan with 1 cup water, 2 teaspoons freshly grated ginger, 6 bruised cardamom pods, 1 cinnamon stick and 1 tablespoon lemon juice; bring to the boil. Reduce heat; simmer, partially covered, for 25 minutes, stirring occasionally, or until liquid has reduced slightly and pears are tender. Serve warm or chilled.

serving suggestion Serve with vanilla yoghurt or homemade muesli.

prep + cook time 25 minutes serves 4

APPLE, RHUBARB & GOJI COMPOTE

Place ½ cup fresh orange juice and 1½ tablespoons Natvia in a medium saucepan over low heat; cook, stirring, until Natvia dissolves. Add 2 large (400g) coarsely chopped pink lady apples, 4cm (1½in) wide strip of orange rind, the seeds scraped from ½ vanilla bean and the pod; simmer, covered, for 5 minutes. Add 1 bunch (500g) trimmed, chopped rhubarb and 2 tablespoons goji berries; simmer gently, covered, for 10 minutes or until fruit is tender and still holding its shape. Serve warm or chilled.

serving suggestion Serve with porridge or yoghurt. To turn into a dessert, add a crumble topping to make a rhubarb and apple crumble.

keeps Store compote in an airtight container in the fridge for up to 1 week.

prep + cook time 35 minutes serves 4

VANILLA-ROASTED NECTARINES & PEACHES

Preheat oven to 220°C/425°F. Grease a medium ovenproof dish with butter. Halve and remove stones from 3 medium (500g) yellow nectarines and 3 medium (450g) yellow peaches; place in dish. Split a vanilla bean lengthways, scrape seeds from halves, using the tip of a knife. Add vanilla bean and seeds to dish with 1½ tablespoons Natvia, 2 x 4cm (1½in) strips lemon rind, 1 tablespoon lemon juice, 2 tablespoons water and a pinch of sea salt flakes; turn fruit to coat. Arrange fruit in a single layer, cut-side up. Bake fruit for 20 minutes or until fruit is tender but still holds its shape. Serve warm or chilled.

serving suggestion Serve with thick Greek-style yoghurt, topped with nuts and seeds.

keeps Store compote in an airtight container in the fridge for up to 1 week.

prep + cook time 25 minutes serves 4

PLUM, RASPBERRY & ROSEMARY COMPOTE

Halve and remove stones from 5 blood plums (450g); cut each half into thirds. Place plums in a large saucepan with ¼ cup water, 1 tablespoon lemon juice, 1 cinnamon stick and 2 sprigs rosemary; bring to the boil. Reduce heat; simmer, covered, for 5 minutes. Uncover; simmer, for a further 5 minutes or until plums are just tender. Stir in ½ cup raspberries and 2 teaspoons Natvia; stir until Natvia dissolves. Remove from heat.

serving suggestion Serve compote with thick Greek-style yoghurt.

keeps Store compote in an airtight container in the fridge for up to 1 week.

prep + cook time 40 minutes serves 6

Berry & fig weekend BREKKIE PUDDING

PLACE THIS SHOW-STOPPING BREKKIE PUDDING IN THE CENTRE OF THE TABLE AT BRUNCH AS THE MAIN ATTRACTION FOR FAMILY OR GUESTS TO HELP THEMSELVES.

- 40g (1½ ounces) butter, softened
- 1 vanilla bean (see tips)
- ½ cup (125ml) water
- 1 cup (230g) fresh dates, pitted
- 2 tablespoons ground turmeric
- 2 tablespoons ground cinnamon
- 5cm (2-inch) piece fresh ginger, chopped coarsely
- 1 cup (120g) almond meal (ground almonds)
- 400ml can coconut cream
- 1½ teaspoons baking powder
- ¼ cup (35g) self-raising flour
- 8 eggs
- ¼ cup (90g) raw honey
- 3 medium fresh figs (180g), cut into wedges
- 150g (4½ ounces) fresh raspberries
- 150g (4½ ounces) fresh blackberries
- 1 cup (150g) fresh cherries, pitted
- 1½ cups (420g) unsweetened coconut yoghurt

1 Preheat oven to 200°C/400°F. Grease a 1.5 litre (6-cup) capacity baking dish with half the butter.

2 Split vanilla bean lengthways, scrape seeds from halves, using the tip of a knife. Process vanilla seeds, the water, dates, turmeric, cinnamon, ginger, almond meal, coconut cream, baking powder and flour until smooth.

3 Whisk eggs in a large bowl until light and frothy. Add turmeric mixture to egg; stir gently to combine. Pour into baking dish.

4 Bake pudding for 25 minutes or until risen and firm. Remove and cool for 15 minutes.

5 Meanwhile, heat remaining butter and the honey in a large frying pan over medium heat; cook figs for 2 minutes each side or until light golden. Add berries and cherries; cook for 1 minute or until berries release their juices.

6 Spread coconut yoghurt over pudding. Top with warm fruit and pan juices.

tips Place the leftover vanilla bean in a zip-top bag and save for another use. Use to flavour roasted fruit or for a decadent hot chocolate, or cut into shorter lengths and slip into a jar of muesli to infuse with a vanilla flavour. To make this dairy-free, use cacao butter instead of regular butter.

prep + cook time 40 minutes serves 4

POWER STACK

- 400g (12½ ounces) medium orange sweet potato (see tips)
- 8 fresh shiitake mushrooms (140g), stems trimmed
- ¼ cup (60ml) olive oil
- 2 teaspoons chopped fresh rosemary
- 1 long fresh red chilli, seeded, chopped
- 2 tablespoons sunflower seeds
- 2 cups (80g) baby kale
- ¼ cup (20g) finely grated parmesan
- 1 tablespoon white vinegar
- 8 fresh eggs
- 3 green heirloom tomatoes (380g), sliced (see tips)
- 4 baby target beetroot (beets) (80g), sliced thinly (see tips)
- ½ cup baby micro cress

LEMON AÏOLI

- 1 egg yolk
- 1 small clove garlic, chopped
- 1 tablespoon finely grated lemon rind
- 1 teaspoon fresh chopped rosemary
- 2 tablespoons lemon juice
- ½ teaspoon raw honey
- ½ cup (125ml) olive oil

1 Preheat oven to 200°C/400°F. Line an oven tray with baking paper.

2 Cut sweet potato into eight 5mm (¼-inch) rounds. Place on tray with mushrooms, 2 tablespoons of the oil, rosemary and chilli; toss to coat. Bake for 25 minutes or until sweet potato is tender.

3 Meanwhile, make lemon aïoli.

4 Heat remaining oil in a medium frying pan over medium heat; cook sunflower seeds, stirring, for 2 minutes or until toasted. Stir in kale, turn off heat; leave for the residual heat to wilt leaves. Add parmesan; season to taste.

5 To poach eggs, half-fill a large, deep-frying pan with water, add vinegar; bring to a gentle simmer. Break 1 egg into a cup. Using a wooden spoon, make a whirlpool in the water; slide egg into whirlpool. Repeat with 3 more eggs. Cook eggs for 3 minutes or until whites are set and the yolks are runny. Remove eggs with a slotted spoon; drain on a paper towel-lined plate. Keep warm. Repeat poaching with remaining eggs.

6 Spoon 2 tablespoons of the aïoli onto each plate. Build two stacks on each plate with sweet potato, tomato, mushrooms then kale mixture. Top each stack with a poached egg, beetroot and micro cress.

lemon aïoli Process egg yolk, garlic, rind, rosemary, juice and honey in a small food processor for 1 minute. With motor operating, gradually add oil, drop by drop at first, then in a slow steady stream until mixture is thick and emulsified. Season to taste. (Makes ⅔ cup)

tips Try to buy a sweet potato with a diameter of 7cm (2¾ inches) as it will provide the base for your stack, and tomatoes of a similar size. If heirloom green tomatoes are hard to find, use red. Target beetroots are available from specialist green grocers and grower's markets. If they're unavailable, use radishes or a little shaved fennel instead.

prep + cook time 1 hour 30 minutes serves 2

Seed crackers WITH SMASHED AVOCADO

- 1 cup (200g) long-grain brown rice
- 2½ cups (625ml) water
- 1 cup (200g) tri-coloured quinoa
- 2 cups (500ml) water, extra
- ¼ cup (g) sesame seeds
- ¼ cup (50g) linseeds (flaxseeds)
- ¼ cup (35g) chia seeds
- ¼ cup (35g) sunflower seeds
- 1 tablespoon finely chopped fresh lemon thyme
- 1 tablespoon finely chopped fresh oregano
- 1 tablespoon finely chopped fresh rosemary
- 1 teaspoon cracked black pepper
- 2 teaspoons onion powder
- 1 medium avocado (250g)
- 1 tablespoon lemon juice
- 2 teaspoons chia seeds, extra
- 45g (1½ ounces) snow pea shoots
- pinch sumac, optional

1 Preheat oven 180°C/350°F.

2 Place brown rice and the water in a small saucepan; bring to the boil. Reduce heat to low; simmer, uncovered, for 25 minutes or until most of the water has evaporated. Remove from heat; stand, covered, for 10 minutes. Fluff with a fork, spread out over an oven tray; cool.

3 Place quinoa and the extra water in same pan; bring to the boil. Reduce heat to low; simmer, uncovered, for 10 minutes or until most of the water has evaporated. Remove from heat; stand, covered, for 10 minutes. Fluff with a fork, spread out over an oven tray; cool.

4 Process the rice with half the quinoa to form a coarse paste; transfer to a large bowl. Add remaining quinoa, seeds, the herbs, pepper and onion powder, season; using your hands, combine well. Divide into four portions.

5 Line four oven trays with baking paper. Remove one of the pieces of baking paper. Flatten a portion of dough over paper, cover with plastic wrap then roll out with a rolling pin to 1mm-thick or as thin as possible. (Don't worry if there are holes, these will give the crackers texture and character.) Discard plastic; carefully lift the paper back onto the tray. Repeat with remaining portions of dough until you have four trays. Score the crackers into 5cm x 10cm (2-inch x 4-inch) lengths or triangles (or leave as whole sheets and break into pieces after baking).

6 Bake crackers for 20 minutes. Cover crackers with a sheet of baking paper and a second tray. Holding the hot tray with oven gloves, flip the crackers over onto the second tray; carefully remove lining paper. Repeat with remaining trays. Cook crackers for a further 20 minutes or until golden and crisp. Cool on trays.

7 To serve, roughly smash avocado with a fork in a small bowl with juice; season to taste. Place 4 crackers on each of two serving plates; top crackers with avocado mixture, extra chia seeds, snow pea shoots and sumac.

tips If the cracker mixture spreads past the paper when you're rolling it just cut those edges off. If you don't have enough oven trays, you can cook the crackers in two batches. Crackers can be stored in an airtight container for up to 1 month.

prep + cook time 30 minutes (+ cooling) serves 4 (makes 4¾ cups)

Grain-free coconut & VANILLA MUESLI

- 2 vanilla beans
- 2½ cups (125g) flaked coconut
- ½ cup (80g) natural almonds, chopped coarsely
- ½ cup (80g) brazil nuts, chopped coarsely
- ½ cup (60g) pecans, chopped coarsely
- ¼ cup (35g) sunflower seeds
- ½ cup (100g) coconut oil, melted
- 2 tablespoons raw honey
- ½ teaspoon sea salt

1 Preheat oven to 160°C/300°F. Grease and line two large oven trays with baking paper.
2 Split vanilla beans in half lengthways; using the tip of a small knife, scrape out seeds. Place seeds and pods in a large bowl with remaining ingredients; stir to combine. Spread mixture evenly between trays.
3 Bake muesli for 20 minutes, stirring occasionally to break into clumps, or until lightly golden. Cool to room temperature.

serving suggestion Serve with milk or yoghurt.

keeps Store muesli in an airtight container in the fridge for up to 4 weeks.

prep + cook time 25 minutes serves 2

Green quinoa WITH SESAME EGGS

- ½ cup (100g) white quinoa, rinsed
- 1 cup (250g) chicken or vegetable stock
- 4 eggs, at room temperature
- 2 teaspoons coconut oil
- 1 small clove garlic, crushed
- 1 small red chilli, chopped finely
- 2 cups (80g) thinly sliced kale (see tips)
- 2 cups (90g) firmly packed thinly sliced silver beet (swiss chard) (see tips)
- 1 tablespoon lemon juice
- ¼ cup finely chopped fresh flat-leaf parsley
- 1 tablespoon white sesame seeds
- 1 tablespoon black sesame seeds
- 1 teaspoon sea salt flakes

1 Place quinoa and stock in a medium saucepan; bring to the boil. Reduce heat to low-medium; simmer gently for 15 minutes or until most of the stock is absorbed. Remove from heat; cover, stand 5 minutes.
2 Meanwhile, cook eggs in a small saucepan of boiling water for 5 minutes. Remove immediately from pan; cool under cold running water for 30 seconds. Peel.
3 Heat coconut oil in a medium saucepan over medium heat, add garlic and chilli; cook stirring, for 2 minutes or until fragrant. Add kale and silver beet; stir until wilted. Stir in quinoa and juice; season to taste.
4 Combine parsley, sesame seeds and salt in a small bowl. Roll peeled eggs in parsley mixture.
5 Serve quinoa topped with eggs.

tips You will need half a bunch of kale and half a bunch of silver beet for this recipe. Wash well before use.

prep + cook time 2 hours 30 minutes (+ standing & cooling) serves 2 (makes 10 slices)

Seedaholic bread
WITH ALMOND SPREAD & PEAR

- » 1½ cups (135g) rolled oats
- » 1½ cups (120g) quinoa flakes
- » 1 cup (150g) sunflower seeds
- » 1 cup (200g) pepitas (pumpkin seeds)
- » ⅔ cup (130g) linseeds (flaxseeds)
- » ½ cup (70g) white chia seeds
- » ½ cup (80g) coarsely chopped almond kernels
- » ½ cup (70g) coarsely chopped hazelnuts
- » ½ cup (40g) psyllium husks
- » 2 teaspoons sea salt flakes
- » 3½ cups (875ml) warm water
- » 2 tablespoons Natvia
- » ⅔ cup (140g) coconut oil, melted
- » ¼ cup (65g) almond spread
- » 1 medium packham pear (250g), sliced thinly
- » 1 tablespoon olive oil

1 Grease a 1.5-litre (6-cup), 14cm x 24cm (5½-inch x 9½-inch) loaf pan; line base and two long sides with baking paper, extending the paper 5cm (2 inches) over the edge.
2 Place dry ingredients, except for Natvia, in a large bowl. Place the water, Natvia and coconut oil in a large jug; stir until dissolved. Pour over dry ingredients; stir to combine; if the mixture is too stiff add extra tablespoons of water, one at a time.
3 Spoon seed mixture into pan; shape with your hands into a loaf shape. Cover surface with plastic wrap; stand at room temperature for 2 hours to allow ingredients to absorb the liquid and set the bread into shape.
4 Preheat oven 170°C/340°F.
5 Bake bread for 30 minutes. Invert bread onto a wire rack on an oven tray; peel away lining paper. Return bread on wire rack to oven on tray; bake a further 1 hour 20 minutes, (cover loosely with foil during the last 30 minutes of cooking time), or until a skewer inserted into the centre comes out clean. Leave for 3 hours or until completely cool before slicing.
6 To serve, spread 4 slices of seedaholic bread with almond spread, top with pear slices; drizzle with olive oil. Divide between two serving plates. Season to taste.

tips Psyllium husks are available from vitamin and health food stores. Position the shelf in the oven so the top of the bread sits in the middle of the oven. If the bread starts to overbrown during baking, cover it loosely with foil.

keeps Bread will keep in an airtight container in the fridge for up to 1 week. Freeze individual slices in zip-top bags for up to 1 month.

prep + cook time 10 minutes serves 2

Refreshing green SMOOTHIE

YOU CAN USE A VARIETY OF GREEN VEGETABLES OR FRUITS, SUCH AS LETTUCE, PEAR OR HONEYDEW MELON.

- » 1 medium lime (90g)
- » 1 medium apple (150g)
- » 1 lebanese cucumber (130g)
- » ½ medium avocado (125g)
- » 1⅓ cups (330ml) coconut water
- » 30g (1 ounce) baby spinach leaves
- » 1 teaspoon finely grated fresh ginger
- » 50g (1½ ounces) baby kale leaves

1 Remove rind with pith from lime; discard. Coarsely chop lime flesh, apple, cucumber and avocado.

2 Blend or process ingredients until smooth. Pour into two glasses; serve immediately.

tips For smoothies it is best to use tender baby kale so you don't need to remove the hard stems. If you like, top the smoothies with white or black chia seeds and toasted shredded coconut, or simply serve the smoothie with crushed ice.

prep + cook time 25 minutes serves 2

Breakfast salad with POACHED EGG & KALE PESTO

- ¾ cup (45g) firmly packed baby leaves (see tip)
- 100g (3 ounces) brussels sprouts, shaved thinly
- 1 cup (150g) crunchy combo sprout mix
- 1 small carrot (80g), cut into matchsticks
- 2 tablespoons toasted sunflower seeds
- 2 tablespoons apple cider vinegar
- 1½ tablespoons avocado oil
- 1 teaspoon raw honey
- 1 tablespoon white vinegar
- 4 eggs
- ½ medium avocado (125g), sliced thinly

KALE PESTO

- ⅓ cup (55g) dry-roasted almonds
- ⅓ cup (50g) roasted cashews
- 2 small cloves garlic
- 2 cups (80g) baby kale, chopped coarsely
- ½ cup (125ml) extra virgin olive oil
- 1½ tablespoons apple cider vinegar
- ¼ cup (20g) finely grated parmesan

1 Make kale pesto.

2 Place baby leaves, brussels sprouts, sprout mix, carrot and seeds in a medium bowl; toss to combine. Whisk cider vinegar, 1 tablespoon of the oil and honey in a small bowl; season to taste. Add dressing to salad; toss to combine.

3 To poach eggs, half-fill a large, deep-frying pan with water, add white vinegar; bring to a gentle simmer. Break 1 egg into a cup. Using a wooden spoon, make a whirlpool in the water; slide egg into whirlpool. Repeat with 3 more eggs. Cook eggs for 3 minutes or until whites are set and the yolks are runny. Remove eggs with a slotted spoon; drain on a paper towel-lined plate.

4 Divide salad between serving bowls; top with eggs and avocado. Spoon pesto on eggs; drizzle with remaining oil.

kale pesto Pulse nuts and garlic in a food processor until coarsely chopped. Add kale, oil and vinegar; pulse to a fine paste. Add parmesan, season with sea salt and cracked pepper; pulse until just combined. (Makes 1¼ cups)

tip We used a baby leaf micro herb mix of sorrel, parsley, coriander (cilantro) and radish.

keeps Leftover pesto can be stored, covered with a light layer of oil, in an airtight container in the fridge for up to 1 week.

prep + cook time 30 minutes serves 2

Sweet potato rösti DUKKAH BRUNCH

- 240g (7½ ounces) purple-skinned white-flesh sweet potato, peeled, grated coarsely
- 1 medium onion (150g), grated coarsely
- 1 egg white
- ⅓ cup (25g) finely grated parmesan
- 1 tablespoon finely chopped fresh flat-leaf parsley
- 1 tablespoon finely chopped fresh dill
- 1 clove garlic, crushed
- 2 tablespoons olive oil
- 20g (¾ ounce) butter
- 1 tablespoon white vinegar
- 4 eggs
- 150g (4½ ounces) hot-smoked salmon, flaked
- ¼ cup (70g) Greek-style yoghurt
- 2 teaspoons dukkah
- 2 tablespoons fresh coriander (cilantro) leaves
- lemon wedges, to serve

1 Preheat oven to 180°C/350°F. Line an oven tray with baking paper.
2 Combine sweet potato and onion in a medium bowl; squeeze out excess liquid, return vegetables to bowl. Stir in egg white, parmesan, herbs and garlic; season.
3 Heat half the oil and half the butter in a large frying pan over medium heat; spoon half the sweet potato mixture into pan, flatten to a 10cm (4-inch) round. Cook for 3 minutes each side or until golden. Drain on paper towel; place on tray, season with salt. Repeat with remaining oil, butter and sweet potato mixture to make 2 rösti.
4 Bake rösti for 10 minutes or until crisp and cooked through.
5 Meanwhile, to poach eggs, half-fill a large, deep-frying pan with water, add white vinegar; bring to a gentle simmer. Break 1 egg into a cup. Using a wooden spoon, make a whirlpool in the water; slide egg into whirlpool. Repeat with 3 more eggs. Cook eggs for 3 minutes or until whites are set and the yolks are runny. Remove eggs with a slotted spoon; drain on a paper towel-lined plate.
6 Divide rösti between plates; top with salmon, eggs and yoghurt. Sprinkle with dukkah and coriander, serve with lemon wedges.

tips Dukkah is a Middle Eastern nut and spice mixture available from supermarkets and delis. You can substitute orange sweet potato or potato for the white sweet potato in the rösti and hot-smoked trout or white fish for the salmon.

prep + cook time 20 minutes serves 2

Mushroom & parmesan FRENCH TOAST

- 2 eggs
- ½ cup (125ml) milk
- 2 teaspoons dijon mustard
- ¼ cup (20g) finely grated parmesan
- 4 x 2cm (¾-inch) thick slices sourdough bread
- ⅓ cup (80ml) olive oil
- 300g (9½ ounces) button mushrooms, sliced thinly
- 1 clove garlic, crushed
- 2 tablespoons fresh thyme leaves
- 2 teaspoons apple cider vinegar
- 10g (½ ounce) butter
- ¼ cup (60g) crème fraîche
- ¼ cup (20g) flaked parmesan
- 1 tablespoon finely chopped fresh chives

1 Using a fork, whisk eggs, milk, mustard and grated parmesan in a shallow dish until combined; season. Soak bread slices in egg mixture for 5 minutes, turning halfway through.

2 Meanwhile, heat 1½ tablespoons of the oil in a large frying pan over medium-high heat; cook half the mushrooms, without stirring, for 1 minute or until browned underneath. Cook, stirring, for a further 2 minutes or until tender. Transfer to a heatproof dish; cover with foil. Repeat process with another 1½ tablespoons of the oil and remaining mushrooms, adding garlic and thyme during the last minute of cooking; stir in vinegar and half the butter. Combine all mushrooms in dish; cover to keep warm.

3 Wipe out the pan; heat remaining oil and remaining butter over medium heat and cook bread for 2 minutes each side or until golden.

4 Serve topped with mushroom mixture, crème fraîche, flaked parmesan and chives.

Power drinks

prep time 10 minutes makes 1 litre

ELECTROLYTE BOOSTER

Blend 2 cups coconut water, 400g (12½ ounces) frozen pineapple (see tip), 1 small (200g) avocado, ½ cup fresh mint leaves, 2 cups firmly packed baby spinach and 2 tablespoons lime juice in a high-speed blender until smooth. Serve over ice.

tip Frozen pineapple is available from supermarkets or you can freeze your own portioned, peeled, cored and chopped pineapple in zip-top bags.

prep time 10 minutes makes 1 litre

JUST LIKE A CHOCOLATE THICKSHAKE

Blend 2 cups unsweetened almond milk, 2 ripe medium (260g) chopped frozen bananas, 1 small (200g) chopped avocado, 1 cup firmly packed baby spinach, 2 tablespoons cacao powder, ⅓ cup vanilla bean whey protein powder (optional) or yoghurt and 1 tablespoon raw honey in a high-speed blender until smooth. Serve over ice, dusted with ¼ teaspoon extra cacao powder.

prep time 10 minutes makes 3 cups

BERRY BERRY LUSCIOUS

Soak 2 tablespoons of goji berries in 1 cup chilled coconut milk blend (see tip) for 10 minutes in a small bowl. Transfer to a high-speed blender; add 2 cups frozen mixed berries, 1 cup firmly packed baby spinach and another cup chilled coconut milk blend. Blend until smooth. Serve over ice, topped with 1 tablespoon each goji berries and mixed berries.

tip We used Pureharvest Coco Quench, a blend of coconut and rice milks; it has a thinner consistency than canned coconut milk, but still has a great coconut milk taste.

prep time 10 minutes (+ cooling) makes 1 litre

GREEN TEA & KIWI SIPPER

Brew 2 green tea bags in 2 cups boiling water for 5 minutes. Discard tea bags. Stir in 1 tablespoon raw honey. Cool in the refrigerator. Place cooled tea in a high-speed blender with 1 cup frozen green grapes, 2 medium (170g) peeled chopped kiwifruit, 1 cup fresh mint leaves and 1 cup firmly packed baby spinach. Blend until smooth. Serve immediately over ice.

tip This drink separates quickly, so it is best made just before serving.

prep + cook time 40 minutes (+ standing) serves 4

Banana pancakes with LABNEH & BLUEBERRY COMPOTE

You will need to start the labneh 2 days ahead, or you can serve the pancakes with Greek-style yoghurt instead.

- 1 medium ripe banana (200g)
- ¼ cup (35g) coconut flour
- ¼ teaspoon bicarbonate of soda (baking soda)
- ¼ teaspoon ground cinnamon
- 2 eggs
- 1 vanilla bean, split lengthways, seeds scraped
- ½ cup (125ml) unsweetened almond milk
- 2 tablespoons coconut oil
- 1 medium banana (200g), extra, sliced thickly
- 2 tablespoons roasted coconut chips

LABNEH

- 500g (1 pound) Greek-style yoghurt
- ½ teaspoon sea salt
- 1 teaspoon finely grated lemon rind

BLUEBERRY COMPOTE

- 1 cup (250ml) apple juice
- ½ cup (75g) coconut sugar
- 2 cups (280g) frozen blueberries

1 Make labneh.

2 Make blueberry compote.

3 Mash banana to a paste in a medium bowl with a fork. Add coconut flour, soda, cinnamon, eggs, vanilla seeds and almond milk; stir to combine.

4 Melt one-third of the coconut oil in a large non-stick frying pan over low-medium heat. Spoon tablespoons of batter into pan, flatten slightly; cook for 2 minutes or until bubbles appear on the surface. Using two spatulas, as mixture is delicate, carefully turn over; cook a further 1 minute or until cooked through. Remove from pan; keep warm. Repeat two more times with remaining coconut oil and batter to make a total of 12 pancakes.

5 Serve pancakes topped with labneh, sliced banana, coconut chips and blueberry compote.

labneh Line a sieve with two layers of muslin (or a clean Chux cloth); place it over a bowl. Stir ingredients together in a small bowl; spoon into the lined sieve. Tie the cloth close to the surface of the yoghurt; refrigerate for 48 hours. (Makes 260g/8½ ounces labneh)

blueberry compote Stir juice and coconut sugar in a medium saucepan over low heat until sugar dissolves. Bring to a simmer; cook for 10 minutes or until reduced to a thin syrup. Add frozen blueberries; stir gently until berries are coated and thawed.

prep + cook time 25 minutes serves 2

Quinoa & pear bircher WITH COCONUT FRUIT SALAD

- 1 tablespoon pepitas (pumpkin seed kernels)
- 1 tablespoon sunflower seeds
- 1 medium pear (230g), grated coarsely
- 1½ cups (120g) quinoa flakes
- ½ cup (125ml) coconut milk
- ½ cup (125ml) unsweetened apple juice

COCONUT FRUIT SALAD

- 1 medium young drinking coconut (900g)
- 50g (1½ ounces) raspberries
- 60g (2 ounces) blueberries
- 1 tablespoon long thin strips of orange rind
- 1 medium orange (240g), peeled, segmented (see tips)

1 Make coconut fruit salad.
2 Stir pepitas and sunflower seeds in a frying pan over medium heat for 2 minutes or until toasted.
3 Combine pear, quinoa flakes, coconut milk, apple juice and reserved coconut water (from coconut fruit salad) in a medium bowl.
4 Divide bircher between two serving bowls; spoon fruit salad on top. Sprinkle with toasted seeds.

coconut fruit salad Insert the tip of a small knife into the soft spot on the base of the coconut, using a twisting action. Place coconut over a glass; drain coconut water. Reserve ½ cup (125ml) for bircher. Wrap coconut in a clean towel, break open with a hammer, or by smashing it onto the floor. Spoon out the soft coconut flesh; slice into thin strips. Combine coconut flesh with remaining ingredients in a small bowl. Cover; refrigerate until required.

tips To segment an orange, cut off the rind with the white pith, following the curve of the fruit. Cut down either side of each segment close to the membrane to release the segment. Young drinking coconuts are available from green grocers and some supermarkets. Look for a freshly squeezed apple juice from single variety apples such as granny smith, as they will have a clean fresh sweet and tart taste.

keeps Store bircher in an airtight container in the fridge for up to 4 days.

prep + cook time 10 minutes serves 2

Super seed bowl
WITH APPLE & YOGHURT

- 2 medium green apples (300g), cut into matchsticks
- 2 tablespoons lemon juice
- ½ cup (125ml) coconut water
- 100g (3 ounces) strawberries, sliced thickly
- ½ cup (140g) Greek-style yoghurt
- 2 tablespoons raw honey

SUPER SEED MIX
- 2 tablespoons sunflower seeds
- 2 tablespoons pepitas (pumpkin seed kernels)
- 1½ tablespoons sesame seeds
- 1½ tablespoons poppy seeds
- 1½ tablespoons chia seeds
- 1½ tablespoons linseeds (flaxseeds)
- 2 tablespoons currants
- 2 tablespoons goji berries

1 Make super seed mix.
2 Combine apple and juice in a medium bowl.
3 Divide apple mixture and half the seed mix between two bowls, add coconut water. Top with strawberries and yoghurt; drizzle with honey and sprinkle with remaining seed mix.
super seed mix Stir sunflower seeds and pepitas in a small frying pan over medium heat for 2 minutes or until lightly golden. Add sesame seeds, poppy seeds, chia seeds and linseeds; stir for 30 seconds or until toasted. Remove from pan; cool. Stir in currants and goji berries. (Makes 1 cup)

tip When in season, you can use pears instead of apples.

keeps Super seed mix can be made ahead. Store seed mix in an airtight container or jar in the fridge for up to 3 months.

prep + cook time 25 minutes serves 2

Baked turkish egg WITH LAMB MINCE

- ¼ cup (60ml) extra virgin olive oil
- 1 medium onion (150g), chopped finely
- 2 cloves garlic, crushed
- ½ teaspoon mixed spice
- ½ teaspoon ground cinnamon
- ¼ teaspoon chilli flakes
- 150g (4½ ounces) minced (ground) lamb
- 1 large tomato (220g), chopped coarsely
- 2 tablespoons lemon juice
- ½ teaspoon stevia granules or norbu (monk fruit sugar)
- 1 tablespoon finely chopped fresh mint
- 1 tablespoon finely chopped fresh flat-leaf parsley
- 4 eggs
- ¼ cup loosely packed fresh micro mint leaves
- ¼ cup loosely packed fresh flat-leaf parsley leaves, extra
- 2 lebanese flatbreads (230g), quartered

CUCUMBER YOGHURT

- ½ lebanese cucumber (130g)
- ½ cup (95g) Greek-style yoghurt
- 1 clove garlic, crushed
- 1 teaspoon finely grated lemon rind

1 Make cucumber yoghurt.

2 Heat 2 tablespoons of the oil in a large frying pan over medium heat; cook onion, garlic, spices and chilli flakes, for 3 minutes or until soft. Add mince; cook, breaking mince up with a wooden spoon, for 5 minutes or until browned. Add tomato, juice and stevia; cook, for 2 minutes. Remove from heat; stir in chopped herbs. Season to taste.

3 Make four indents in mince mixture with the back of a spoon. Carefully crack eggs into indents; season eggs. Cook, covered, over medium heat for a further 6 minutes or until egg whites have set but yolks are still runny.

4 Drizzle baked eggs with remaining oil; top with cucumber yoghurt, micro mint and extra parsley. Serve with flatbread.

cucumber yoghurt Coarsely grate cucumber; squeeze out excess water. Combine cucumber with remaining ingredients in a small bowl; season to taste.

tips This is a great dish for a group, just multiply the recipe. You can use minced beef, pork or chicken instead of the lamb, if you like.

prep + cook time 15 minutes (+ refrigeration) serves 4 (makes 1 litre)

PORRIDGE SHAKE

You will need to start this recipe a day ahead.

- » 1 vanilla bean
- » 1 litre (4 cups) unsweetened almond milk
- » 1 cup (90g) rolled oats
- » 1 tablespoon raw honey
- » ½ teaspoon sea salt
- » 1 tablespoon rolled oats, extra
- » ⅓ cup (24g) flaked almonds
- » ½ teaspoon ground cinnamon

1 Split vanilla beans in half lengthways; using the tip of a small knife, scrape out seeds. Combine vanilla seeds and pod with almond milk, oats and honey in a medium jug. Cover; refrigerate overnight.

2 Preheat oven to 180°C/350°F. Place extra oats on an oven tray; roast for 5 minutes. Add almonds; roast for another 5 minutes or until lightly golden.

3 Discard vanilla bean from milk mixture. Blend or process milk mixture until smooth; stir in salt.

4 Pour shake into four glasses, top with roasted almond mixture; sprinkle with cinnamon. Serve immediately.

tips This recipe is perfect for a breakfast on the go, simply pour into a bottle, jar or jug with a lid and away you go. For a quick version, leave out the oats (and the overnight refrigeration); blend chilled milk, vanilla seeds, honey and salt together. Serve immediately.

prep + cook time 15 minutes makes 2

Banana & chocolate-almond TOASTIE

- 1 tablespoon Natvia
- 4 square slices sourdough bread (180g) (see swap out)
- 20g (1oz) butter, softened
- ¼ cup (70g) almond spread
- 1 teaspoon cacao powder
- 1 medium banana (200g), sliced thinly
- ¼ teaspoon ground cinnamon

1 Preheat a jaffle or sandwich maker.
2 Process Natvia in a spice grinder until consistency of icing sugar.
3 Spread one side of each bread slice with butter.
4 Stir almond spread, cacao and 2 teaspoons powdered Natvia in a small bowl to form a smooth thick paste (reserve any remaining Natvia for another use).
5 Place two slices of bread buttered-side-down on a board; spread half the almond spread mixture on each slice, then top with banana, leaving a 1cm (½-inch) border. Top with remaining bread slices, buttered-side-up.
6 Cook sandwiches in jaffle maker for 5 minutes or until golden. Serve toastie cut in half, dusted with cinnamon.

swap out You can use any bread you prefer – wholemeal, wholegrain and rye would all taste great, just make sure the slices are square to fit the jaffle maker. You can substitute any nut butter of your choice for the almond spread; try with homemade chocolate hazelnut spread (see page 323). Other great alternatives are coconut butter or ricotta, especially if you have a nut allergy.

prep + cook time 30 minutes serves 4

Strawberry & almond SWEET FRITTATA

- 250g (8 ounces) strawberries, hulled
- 1 tablespoon coconut sugar
- 1 vanilla bean
- 6 eggs
- 2 tablespoons coconut sugar, extra
- ⅓ cup (40g) almond meal (ground almonds)
- 10g (½ ounce) butter
- 100g (3 ounces) firm ricotta, crumbled coarsely
- ⅓ cup (55g) dry-roasted almonds, chopped coarsely

1 Thinly slice half the strawberries; cut remaining strawberries in half. Combine halved strawberries with coconut sugar in a small bowl. Reserve sliced strawberries.

2 Split vanilla bean lengthways; using the tip of a knife, scrape the seeds. Reserve vanilla pod for another use (see tips).

3 Place vanilla seeds, eggs, extra coconut sugar and almond meal in a bowl; whisk until combined.

4 Preheat grill (broiler) to high.

5 Melt butter in a 24cm (9½-inch) non-stick ovenproof frying pan over medium heat. Add egg mixture, top with sliced strawberries, ricotta and half the chopped almonds. Reduce heat to low; cook, for 8 minutes or until half set. Place pan under grill for a further 8 minutes or until ricotta is lightly browned and mixture just set.

6 Top with halved strawberries and remaining chopped almonds. Drizzle with some honey and sprinkle with black chia seeds, if you like. Serve immediately.

tip The unused vanilla pod can be wrapped and frozen for up to 1 year. Use in recipes where a vanilla bean is called for.

swap out You can use macadamias and hazelnuts instead of the almonds, if you like.

Make & Save

PORTABLE FOOD

prep time 30 minutes (+ fermentation) makes 1 litre

Water kefir SODA

You will need to start this recipe 4 days ahead.

- 2 tablespoons raw sugar
- ¼ cup (60ml) boiling water
- 1 litre (4 cups) bottled filtered water
- 1 tablespoon hydrated water kefir grains (see tips)
- 1 slice lemon
- 1 dried apricot or fig

1 Sterilise a 1.25 litre (5 cup) glass jar. (For details on 'how to sterilise' see page 485.)
2 Place sugar and the boiling water in sterilised jar; stir until sugar dissolves. Add the filtered water. Check the mixture is now at room temperature; if not, leave to cool further.
3 Add kefir grains, lemon slice and dried fruit; cover top of jar with muslin and secure with an elastic band or kitchen string (this allows kefir to breathe and prevents contamination). Leave jar on a work bench at a stable room temperature for at least 72 hours (see tips).
4 After first ferment, strain liquid into a sterilised 1 litre (4-cup) glass jar or bottle with a tight-fitting lid; add one of the suggested flavour combinations opposite. Seal; leave jar on a work bench at a stable room temperature to ferment for a further 12-24 hours.
5 Refrigerate after second ferment to slow down fermentation process. Strain flavourings before serving.

tips Water kefir grains are available from health food stores or are readily available to purchase online. Freeze leftover grains for up to 12 months. In warmer months kefir will ferment faster. Taste it after 24 hours; it should taste slightly sour. The longer it is left, the more the sugar will be converted to carbon dioxide, and the more sour the taste will be.

keeps Store in the fridge for up to 2 weeks.

FLAVOUR COMBINATIONS

Beetroot
Add 2 thin slices fresh beetroot, cut into julienne, to the strained kefir liquid before second fermenting.

Green apple & spirulina
Add 3 thin slices green apple and ⅛ teaspoon spirulina to the strained kefir liquid before second fermenting.

Fresh turmeric & ginger
Peel and slice a 3cm (1¼-inch) piece fresh turmeric and a 3cm (1¼-inch) piece ginger; add to the strained kefir liquid before second fermenting.

Raspberry
Add 8 fresh raspberries to the strained kefir liquid before second fermenting.

Pineapple & passionfruit
Add one 2cm x 5cm (¾-inch x 2-inch) piece of peeled pineapple and the pulp of 1 passionfruit to the strained kefir liquid before second fermenting.

TRADITIONALLY, KEFIR IS A FERMENTED MILK PRODUCT OF RUSSIAN ORIGIN MADE BY USING A CULTURE OF KEFIR GRAINS, COMPRISING OF A NUMBER OF DIFFERENT BACTERIA AND YEASTS. THE YEASTS FERMENT THE SUGAR IN MILK TO CREATE CARBON DIOXIDE AND ALCOHOL. THESE KEFIR GRAINS CAN BE USED WITH OTHER LIQUIDS TO CREATE AN EFFERVESCENT MIXTURE, HOWEVER, FOR THIS TO WORK SOME SUGAR NEEDS TO BE PRESENT, WHICH IS THEN MOSTLY CONVERTED TO CARBON DIOXIDE, PRODUCING A REFRESHING HEALTHY, SPARKLING DRINK.

prep + cook time 1 hour (+ standing) makes 18

PB & J chickpea COOKIES

BISCUITS HAVE A REPUTATION FOR BEING FAT AND SUGAR TRAPS BUT NOT THESE GUYS! WHILE THEY DO OF COURSE CONTAIN SOME FAT, THE FAT IN NUTS IS CONSIDERED TO BE A 'GOOD FAT'. ADD TO THAT THE PROTEIN POWER OF CHICKPEAS AND CHIA SEEDS, AND YOU HAVE A GREAT PICK-ME-UP COOKIE FOR MID-MORNING LULLS, 3PM SLUMPS, OR POST-WORK OUT.

- 2 tablespoons Natvia
- 400g (12½ ounces) can chickpeas
- ½ cup (140g) crunchy natural peanut butter
- 1 teaspoon pure vanilla extract
- 1 teaspoon baking powder
- ½ teaspoon sea salt

RASPBERRY CHIA JAM

- 2 teaspoons Natvia
- ½ cup (75g) frozen raspberries, thawed
- 1 tablespoon water
- 1 tablespoon white chia seeds

1 Make raspberry chia jam.
2 Preheat oven to 180°C/350°F. Line two oven trays with baking paper.
3 Blend Natvia in a high speed blender until consistency of icing sugar.
4 Drain chickpeas over a bowl; reserve ¼ cup (60ml) liquid (aquafaba, see tip). Process drained chickpeas, aquafaba, peanut butter, powdered Natvia, vanilla, baking powder and salt, scraping down side of the food processor bowl several times, until smooth.
5 Using damp hands, roll tablespoonfuls of mixture into balls, place on trays; flatten with the palm of your hand into a 5cm (2-inch) round. Spoon 1 teaspoon raspberry chia jam onto centre of each cookie, spread jam leaving a ½ cm boarder.
6 Bake cookies for 18 minutes or until lightly browned and a cookie can be gently pushed without breaking. Cool on tray.
raspberry chia jam Process Natvia in a spice grinder until consistency of icing sugar. Blend or process raspberries, powdered Natvia and the water until pureed. Transfer to a bowl; stir in chia seeds. Cover with plastic wrap; refrigerate for at least 1 hour until thickened to a jam-like consistency.

tip Aquafaba is the drained liquid from canned legumes. You can keep aquafaba in the fridge for 2 days or freeze for up to 2 months.

keeps Store cookies in an airtight container in the fridge for up to 4 days.

prep + cook time 15 minutes makes 1⅓ cups

STICKY CHAI TEA

- 2 tablespoons cardamom pods
- 4 cinnamon sticks, broken into pieces
- 8 star anise
- 2 teaspoons fennels seeds
- ⅔ cup (70g) roasted dandelion (see tip)
- 2 tablespoons finely grated fresh ginger
- 2 teaspoons ground turmeric
- 1 teaspoon vanilla bean paste
- ⅓ cup (115g) honey
- 2 tablespoons lemon juice

1 Heat a small frying pan over medium heat. Add cardamom, cinnamon, star anise and fennel seeds; cook, stirring continuously for 2 minutes or until lightly toasted. Grind using a mortar and pestle until crushed finely.
2 Place roasted dandelion in a small bowl; stir through toasted spices, ginger, turmeric and vanilla.
3 Place honey in a small heatproof cup; sit cup in a small bowl of boiling water, stir until thin and runny. Stir honey and lemon juice through dandelion mixture. Transfer chai mix to a small screw-top jar; seal and refrigerate.

tip Roasted dandelion is made from the roasted roots and leaves of the dandelion plant. It is available from some supermarkets, health food stores and online.

try this Make a delicious dandy chai for two. Place 1 teaspoon of chai mix and 1 cup water in a small saucepan. Bring to the boil; remove from heat. Add 1 cup of your favourite milk, return pan to medium heat; cook, stirring, until mixture boils. Immediately remove from heat; steep for 3 minutes. Pour into your favourite mugs; serve sprinkled with ground cinnamon.

keeps Store in the fridge for up to 1 month.

prep + cook time 40 minutes makes 25

Rosemary & cacao CRACKERS

- 1½ cups (180g) almond meal (ground almonds)
- 2 tablespoons cacao powder
- 1 teaspoon finely chopped fresh rosemary
- 1 teaspoon sea salt flakes
- 1 tablespoon extra virgin olive oil
- 1 egg
- 1 teaspoon extra virgin olive oil, extra
- 1 tablespoon fresh rosemary leaves, extra

1 Preheat oven to 180°C/360°F.

2 Combine almond meal, sifted cacao, rosemary and ½ teaspoon salt in a large bowl. Whisk oil and egg together in a small bowl, add to cacao mixture; using clean hands, combine well to form a dough.

3 Shape dough into a ball; place between two sheets of baking paper. Roll out to a 2mm (⅛ inch) thick, 20cm x 30cm (8-inch x 12-inch) rectangle. Transfer dough on paper to a large oven tray; remove top sheet of baking paper.

4 Using a sharp knife, trim the edges of the dough straight; cut into five lengthways and crossways to make 25 pieces, 4cm x 6cm (1½-inch x 2½-inch) in size. Brush with extra olive oil. Sprinkle with extra rosemary and remaining salt.

5 Bake crackers, rotating tray halfway through cooking time, for 20 minutes or until golden. Cool on tray.

try this with a sugar-free dip or your favourite cheese, such as parmesan, brie or cheddar.

keeps Store crackers in an airtight container for up to 5 days.

prep time 1 hour (+ standing & freezing) makes 15 sandwiches

Coconut & vanilla ICE-CREAM SANDWICHES

You will need to start this recipe 2 days ahead.

- ⅔ cup (160ml) coconut cream
- 1 cup (150g) raw cashews
- 3 young drinking coconuts (3.6kg)
- ½ cup (125ml) rice malt syrup
- ¼ cup (60ml) coconut cream, extra
- 3 teaspoons pure vanilla extract
- 1 vanilla bean, split lengthways, seeds scraped
- 200g (7 ounces) dark (semi-sweet) vegan chocolate, chopped coarsely
- 1 tablespoon coconut oil, melted, extra

CHOCOLATE BISCUITS

- ¾ cup (120g) natural almonds
- ¾ cup (130g) activated buckwheat groats
- ⅔ cup (50g) desiccated coconut
- ½ cup (50g) cacao powder
- ⅓ cup (80ml) pure maple syrup
- ¼ cup (50g) coconut oil, melted
- ½ teaspoon pure vanilla extract

1 To make the coconut ice-cream, pour coconut cream into an ice-cube tray and freeze overnight.
2 Meanwhile, place cashews in a medium bowl; cover with cold water. Stand for 4 hours or overnight. Drain cashews, rinse under cold water; drain well.
3 Line an 18cm x 28cm (7¼-inch x 11¼-inch) slice pan with plastic wrap, extending the plastic 5cm (2 inches) over the sides.
4 Place a coconut on its side on a chopping board; carefully cut off the dome-shaped top with a cleaver – you will need to use a bit of force. Drain coconut water into a large jug. Spoon out the soft flesh. Repeat with remaining coconuts; you should have about 3 cups (270g) coconut flesh.
5 Blend coconut flesh with drained cashews, syrup, extra coconut cream, vanilla extract and seeds until as smooth as possible, using a high-powered blender if available; this type of blender will produce a very smooth consistency. Add coconut cream ice-cubes; blend until well combined. Pour into lined pan. Freeze overnight or until firm.
6 Make chocolate biscuits.
7 Remove ice-cream from pan. Cut into 15 rounds using a 5cm (2-inch) cutter. Place a round of ice-cream on half the biscuits, flatten slightly and sandwich with a second biscuit.
8 Place chocolate in a small heatproof bowl over a saucepan of gently simmering water (don't allow bowl to touch water); stir until just melted. Add extra coconut oil; stir to combine. Pour melted chocolate into a small deep bowl.
9 Dip ice-cream sandwiches into melted chocolate to half-coat. Allow excess chocolate to drain off, place on a tray lined with baking paper (or balance on egg rings, choc-dipped half facing up); freeze for 10 minutes or until chocolate is set.
chocolate biscuits Process all ingredients until coarse crumbs form and mixture starts to come together. Roll between two sheets baking paper until about 3mm (⅛-inch) thick. Place on oven tray. Freeze for 15 minutes or until firm. Cut into 30 rounds using a 5cm (2-inch) cutter, re-rolling scraps. Return biscuits to tray, cover with plastic wrap; freeze until needed.

prep time 5 minutes (+ standing) makes 1½ cups

Instant stonefruit & PASSIONFRUIT CHIA JAM

THIS IS NOT A PROPER JAM, BUT THAT'S A GOOD THING, SINCE IT MEANS IT'S FAST, FOOLPROOF AND HAS A FRACTION OF THE SUGAR. RATHER THAN RELYING ON THE INTERACTION BETWEEN PECTIN AND SUGAR TO CREATE A GEL, THE NATURAL THICKENING QUALITIES OF CHIA SEEDS PROVIDE A JAM-LIKE QUALITY.

- » 2 tablespoons white chia seeds
- » ⅓ cup (80ml) water
- » 1 tablespoon Natvia
- » 2 ripe peaches or nectarines (300g), chopped coarsely (see tip)
- » ½ vanilla bean, split lengthways, seeds scraped
- » 2 passionfruit, halved, pulp removed

1 Place chia seeds in a small bowl, stir in the water; stand for 5 minutes.
2 Process Natvia in a spice grinder until consistency of icing sugar.
3 Place fruit in a bowl; crush with the back of a fork. Add chia seed mixture and remaining ingredients; stir until combined.

tip Peaches, nectarines, apricots and even plums are all suitable fruit for making this jam.

keeps Store chia jam in an airtight container in the fridge for up to 1 week or freezer for up to 1 month.

try this
Spooned over thick sugar-free coconut or Greek-style yoghurt, with sliced nectarine or peach.
Swirled through a multi-grain porridge.
Spread over ricotta on grainy bread.

prep time 10 minutes (+ standing) makes 1½ cups

Smoked 'cheese' SPREAD

WE'VE CREATED THIS RECIPE WITH VEGANS AND THE DAIRY INTOLERANT IN MIND. THE CHEESE SPREAD IS MULTI-PURPOSE, SEE 'TRY THIS' FOR SUGGESTED USES.

You will need to start this recipe a day ahead.

- ½ cup (75g) raw cashews
- ½ cup (70g) raw macadamias
- 1 tablespoon lemon juice
- 2 tablespoons nutritional yeast flakes
- 1½ teaspoons apple cider vinegar
- 1½ teaspoons smoked paprika
- 1 teaspoon ground turmeric
- ¼ teaspoon onion powder
- ½ teaspoon garlic powder
- ½ cup (125ml) almond and cashew milk
- 1 teaspoon white (shiro) miso paste

1 Place cashews and macadamias in two separate small bowls; cover with cold water. Stand, covered, for 4 hours or overnight. Drain nuts, rinse under cold water; drain well.
2 Blend drained nuts with remaining ingredients, using a high-powered blender if available; this type of blender will produce a very smooth consistency.

tip Nutritional yeast is deactivated yeast that is a complete protein, as it contains 18 amino acids, including the nine that are essential for good health. It is generally fortified with B12, an important nutrient for vegans that is lacking in a meat-free diet. It is available from health food stores.

try this Spoon spread over oven-baked tortillas; serve topped with sugar-free dill pickles, pickled jalapeños, lime wedges and coriander (cilantro).

keeps Store in an airtight container in the fridge for up to 3 weeks.

prep time 5 minutes makes 1 cup (250ml)

Sesame ginger DIPPING SAUCE

- 70g (2½-ounce) piece fresh ginger, grated finely
- ¼ cup (70g) unhulled tahini
- 2 tablespoons sesame oil
- 2 tablespoons tamari
- 2 tablespoons apple cider vinegar
- 2 tablespoons yacon syrup (see tip) or coconut nectar
- ½ fresh long red chilli, seeded, sliced thinly, optional

1 Press grated ginger through a sieve over a small bowl; you need 2 tablespoons ginger juice. Discard pulp.

2 Combine ginger juice with tahini, sesame oil, tamari, vinegar and yacon syrup in a small bowl; stir until smooth. Add chilli, if you like.

tip Yacon syrup is available from some health food stores. It has a consistency similar to rice malt syrup, with a distinct treacle-like flavour and a mild level of sweetness.

try this as a dipping sauce for rice paper rolls or as a dressing on salads, slaws, kelp noodles and steamed vegetables.

keeps Store in a sealed glass jar in the fridge for up to 1 week.

prep + cook time 1 hour 20 minutes (+ standing) serves 6

Cheesy parsnip TEFF BREAD

- 3 cups (375g) grated parsnip
- 1½ cups (240g) ivory teff flour (see tips)
- 1½ cups (180g) grated vintage cheddar
- 1½ teaspoons baking powder
- 3 eggs
- ¾ cup (180ml) milk
- ⅓ cup (80ml) olive oil

1 Preheat oven to 180°C/350°F. Grease a 7cm x 25cm (2¾-inch x 10-inch) loaf pan or 1.25 litre (5 cup) terrine mould. Line base and long sides with baking paper, extending the paper 5cm (2 inches) over long sides.

2 Combine parsnip, teff, cheddar and baking powder in a large bowl. Season. Whisk eggs, milk and oil in a small bowl; stir through parsnip mixture. Spoon into tin; smooth top.

3 Bake for 1 hour 10 minutes or until a skewer inserted into the centre comes out clean; cover loosely with foil halfway through cooking if it starts to overbrown. Stand loaf in pan for 15 minutes before turning, top-side up, onto a wire rack to cool. Slice and toast to serve.

tips Teff flour is derived from the seeds of a hardy grass. It is available from some supermarkets, delis and health food stores. You can use a loaf pan that is slightly longer and narrower, or wider and shorter, as long as the capacity of the pan is close to 5 cups. To check your pan, fill a jug with 5 cups of water and pour into the pan.

try this with different toppings, such as boiled eggs seasoned with salt and pepper, sprinkled with parsley sprigs. For more ideas, see page 113.

keeps Store bread, wrapped in plastic wrap in an airtight container, for up to 3 days.

Teff bread toppings

prep + cooking time 5 minutes serves 2

AVOCADO, GOAT'S CHEESE & PISTACHIO DUKKAH

Top toasted sliced teff bread (see page 110) with a quarter of a sliced avocado, 2 tablespoons marinated goat's cheese, a sprinkle of pistachio dukkah and a few dill sprigs.

prep + cooking time 5 minutes serves 2

SMASHED AVOCADO, KIMCHI & SEEDS

Mash a quarter of an avocado in a small bowl; season to taste. Spread on a slice of toasted teff bread (see page 110), then top with your favourite kimchi and a few pepitas (pumpkin seed kernels) and sunflower seeds.

tip We used Green St Kitchen's black miso and garlic kimchi.

prep time 45 minutes (+ fermentation)

Golden & red SAUERKRAUT

FERMENTATION IS CURRENTLY IN THE SPOTLIGHT DUE TO ITS MEDICINAL AND DIGESTION-ENHANCING BENEFITS. FERMENTED FOODS LIKE SAUERKRAUT CAN CONTRIBUTE TO IMPROVED DIGESTION BY PROVIDING AN ABUNDANCE OF LACTIC ACID BACTERIA, YEASTS AND MOULDS.

GOLDEN SAUERKRAUT

» 1 small white cabbage (1.2kg)
» 3 medium carrots (360g), peeled
» 2 cloves garlic, crushed
» 5cm (2-inch) piece ginger, grated finely
» 5cm (2-inch) piece turmeric, grated finely
» 2 teaspoons caraway seeds
» 2 teaspoons fennel seeds
» 1 tablespoon sea salt

RED SAUERKRAUT

» 1 small red cabbage (1.2kg)
» 2 medium beetroot (beets) (350g), peeled
» 2 cloves garlic, crushed
» 2 teaspoons cumin seeds
» 2 teaspoons juniper berries
» 1 tablespoon sea salt

1 Sterilise two 1.5 litre (6-cup) jars. (For details on 'how to sterilise', see page 485.)
2 For both golden and red sauerkraut, wash exterior of each cabbage, carrot and beetroot well. Pull off two outer layers from each cabbage and reserve.
3 Using a food processor fitted with a fine slicing attachment, slice white cabbage. Change the attachment to a coarse grater; grate carrot. Transfer to a large bowl. Wash food processor bowl; using the fine slicing attachment, slice red cabbage. Using the coarse grater attachment, grate beetroot. Transfer red vegetables to a second large bowl. (If you don't have a food processor with attachments, thinly slice the cabbage with a sharp cook's knife and grate the carrot and beetroot coarsely using a box grater.)
4 Add remaining golden sauerkraut ingredients to the first bowl and remaining red sauerkraut ingredients to the second bowl. Wearing plastic gloves, massage vegetables in each bowl for 15 minutes or until they release their moisture and soften. (Wash gloves in between mixing to avoid transferring flavours and colours between each bowl.)
5 Spoon each sauerkraut mixture tightly into a sterilised jar, pressing it down firmly to remove air pockets and to ensure that the top is covered by cabbage juice. Fold reserved white cabbage leaves in half; place over golden sauerkraut. Repeat with reserved red cabbage leaves for red sauerkraut. Make sure there is about a 1cm (½-inch) gap at the top of the jars for juices to gather. Seal jars.
6 Leave jars to ferment at room temperature for 3-4 weeks (see tips). When sauerkraut is ready it will have an acidic taste and a soft but not mushy texture. Discard the folded cabbage leaves; store sauerkraut in the fridge to halt the fermentation process.

keeps Once fermented, store in the fridge for up to 3 months.

WECK

prep time 10 minutes (+ standing) makes 1 cup

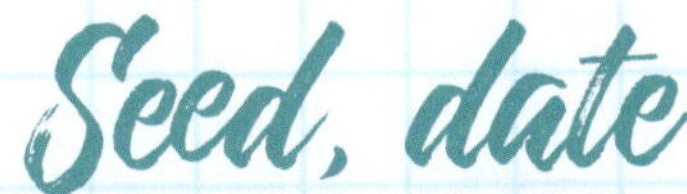

Seed, date & TAHINI SPREAD

- 1 cup (230g) fresh dates, pitted
- ⅓ cup (90g) tahini
- 2 teaspoons sesame seeds
- 2 teaspoons linseeds (flaxseeds)
- 1 teaspoon poppy seeds
- ⅛ teaspoon sea salt flakes

1 Place dates in a small heatproof bowl, cover with boiling water; stand 5 minutes. Drain; reserve 2 tablespoons liquid. Blend or process dates with reserved liquid, tahini, seeds and salt until smooth.

2 Spoon the mixture into a jar and refrigerate.

VARIATION

For a chocolate spread, blend in 1 tablespoon cacao powder with all the ingredients.

try this

Folded through coconut or Greek-style yoghurt for a natural sweet treat.
Spread over pancakes or toast in place of jam.
Stirred into a banana smoothie.
Blended with ricotta as a topping for cakes.

keeps Store spread in an airtight jar in the fridge for up to 6 weeks.

prep time 5 minutes makes 1 cup

MAYONNAISE

THIS AMAZING MAYO IS A BIT OF A GAME-CHANGER FOR VEGANS OR THOSE ALLERGIC TO EGGS WHO HAVE STRUGGLED TO FIND A DECENT MAYO COMPARABLE IN TASTE TO EGG MAYONNAISE.

- ¼ cup (60ml) aquafaba (liquid from canned chickpeas, see tip)
- 1 tablespoon apple cider vinegar
- ½ teaspoon sea salt flakes
- ½ teaspoon dijon mustard
- 1 cup (250ml) sunflower oil

1 Blend aquafaba, vinegar, salt and mustard in a small blender (do not use a food processor) until smooth. With the motor operating, add oil in a slow, steady stream until thick and creamy.
2 Spoon vegan mayonnaise into a jar and refrigerate.

VARIATIONS
lemon aïoli Substitute lemon juice for vinegar and stir in 1 crushed clove garlic and 1 teaspoon finely grated lemon rind at the end.
chipotle Stir in 1 teaspoon Tabasco chipotle hot sauce (or to taste) and 1 teaspoon ground cumin at the end.
green genius Blend in ¼ cup blanched chopped spinach leaves and 2 tablespoons coarsely chopped fresh dill.

tip Aquafaba (bean water) is the drained liquid from canned legumes; we prefer to use chickpeas (garbanzo beans). A 420g (13½-ounce) can will generally provide ½ cup (125ml) aquafaba. Leftover aquafaba will keep refrigerated for up to 2 days.

keeps Store mayonnaise in an airtight container in the fridge for up to 1 month.

Chicken
Fish
Vegetable
Beef

Basic broths

HOT BROTH IS A GREAT HEALTHY ALTERNATIVE TO TEA OR COFFEE. BROTHS CAN BE MADE UP TO 3 DAYS AHEAD; KEEP, COVERED, IN THE REFRIGERATOR, OR FREEZE FOR UP TO 3 MONTHS.

prep + cook time 6¼ hours (+ cooling & refrigeration) makes 3 litres (12 cups)

CHICKEN BROTH

Place 2kg (4lbs) chicken bones, 2 tablespoons apple cider vinegar, 2 coarsely chopped medium brown onions, 2 coarsely chopped trimmed celery stalks, 2 coarsely chopped medium carrots, 8 peeled cloves garlic, 6 stalks fresh flat-leaf parsley, 2 teaspoons black peppercorns and 5 litres (20 cups) water in a large heavy-based saucepan; bring to the boil. Reduce heat to low; simmer for 6 hours, skimming the surface occasionally. Strain stock through a muslin-lined sieve into a heatproof bowl; discard solids. Season with sea salt. Cool. Cover; refrigerate until cold. Skim and discard surface fat before using.

prep + cook time 2¼ hours (+ cooling & refrigeration) makes 3 litres (12 cups)

VEGETABLE BROTH

Place 4 coarsely chopped onions, 2 coarsely chopped large carrots, 8 coarsely chopped trimmed celery stalks, 2 coarsely chopped large parsnips, 8 peeled cloves garlic, 6 stalks fresh flat-leaf parsley, 2 teaspoons black peppercorns and 4 litres (16 cups) water in a large heavy-based saucepan; bring to the boil. Reduce heat to low; simmer for 1½ hours. Add 200g (6½oz) coarsely chopped cup mushrooms and 4 coarsely chopped tomatoes; simmer for a further 30 minutes. Strain stock through a muslin-lined sieve into a heatproof bowl; discard solids. Season with sea salt. Cool. Cover; refrigerate until cold.

prep + cook time 45 minutes (+ cooling & refrigeration) makes 2 litres (8 cups)

FISH BROTH

Place 1.5kg (3lbs) fish bones, 3 litres (12 cups) water, 1 chopped brown onion, 2 coarsely chopped trimmed celery stalks, 6 stalks fresh flat-leaf parsley and 1 teaspoon black peppercorns in a large heavy-based saucepan; bring to the boil. Reduce heat to low; simmer for 30 minutes. Strain stock through a muslin-lined sieve into a heatproof bowl; discard solids. Season with sea salt and 2 tablespoons lemon juice. Cool. Cover; refrigerate until cold. Skim and discard any surface fat before using.

prep + cook time 17 hours (+ cooling & refrigeration) makes 2 litres (8 cups)

SLOW-COOKER BEEF BONE BROTH

Preheat oven to 220°C/450°F. Place 1kg (2lbs) beef bones (cut into short lengths by your butcher) in a roasting pan; roast for 30 minutes or until golden. Transfer to a 5 litre (20-cup) slow cooker set on lowest setting. Add 1 quartered medium brown onion, 2 coarsely chopped, trimmed celery stalks, 3 sprigs fresh thyme, 2 teaspoons black peppercorns and 3.5 litres (14 cups) filtered water; it should fill to 1cm (½-inch) from top. Add 1 tablespoon apple cider vinegar; cook, covered, for 16 hours. Strain stock through a muslin-lined sieve into a heatproof bowl; discard solids. Cool. Cover; refrigerate for 12 hours.

tip Broth may turn to jelly; this is due to the gelatine from bones. Skim and discard surface fat before using, or refrigerate fat for up to 3 days and use instead of oil when roasting vegetables.

prep + cook time 25 minutes (+ standing) makes 2 cups

GOODNESS SMASH

This versatile smash can be used to power-up loads of meals and snacks.

- » 500g (1 pound) frozen broad (fava) beans
- » 1 clove garlic, crushed
- » 1 medium avocado (250g), sliced
- » 2 tablespoons lemon juice
- » 1 nori (seaweed) sheet, crumbled coarsely
- » 1 tablespoon sesame seeds, toasted
- » ½ teaspoon sesame oil

1 Place beans in a large bowl with enough boiling water to cover; stand for 1 minute. Drain; cool under cold running water. Peel skins. Pulse peeled beans just until chopped coarsely.
2 Transfer beans to a medium bowl. Add remaining ingredients; stir to combine. Mash lightly with a fork until avocado is mashed coarsely; season to taste.

try this
Spooned over roasted sweet potato wedges, with mint leaves and lime wedges.
Dolloped over cooked eggs for breakfast.
Stirred through warm or cold soba or green tea noodles.
Spread over rosemary and cacao crackers (see page 101).
With a little extra chopped fresh mint and lemon juice stirred in, for a little more zing.

keeps Cover surface with plastic wrap and store in an airtight container in the fridge for up to 2 days.

prep + cook time 15 minutes makes 1 cup

Salted caramel SAUCE

- 160g (5 ounces) fresh dates, pitted, chopped coarsely
- 270ml (8½ ounces) coconut cream
- ½ vanilla bean, split lengthways, seeds scraped
- ¾ teaspoon fine sea salt

1 Blend all ingredients using a high-powered blender if available; this type of blender will produce a very smooth consistency.
2 Transfer mixture to a small saucepan. Cook, stirring continuously over low heat, for 10 minutes or until thickened.

tip You can add 2 teaspoons cacao powder to the sauce for a hint of chocolate, if you like.

try this
Drizzled over coconut and vanilla ice-cream (see page 102), scooped into halved coconuts, topped with flaked coconut.
Dolloped over a stack of feather-light pancakes.
Swirled through frozen sugar-free yoghurt.
Thinned with a little water to drizzle.
Straight from the jar!

keeps Store salted caramel sauce in an airtight container in the fridge for up to 1 week.

prep time 10 minutes (+ standing) makes 2 litres (8 cups)

Pineapple GINGER BEER

You will need a 25cm (10-inch) piece muslin and to start this recipe 2 days ahead.

- 1 medium pineapple (1.25kg)
- 150g (4½ ounces) fresh ginger, peeled, chopped coarsely
- ½ cup (75g) raisins
- 1 cup (240g) rice malt syrup
- ¼ cup (60ml) lemon juice
- 1.75 litres (7 cups) water
- ¼ teaspoon dried yeast

1 Peel and coarsely chop pineapple, including core.
2 Process pineapple and ginger until chopped finely. Combine with remaining ingredients in a large stainless steel or glass bowl. Cover bowl with muslin; secure with kitchen string. Set aside at room temperature for 36 hours or until mixture is fizzy.
3 Strain into airtight sterilised bottles (see page 485) and refrigerate.

tips You could use a clean plastic bucket to brew the ginger beer if you don't have a large enough bowl. The number of days it takes to become fizzy will vary slightly, depending on room temperature.

keeps Store the ginger beer in the fridge for up to 2 months. Take care when opening, as it will fizz up.

OLÉ!

prep + cook time 40 minutes (+ standing) makes 3 cups

CHILLI SAUCE

PURCHASED SAUCES CAN BE A BIG SUGAR TRAP. OUR VERSION HERE DIALS THE SUGAR BACK, WHILE STILL PACKING A GOOD CHILLI PUNCH. IF YOU WANT TO REDUCE THE HEAT A LITTLE, REMOVE THE SEEDS FROM ALL THE CHILLIES. HOWEVER, BE AWARE THE HEAT LEVEL OF CHILLIES CAN VARY SIMPLY DUE TO GROWING CONDITIONS AND EVEN SEEDING MAY HAVE NO IMPACT ON HEAT REDUCTION.

» 4 bulbs garlic, cloves separated, unpeeled
» 400g (13 ounces) fresh long red chillies, half seeded, all chopped coarsely (see notes above)
» 2 cups (500ml) rice wine vinegar
» ¼ cup (90g) honey
» 2 tablespoons sea salt flakes
» 2 teaspoons cornflour (cornstarch)
» 1 tablespoon tamari

1 Place garlic in a medium saucepan, cover with cold water, bring to the boil; simmer for 1 minute. Scoop garlic from water with a slotted spoon. Rinse under cold water, drain; peel skins. Return to boiling water for 30 seconds; drain again. (Cooking the first time will assist with peeling, blanching the second time helps mellow the garlic flavour.)
2 Combine garlic, chilli and vinegar in same medium saucepan. Bring to the boil; boil for 4 minutes or until chilli is just tender. Remove from heat; stand 10 minutes to cool.
3 Blend or process chilli mixture, honey, salt and cornflour until smooth.
4 Strain chilli mixture through a fine sieve back into same saucepan; discard solids. Bring chilli mixture to the boil. Reduce heat to medium; simmer, stirring occasionally, for 10 minutes or until thickened slightly, to allow flavours to develop. Stir in tamari; cool.

try this
For healthy nachos, spoon over corn chips, guacamole, grilled corn kernels and mixed halved cherry tomatoes and serve with coriander sprigs and lime wedges.
Drizzled over sweet potato hash to complement the sweetness of the potatoes.
Brushed over uncooked prawns with a mix of crushed garlic and lemon grass before grilling.
Stirred through fried brown rice or other rice dishes.

keeps Store in an airtight jar in the fridge for up to 4 months.

Lunch or Dinner

SATISFYING MEAL IDEAS

prep + cook time 1 hour 30 minutes (+ refrigeration) serves 6

Quinoa-crusted KALE & FIG TART

- ¾ cup (150g) tri-coloured quinoa, rinsed
- 1½ cups (120g) finely grated pecorino cheese
- 3 eggs
- 1 teaspoon sea salt flakes
- 1 tablespoon olive oil
- 1 clove garlic, crushed
- 3 cups (70g) firmly packed coarsely chopped kale
- ¼ cup (60ml) water
- 1 tablespoon dijon mustard
- ¾ cup (180ml) pouring cream
- 10 medium figs (600g), torn in half
- 1 cup (40g) loosely packed rocket (arugula) leaves
- ¼ cup (35g) roasted hazelnuts, halved

YOGHURT DRESSING

- ⅓ cup (95g) Greek-style yoghurt
- 1 teaspoon raw honey
- 2 teaspoons chopped fresh tarragon
- ½ clove garlic, crushed

1 Grease an 11cm x 35cm (4½-inch x 14-inch) rectangular loose-based tart tin.
2 Cook quinoa in a saucepan of boiling water for 12 minutes or until tender; drain well. Cool.
3 Process quinoa and half the pecorino until quinoa is finely chopped. Add 1 egg and half the salt; process until mixture forms a coarse dough. Press mixture evenly over base and sides of tart tin. Refrigerate for 30 minutes or until firm.
4 Meanwhile, preheat oven to 200°C/400°F.
5 Bake tart shell for 30 minutes or until golden. Remove from oven; reduce temperature to 180°C/350°F.
6 Meanwhile, heat oil in a medium frying pan over medium heat; cook garlic for 30 seconds. Add kale; cook, stirring, for 30 seconds. Add the water; cook, covered, for 3 minutes. Remove from heat; stand, covered, for 1 minute. Cool; drain away any excess liquid.
7 Place kale mixture in a medium bowl with remaining eggs and salt, half the remaining pecorino, the mustard and cream; whisk to combine. Spread mixture evenly into tart shell; sprinkle with remaining pecorino.
8 Bake tart for 30 minutes or until filling is set. Meanwhile, place figs, cut-side up, on an oiled oven tray; bake alongside tart, for 30 minutes or until just soft.
9 Make yoghurt dressing.
10 Serve tart topped with figs, rocket and hazelnuts; drizzle with dressing.
yoghurt dressing Combine ingredients in a small bowl; season to taste.

prep + cook time 35 minutes makes 12

SWEET POTATO SLIDERS

The sweet potatoes need to be about 7cm (2¾ inches) in diameter, as they will serve as the 'buns' for the sliders.

- » 3 purple-skinned white-fleshed sweet potatoes (1kg), unpeeled
- » ¼ cup (60ml) olive oil
- » 12 large green king prawns (shrimp) (300g), peeled, deveined, with tails intact
- » 2 cups (50g) watercress sprigs
- » ¼ cup fresh micro sorrel leaves
- » ¼ cup fresh coriander (cilantro) leaves
- » 1 tablespoon extra virgin olive oil
- » 1 tablespoon lemon juice
- » 1 medium avocado (250g)

CRAB FILLING

- » 200g (6½ ounces) cooked crab meat
- » ½ cup (60g) crème fraîche
- » ½ clove garlic, crushed
- » 1 green onion (scallion), chopped finely
- » 1 tablespoon finely chopped fresh chives
- » 1 tablespoon nigella seeds
- » 2 tablespoons horseradish cream
- » 1 tablespoon lemon juice

1 Cut eight 8mm (½-inch) thick rounds, from each sweet potato (you need 24 rounds in total); discard tapered ends. Brush rounds with 2 tablespoons of the olive oil; season. Cook rounds, in batches, on a heated chargrill plate (or barbecue) for 6 minutes each side or until cooked through. Remove from heat; keep warm.
2 Make crab filling.
3 Coat prawns in remaining olive oil; season. Cook prawns on heated chargrill plate for 1 minute each side or until just cooked through. Remove from heat; cover to keep warm.
4 Place watercress, sorrel and coriander in a small bowl with extra virgin olive oil and juice. Season; toss to combine. Mash avocado in a small bowl.
5 Place 12 sweet potato rounds on a board; top each with crab filling, a prawn, mashed avocado and watercress salad. Top with remaining sweet potato rounds.
crab filling Combine ingredients in a small bowl; season.

tip We used crème fraîche in the crab filling rather than a commercial aïoli or mayonnaise, as they tend to contain refined sugars.

prep + cook time 35 minutes serves 4

Lamb & walnut pittas
WITH TURKISH SALAD

- 2 tablespoons olive oil
- 250g (8 ounces) minced (ground) lamb
- 2 teaspoons cumin seeds
- 1 clove garlic, crushed
- 3 teaspoons finely chopped fresh rosemary
- ⅓ cup (35g) coarsely chopped walnuts
- ¾ cup (195g) tomato passata
- 4 wholemeal pitta pocket breads
- ½ cup (140g) Greek-style yoghurt
- 2 tablespoons fresh flat-leaf parsley
- 1 tablespoon fresh mint leaves
- 4 lemon wedges

TURKISH SALAD

- 1 cup loosely packed fresh flat-leaf parsley leaves
- 1 cup loosely packed fresh mint leaves
- ¼ cup (40g) pomegranate seeds
- ½ small red onion (50g), sliced thinly
- 80g (2½ ounces) fetta, crumbled

1 Preheat oven to 220°C/425°F. Line two oven trays with baking paper.

2 Heat 1 tablespoon oil in a medium frying pan over high heat. Add lamb, cumin, garlic, rosemary and walnuts; cook, breaking up any lumps with a wooden spoon, for 5 minutes or until browned. Add passata; cook for 1 minute or until warmed through. Season to taste.

3 Place pitta breads on trays, top evenly with lamb mixture; drizzle with remaining oil. Bake pittas for 10 minutes or until crisp and golden.

4 Make turkish salad.

5 Process yoghurt and herbs until smooth; season to taste. Top pittas with salad, drizzle with yoghurt mixture and serve with lemon wedges.

turkish salad Combine all ingredients in a medium bowl. Season to taste.

sugar alert! Check the pitta bread packet label for sugar amounts. Authentic pitta includes an absolute minimum of sugar, while widely available commercial brands can include more. Tomato passata is pureed and sieved Italian tomatoes. Sold in bottles, it contains no added sugar, unlike bottled pasta sauce.

prep + cook time 2 hours 25 minutes serves 6 (makes 10 cups)

Quinoa & brown rice CHICKEN CONGEE

- 1 cup (200g) medium-grain brown rice, rinsed
- 2.5 litres (10 cups) water
- ¼ cup (50g) black or tri-coloured quinoa, rinsed
- 1 litre (4 cups) chicken stock
- 2 green onions (scallions), sliced thinly on the diagonal
- 2 cloves garlic, chopped finely
- 1 tablespoon finely grated ginger
- ½ teaspoon ground white pepper
- 1 tablespoon sesame oil
- 300g (9½ ounces) chicken breast fillet
- ¼ cup (40g) roasted almonds, chopped coarsely
- ¼ cup fresh coriander (cilantro) sprigs
- 2 tablespoons tamari
- extra sesame oil, to serve

1 Place brown rice and the water in a large saucepan; cover with a lid and bring to the boil. Reduce heat to medium; simmer, covered, for 1 hour. Add quinoa, stock, white part of the green onion, garlic, ginger, pepper, sesame oil and salt to taste. Cook, covered, stirring occasionally, for 30 minutes.

2 Add chicken to congee; cook, covered, for 12 minutes or until cooked through. Remove chicken with a slotted spoon; rest, loosely covered with foil, for 10 minutes. Shred chicken into bite-sized pieces.

3 Meanwhile, cook congee, uncovered, stirring occasionally, for a further 30 minutes or until rice has broken down and mixture is a soupy consistency. Add a little boiling water for a thinner consistency, if you like.

4 Ladle congee among bowls, top with chicken, remaining green onion, almonds and coriander sprigs. Serve drizzled with tamari and extra sesame oil.

prep + cook time 30 minutes (+ refrigeration) serves 6

Green gazpacho WITH PISTACHIO CROÛTONS

- 1 medium avocado (250g), chopped
- 50g (1½ ounces) baby spinach
- 360g (11½ ounces) honeydew melon, chopped coarsely
- ¼ cup loosely packed fresh basil leaves
- 2 cloves garlic, crushed
- 10 green onions (scallions), white part only, chopped coarsely
- 200g (6½ ounces) seedless green grapes
- 2 fresh long green chillies, chopped coarsely
- 750g (1½ pounds) green heirloom tomatoes, chopped coarsely
- 1 telegraph cucumber (400g), chopped coarsely
- 2 tablespoons white wine vinegar
- ¼ cup (60ml) extra virgin olive oil
- 8 ice cubes
- ¼ cup small fresh basil leaves, extra

PISTACHIO CROÛTONS

- ¼ cup (60ml) olive oil
- 1 clove garlic, crushed
- 4 slices seeded rye bread (260g), cut into 1cm (½-inch) cubes
- ¼ cup (35g) pistachios, chopped

1 Make pistachio croûtons.

2 Blend avocado, spinach, melon, basil, garlic, green onion, grapes, chilli, tomato and cucumber, in two batches. Strain through a fine sieve over a large bowl, pressing down to extract as much liquid as possible. Discard solids. Whisk in vinegar, half the oil and the ice cubes; season to taste. Refrigerate for 30 minutes or until chilled.

3 Serve gazpacho in chilled bowls or glasses, topped with pistachio croûtons, extra basil leaves and remaining oil.

pistachio croûtons Heat oil in a small frying pan over medium heat; cook garlic for 30 seconds. Add bread and pistachios; cook, stirring, for 5 minutes or until golden. Remove from pan; cool.

keeps The gazpacho can be made up to 2 days ahead, store in an airtight container in the fridge; stir before serving.

prep + cook time 25 minutes (+ cooling) serves 4

Fennel, apple & PISTACHIO CHICKEN SALAD

WHEN POACHING CHICKEN, IT IS EASY TO OVERCOOK IT AND MAKE IT TOUGH. THE SECRET TO KEEPING IT TENDER AND MOIST IS TO FINISH OFF THE COOKING IN THE GENTLE RESIDUAL HEAT OF THE PAN. THIS METHOD ALSO WORKS WELL WHEN YOU ARE COOKING FISH.

- 2 cups (500ml) chicken stock
- 2 cups (500ml) water
- 4 thin slices lemon
- 4 cloves garlic, bruised (see tips)
- 6 fresh thyme sprigs
- 2 x 200g (6½-ounce) free-range chicken breasts
- ½ cup (125ml) lemon juice
- 1 tablespoon dijon mustard
- ⅓ cup (80ml) extra virgin olive oil
- 1 small bulb fennel (130g), sliced thinly
- 1 medium apple (150g), sliced thinly
- 1 cup (40g) trimmed watercress
- 1 cup firmly packed fresh flat-leaf parsley leaves
- 1 cup firmly packed torn fresh mint
- 1 medium avocado (250g), sliced thinly
- ½ cup (60g) pistachios, chopped coarsely

1 Place stock, the water, lemon slices, garlic and thyme in a medium saucepan over medium heat. Add chicken; bring to the boil. Reduce heat; simmer for 4 minutes. Cover pan, turn off heat; set aside to cool to room temperature. Remove chicken; shred coarsely. (Reserve poaching liquid for another use; see tips.)

2 Whisk juice and mustard in a small bowl until combined; gradually whisk in oil until combined. Season to taste.

3 Combine fennel, apple, watercress, herbs and avocado in a large bowl. Add chicken and dressing; toss to combine. Season to taste. Serve salad topped with pistachios.

tips To bruise garlic, place the flat side of a cook's knife on the unpeeled clove; using the heel of your other hand push down on the knife to flatten it. Remove the skin. Store the reserved poaching liquid in the refrigerator for up to 3 days.

prep + cook time 1 hour (+ standing & refrigeration) serves 6

Quinoa, kale & fetta PATTY WRAPS

PREPARED RELISHES AND CHUTNEYS CONTAIN VAST AMOUNTS OF SUGAR SO THERE IS GOOD REASON TO MAKE YOUR OWN. OUR QUICK VERSION USES THE NATURAL SWEETNESS OF BEETROOT.

- ¾ cup (150g) white quinoa, rinsed
- 1¼ cups (310ml) water
- 1 small zucchini (90g), grated coarsely
- 1 teaspoon fine sea salt
- 120g (4 ounces) fetta, crumbled coarsely
- ¾ cup (80g) parmesan, grated finely
- 3 eggs, beaten lightly
- 1 cup (35g) loosely packed shredded curly kale
- ⅓ cup coarsely chopped fresh flat-leaf parsley
- ½ cup (35g) day-old sourdough breadcrumbs
- 1 clove garlic, crushed
- 2 teaspoons finely grated lemon rind
- ¼ cup (60ml) olive oil
- 4 wholegrain barley wraps (180g)
- ½ cup (140g) Greek-style yoghurt
- 1 medium lemon (140g), cut into wedges

BEETROOT RELISH

- 1 teaspoon cumin seeds
- 1 medium beetroot (beet) (175g), cut into thin matchsticks
- ¼ cup (60ml) sherry vinegar
- ½ medium red onion (75g), sliced thinly
- 2 tablespoons extra virgin olive oil
- 1 tablespoon fresh thyme leaves

1 Place quinoa and the water in a small saucepan over medium heat; bring to the boil. Reduce heat to low; cook, covered, for 15 minutes or until water is absorbed. Remove from heat; stand covered, for 10 minutes. Spread over a tray; cool.
2 Combine zucchini and salt in a small sieve over a small bowl; stand for 30 minutes.
3 Meanwhile, make beetroot relish.
4 Squeeze zucchini to remove excess liquid. Combine zucchini, quinoa, fetta, parmesan, egg, kale, parsley, breadcrumbs, garlic and rind in a medium bowl; season. Cover; refrigerate for 1 hour.
5 Preheat oven to 160°C/325°F. Line an oven tray with baking paper.
6 Using damp hands, shape firmly packed ⅓-cups of mixture into patties; place on tray. Cover; refrigerate for 1 hour to firm.
7 Heat half the oil in a large frying pan over medium heat; cook half the patties, for 3 minutes each side or until golden and cooked through. (Take care turning the patties as the mixture is quite delicate.) Transfer to the oven tray; keep warm in the oven. Repeat with remaining oil and patties.
8 Serve quinoa patties with beetroot relish, wraps, yoghurt and lemon wedges.
beetroot relish Stir cumin seeds in a small frying pan over medium heat for 30 seconds or until fragrant and toasted. Pound seeds using a mortar and pestle until coarsely crushed. Transfer to a medium bowl; add remaining ingredients; stir until combined. Season to taste.

keeps Patties can be made up to 2 days ahead; cover and refrigerate until required.

prep + cook time 40 minutes serves 4

Zucchini & ricotta fritters WITH CARROT RELISH

- 600g (1¼ pounds) zucchini, grated coarsely
- 1 tablespoon sea salt flakes
- 2 cloves garlic, crushed
- 2 green onions (scallions), chopped finely
- 2 tablespoons coarsely chopped fresh mint
- 2 eggs
- 2 teaspoons finely grated lemon rind
- ¾ cup (90g) almond meal (ground almonds)
- ½ cup (120g) firm ricotta
- ¼ cup (60ml) olive oil
- 100g (3 ounces) baby rocket (arugula)

CARROT RELISH

- 2 tablespoons olive oil
- 2 cloves garlic, crushed
- ¼ teaspoon chilli flakes
- 3 medium carrots (360g), cut into thin matchsticks
- ¼ cup (40g) currants
- 2 tablespoons norbu (monk fruit sugar)
- ¼ cup (60ml) red wine vinegar
- ½ cup (125ml) water
- 1 teaspoon ground cardamom
- 400g (12½ ounces) vine-ripened tomatoes, seeded, chopped coarsely

1 Combine zucchini and salt in a medium bowl. Stand for 15 minutes.

2 Meanwhile, make carrot relish.

3 Squeeze excess liquid from zucchini. Combine zucchini with garlic, green onion, mint, eggs, rind, almond meal and ricotta in a medium bowl; season.

4 Heat half the oil in a large frying pan over medium heat. Pour heaped ¼-cups fritter mixture into pan; cook for 3 minutes each side or until golden and cooked through. Remove from pan; cover to keep warm. Repeat with remaining oil and fritter mixture to make a total of 12 fritters.

5 Serve fritters topped with relish and rocket.

carrot relish Heat oil in a large frying pan over medium-high heat; cook garlic and chilli flakes for 30 seconds. Add carrot; cook for 3 minutes. Stir in currants, norbu, vinegar, the water and cardamom; cook for 6 minutes or until liquid has evaporated. Stir in tomatoes; cook a further 2 minutes or until softened slightly. Season. Cool.

keeps The relish can be stored for up to 2 weeks in an airtight container in the fridge.

Shakshuka

prep + cook time 25 minutes serves 2

BASIC SHAKSHUKA

Finely chop 8 stalks of fresh flat-leaf parsley; reserve parsley leaves. Heat 2 tablespoons olive oil in a large 28cm (11¼-in) wide, 26cm (10½-in) base frying pan, over medium heat. Add chopped stalks, 1 finely chopped medium onion, 2 cloves crushed garlic, 1½ teaspoons sea salt flakes, 1 teaspoon cracked black pepper, 1½ teaspoons ground cumin and 1½ teaspoons smoked paprika; cook, stirring for 3 minutes or until soft. Add 800g (1lb) canned tomatoes; reduce heat to low, simmer for 8 minutes. Make four indents in the sauce and break in 4 eggs; season. Reduce heat to low; cook, covered, for 6 minutes or until egg whites are just set. Chop parsley leaves: sprinkle over shakshuka to serve.

prep + cook time 25 minutes serves 2

WHITE BEAN SHAKSHUKA WITH AVOCADO

Make shakshuka using the ingredients and method for basic recipe (see left), except: substitute ½ teaspoon crushed fennel seeds for smoked paprika; fresh coriander (cilantro) stalks for parsley; and add 400g (12½oz), canned cannellini beans, drained and rinsed, with the canned tomatoes. While shakshuka is cooking, dice flesh from 1 medium avocado; combine with 1 tablespoon lime juice. Top cooked shakshuka with avocado mixture and 1 tablespoon coarsely chopped fresh coriander (cilantro) leaves; season with sea salt and freshly ground black pepper.

prep + cook time 25 minutes serves 2

SPICY EGGPLANT SHAKSHUKA

Cut 1 medium eggplant into 1cm (¾-in) cubes. Heat ½ cup olive oil in a 28cm (11¼-in) wide, 26cm (10½-in) base frying pan over medium heat. Add eggplant, 2 tablespoons finely chopped flat-leaf parsley stalks, 1 finely chopped medium onion, 2 cloves crushed garlic, ½ teaspoon chilli flakes and 1½ teaspoons each ground cumin and smoked paprika. Cook, stirring, for 6 minutes or until eggplant is soft. Add 800g (1½lb) canned tomatoes, reduce heat to low; simmer for 8 minutes, stirring occasionally. Make four indents in eggplant mixture; break in 4 eggs and season to taste. Reduce heat to low. Cook, covered, for 6 minutes or until eggs begin to set. Process ½ cup plain Greek-style yoghurt, ¼ cup chopped fresh flat-leaf parsley and 2 pickled japaleño chillies in a small food processor until smooth. Drizzle over shakshuka, top with 2 tablespoons chopped flat-leaf parsley; season.

prep + cook time 30 minutes serves 4

GREEN GOODNESS SHAKSHUKA

Heat 2 tablespoons olive oil in a large frying pan over medium heat; cook 1 thinly sliced medium leek (350g), 1 clove thinly sliced garlic, 1 trimmed, thinly sliced baby fennel (130g), reserving fronds, and 150g (4½oz) coarsely chopped green kale, stirring occasionally, for 5 minutes or until vegetables soften. Stir in ½ cup (125ml) vegetable stock; bring to a simmer. Using the back of a spoon, make eight shallow indents in the mixture; break in 8 eggs. Reduce heat to low; cook, covered, for 6 minutes or until egg whites are set and yolks remain runny, or until cooked to your liking. Season. Top shakshuka with ½ cup (125g) drained labne and ¼ cup (60g) halved spicy green olives; sprinkle with a pinch of sumac and reserved fennel fronds. Serve with char-grilled pitta bread, if you like.

tip You can use silver beet (swiss chard) or spinach instead of the kale, if you prefer.

prep + cook time 1 hour 15 minutes serves 4

Simple satay SALAD JARS

- » ½ bunch kale (150g)
- » 2 teaspoons olive oil
- » ⅓ cup (50g) black rice (see tip)
- » 2 tablespoons coconut oil
- » 1 shallot, chopped finely
- » 1 clove garlic, crushed
- » 2 teaspoons finely grated fresh ginger
- » 1 fresh small red chilli, seeded, chopped finely
- » ½ cup (140g) smooth peanut butter
- » 1 tablespoon tamari
- » 2 teaspoons honey
- » 270ml can coconut milk
- » 2 tablespoons lime juice
- » 300g (9½ ounces) soft tofu, crumbled
- » ¼ medium red cabbage (160g), shredded thinly
- » 1 large carrot (180g), julienned

1 Preheat oven to 120°C/250°F fan-forced. Line an oven tray with baking paper.

2 Tear leaves from kale, toss with olive oil; season to taste. Place on tray; roast for 30 minutes or until dry and crisp.

3 Meanwhile, cook rice in a saucepan of boiling salted water for 35 minutes or until tender; drain.

4 Heat 1 tablespoon of the coconut oil in a small saucepan over medium heat. Cook shallot, garlic, ginger and chilli, stirring, for 2 minutes or until soft. Stir in peanut butter, tamari and honey until smooth. Add coconut milk and lime juice; stir to combine. Simmer gently over low heat for 5 minutes or until thickened.

5 Heat remaining coconut oil in a small saucepan over high heat. Add tofu; cook, stirring continuously, for 5 minutes or until warmed through. Season to taste.

6 Layer satay sauce, cabbage, tofu, rice and carrot evenly in four 1-cup (250ml) jars. Serve topped with crisp kale.

tip Black rice is available from supermarkets. It has a nutty taste and slightly firmer texture than white rice. Once cooked, it takes on a purple hue. Substitute with cooked quinoa, if you like.

prep + cook time 35 minutes serves 4

Chilli lime snapper WITH CORN SALSA SALAD

- » ¼ cup (60ml) olive oil
- » 1 clove garlic, sliced thinly
- » 1 fresh long green chilli, seeded, chopped finely
- » 1 teaspoon finely grated lime rind
- » 4 x 180g (5½-ounce) boneless, skinless snapper fillets
- » 2 corn cobs (250g), husks removed
- » 6 red radishes (90g), sliced thinly
- » 45g (1½ ounces) snow pea sprouts, trimmed
- » 1 green onion (scallion), sliced thinly
- » ¼ cup fresh coriander (cilantro) leaves
- » 1 tablespoon lime juice
- » 1 tablespoon white balsamic vinegar or white vinegar
- » 1 tablespoon olive oil, extra
- » 1 medium avocado (250g), sliced
- » lime cheeks, to serve

1 Combine 2 tablespoons of the oil with garlic, chilli and rind in a large bowl; add snapper, turn to coat. Set aside.

2 Brush corn cobs with remaining oil; cook on a heated chargrill plate (or barbecue), turning every 2 minutes, for 8 minutes or until corn is cooked and lightly charred. Cool.

3 Place radish, sprouts, green onion and coriander in a bowl of iced water to crisp.

4 Cut kernels from cooled cobs; place in a large bowl with juice, vinegar and extra oil. Remove radish mixture from water with a slotted spoon; drain on paper towel. Add to corn mixture, season to taste; toss gently to combine.

5 Line the chargrill plate with baking paper (ensure paper doesn't extend over the edge); cook snapper on heated plate, for 2 minutes each side or until just cooked through.

6 Serve snapper with corn salsa salad, avocado and lime cheeks.

swap out You can use any fish fillets you like or even prawns for this recipe.

prep + cook time 1 hour serves 6 (makes 30 falafel)

Seeded cauliflower FALAFEL

- ½ cup (100g) pepitas (pumpkin seed kernels)
- ½ cup (75g) sunflower seeds
- ¼ cup (35g) sesame seeds
- 2 tablespoons linseeds (flaxseeds)
- 700g (1½ pounds) cauliflower, cut into florets
- 2 cloves garlic, crushed
- 1½ tablespoons cumin seeds, crushed
- 1½ tablespoons coriander seeds, crushed
- ½ cup loosely packed fresh mint leaves
- ½ cup loosely packed fresh flat-leaf parsley leaves
- ½ cup (140g) tahini
- 2 tablespoons psyllium husks (see tips)
- 2 tablespoons lemon juice
- ¼ cup (60ml) water
- rice bran oil, for deep-frying

SALAD

- 1 small red onion (100g), sliced thinly into rings
- 250g (8 ounces) grape tomatoes, sliced crossways
- ¼ cup (60ml) red wine vinegar
- 140g (4½ ounces) Persian fetta

HUMMUS

- 400g (12½ ounces) canned chickpeas (garbanzo beans), undrained, reserve ¼ cup to serve
- ¼ cup (70g) tahini
- 1 clove garlic
- 1½ tablespoons lemon juice
- 1 teaspoon cumin seeds, crushed

1 Make salad and hummus.
2 Heat a medium frying pan over medium-high heat, add pepitas, sunflower seeds, sesame seeds and linseeds; cook, stirring, for 2 minutes or until sesame seeds are golden.
3 Process toasted seeds with cauliflower and remaining ingredients (except rice bran oil) to a coarse paste; season well. Line an oven tray with baking paper. Using a dessert spoon, scoop up a mound of mixture. Hold a second dessert spoon the same size upside down and drag it over the falafel mixture in an arc shape as you reach the other side, bring the top of the spoon under the scoop of falafel mixture transferring it onto it in the process. Using the first spoon, push the quenelle-shaped falafel onto the tray. Repeat with the remaining mixture.
4 Fill a medium saucepan two-thirds full with oil, heat to 160°C/325°F (or until oil sizzles when a small cube of bread is added). Fry, six falafel at a time, for 5 minutes or until dark golden and cooked through. Drain on paper towel.
5 Spoon hummus onto plates, top with reserved chickpeas, falafel and salad. Sprinkle with extra mint and parsley, if you like. Season to taste.
salad Place onion, tomatoes and vinegar in a small bowl; stand for 30 minutes. Stir in fetta.
hummus Process chickpeas and canning liquid with remaining ingredients for 3 minutes or until smooth. Season to taste.

tips Psyllium husks are obtained from the seeds of a plant native to India. They are useful for their binding qualities and are a good source of dietary fibre. Buy at vitamin and health food shops.

prep + cook time 50 minutes serves 4

Healthy brown rice KEDGEREE

- 1.5 litres (6 cups) water
- 3 x 200g (6½-ounce) skinless, boneless salmon fillets
- 2 cups (400g) medium-grain brown rice
- 4 eggs, at room temperature
- ¼ cup (60ml) olive oil
- 1 medium brown onion (150g), chopped finely
- 2 cloves garlic, crushed
- 1 teaspoon finely grated fresh ginger
- 1½ tablespoons jalfrezi curry paste (see tip)
- 2 tablespoons water, extra
- 1 cup (50g) loosely packed baby spinach
- 1 fresh long red chilli, sliced thinly
- ½ cup loosely packed fresh coriander (cilantro)
- 2 medium limes (180g), cut into cheeks
- ½ cup (140g) Greek-style yoghurt

1 Bring the water to the boil in a medium saucepan over high heat. Add salmon; reduce heat to low, simmer for 5 minutes or until salmon is just cooked. Remove salmon from water; keep warm. Reserve cooking water.
2 Add rice to reserved cooking water; bring to the boil. Reduce heat; simmer, uncovered, for 25 minutes or until tender. (If the rice becomes too dry during cooking, add ½ cup water.)
3 Meanwhile, place eggs in a small saucepan of cold water; bring to the boil. Boil for 7 minutes; drain, rinse under cold running water. Peel eggs; cut in half.
4 Heat 2 tablespoons of the oil in a large, deep frying pan over medium heat; cook onion, stirring occasionally, for 8 minutes or until onion has softened. Add garlic, ginger and curry paste; cook for 4 minutes or until paste has darkened slightly. Fold through rice with remaining oil, the extra water, spinach, flaked salmon and eggs; cook for 2 minutes or until spinach is wilted and salmon is heated through. Season to taste.
5 Top kedgeree with chilli, coriander and lime cheeks; serve with yoghurt.

tip Jalfrezi curry paste is available from Asian food stores.

prep + cook time 35 minutes serves 4

Zucchini noodle BEEF PHO

USE OUR BEEF BONE BROTH RECIPE ON PAGE 121 AS THE BASE FOR THIS AROMATIC VIETNAMESE SOUP OR, IF PREFERRED, USE A GOOD-QUALITY PURCHASED BROTH OR STOCK.

- 1 litre (4 cups) beef bone broth (see notes above)
- 2 cups (500ml) water
- 5cm (2-inch) piece fresh ginger, sliced thinly
- 2 cloves garlic, sliced thinly
- 1 star anise
- 2 cinnamon sticks, broken
- 2 tablespoons fish sauce
- ½ teaspoon unrefined sugar (see tips)
- 4 small zucchini (360g), spiralised into noodles (see tips)
- 400g (12½-ounce) piece beef fillet, sliced thinly
- 1 fresh long red chilli, sliced thinly
- 1 cup (80g) bean sprouts
- 1 cup fresh thai basil leaves
- 1 cup fresh mint leaves
- 1 cup fresh coriander (cilantro) leaves
- 4 green onions (scallions), sliced thinly

1 Place broth, the water, ginger, garlic, spices, fish sauce and sugar in a large saucepan; bring to the boil. Reduce heat to low-medium; simmer for 20 minutes. Strain through a fine sieve into a large heatproof bowl; discard solids.
2 Divide zucchini noodles among bowls; top with raw sliced beef and ladle over hot stock. Serve topped with chilli, bean sprouts, herbs and green onion.

tips To balance out flavours, a little sweetener is required; add the unrefined sweetener of your choice. Spiralisers are available from kitchen and homeware stores. Alternatively, you can cut the zucchini into julienne (matchsticks), using a mandoline or sharp knife.

prep + cook time 1 hour 10 minutes serves 2

Super greens CHICKEN SALAD

For four or six people, simply double or triple the recipe to suit your needs.

» 175g (5½ ounces) broccolini
» 220g (7 ounces) green beans, halved lengthways
» 110g (3½ ounces) snow peas
» 3 cups (750ml) water
» 2 cloves garlic
» 2cm (¾-inch) piece fresh ginger, sliced
» 200g (6½-ounce) chicken breast fillet
» 1½ tablespoons matcha (green tea) powder

WASABI PUFFS

» 1 egg white
» 1 tablespoon tamari
» 1 teaspoon wasabi paste
» ¼ teaspoon sea salt flakes
» 1 cup (35g) puffed rice
» 1 cup (140g) slivered almonds
» 1 tablespoon black sesame seeds
» 1 nori (seaweed) sheet, cut into thin strips

AVOCADO DRESSING

» 1 medium avocado (250g)
» 3 teaspoons unhulled tahini
» 1½ tablespoons olive oil
» 1½ tablespoons lime juice
» 1 teaspoon sesame oil

1 Make wasabi puffs.
2 Cook broccolini and beans in a saucepan of boiling water for 3 minutes; add snow peas, cook for a further 1 minute or until vegetables are just tender. Drain, cool under cold running water; drain.
3 Place the water, garlic and ginger in a small saucepan; bring to the boil. Add chicken, return to the boil; reduce heat to low. Add matcha; cook, covered, for 10 minutes or until chicken is cooked through. Cool chicken in liquid for 10 minutes; remove and slice thinly. Discard the cooking liquid.
4 Meanwhile, make avocado dressing.
5 Arrange vegetables and chicken on a platter or large plate, top with a generous spoonful of avocado dressing; scatter with wasabi puffs. Serve with remaining dressing.

wasabi puffs Preheat oven to 150°C/300°F. Line an oven tray with baking paper. Whisk egg white, tamari, wasabi and salt in a small bowl until combined. Place rice, almonds and seeds in a medium bowl; pour over wet mixture. Spread wasabi mixture evenly over lined oven tray. Roast for 20 minutes or until crisp. Cool; stir in nori.

avocado dressing Process all ingredients until combined and as smooth as possible. Season to taste. (Makes ¾ cup)

keeps Store wasabi puffs in an airtight container in the pantry for up to 2 weeks.

prep + cook time 35 minutes serves 4

Broad bean TARTINE

- 200g (6½ ounces) cherry truss tomatoes
- 100g (3 ounces) mixed cherry tomatoes, halved
- ⅓ cup (80ml) olive oil
- 300g (9½ ounces) frozen broad (fava) beans
- 4 large thick slices seeded rye sourdough (260g)
- 1 buffalo mozzarella (250g), torn into pieces
- ¼ cup loosely packed fresh baby mint leaves
- 2 tablespoons fresh oregano leaves
- 1 teaspoon finely grated lemon rind (see tip)
- 1 clove garlic, crushed
- 1 tablespoon sherry vinegar
- 80g (2½ ounces) prosciutto
- ½ cup snow pea tendrils

1 Preheat oven to 200°C/400°F. Line an oven tray with baking paper.

2 Make a small cut in the base of each whole tomato; squeeze out seeds. Combine all tomatoes with 1 tablespoon of the oil in a medium bowl; season. Place on tray; roast for 10 minutes or until tomatoes are blistered and softened.

3 Meanwhile, cook broad beans in a saucepan of boiling water for 1 minute; drain, cool under cold running water. Peel away the skins.

4 Brush bread slices with 2 tablespoons of the olive oil; season. Place bread on a hot chargrill plate (or under the grill), for 2 minutes each side or until lightly charred.

5 Place broad beans and roasted tomatoes in a medium bowl with mozzarella, herbs, rind, garlic, vinegar and remaining oil; season. Toss to combine.

6 Just before serving, place prosciutto, broad bean salad and snow pea tendrils on grilled bread.

tip If you have one, use a zester to cut the lemon rind into long thin strips.

prep + cook time 35 minutes serves 4

Hawaiian brown rice POKE BOWL

POKE, PRONOUNCED POH-KEY, IS A TRADITIONAL HAWAIIAN DISH OF MARINATED RAW FISH AND RICE. AS WITH ANY RAW FISH DISH, IT'S IMPORTANT THAT THE SEAFOOD IS IMPECCABLY FRESH. WE SERVED THIS IN HOLLOWED OUT HALVED COCONUTS.

- » 1 cup (200g) brown rice
- » 3 cups (750ml) water
- » 2 teaspoons white sesame seeds
- » 2 teaspoons black sesame seeds
- » ⅓ cup (80ml) soy sauce
- » 2 teaspoons rice wine vinegar
- » 2 teaspoons sesame oil
- » 500g (1 pound) sushi-grade tuna, cut into 1.5cm (¾-inch) cubes
- » 2 green onions (scallions), sliced thinly
- » 1 medium (250g) avocado, diced
- » 250g (8 ounces) seaweed salad (see tip)
- » 1 lebanese cucumber (130g), sliced

1 Place rice in a sieve; rinse under cold running water until water runs clear. Place rice and the water in a medium saucepan; bring to the boil over medium-high heat. Reduce heat to low; cook, covered, for 25 minutes or until rice is tender and water is absorbed.

2 Meanwhile, place a small frying pan over medium heat; cook sesame seeds, stirring continuously for 2 minutes or until golden.

3 Whisk soy sauce, vinegar, sesame oil and three-quarters of the sesame seeds in a medium jug. Toss tuna and three-quarters of the green onion with half of the soy dressing, cover with plastic wrap; marinate in the fridge for at least 5 minutes.

4 Divide brown rice evenly among bowls. Stir avocado gently into tuna mixture. Top rice with tuna mixture, seaweed salad and cucumber slices. Serve poke drizzled with remaining dressing, sprinkled with remaining sesame seeds and green onion.

tip Seaweed salad is available from fishmongers, sushi bars and salad bars.

prep + cook time 2 hours 20 minutes (+ refrigeration) serves 6

Honey-roasted hainanese CHICKEN RICE BANQUET

You will need to start this recipe the day before.

- 1.6kg (3¼-pound) whole chicken
- 2 tablespoons rock salt
- 2 green onions (scallions), cut into 5cm (2-inch) lengths
- 50g (1½-ounce) piece ginger, sliced
- 2 tablespoons raw honey
- 2 teaspoons chinese five-spice powder
- ¼ teaspoon ground white pepper
- 2 tablespoons rice wine vinegar
- 2 tablespoons light soy sauce
- 1 lebanese cucumber (130g)
- 1 tablespoon rice wine vinegar, extra
- 1 cup loosely packed coriander (cilantro) sprigs
- sliced fresh long red chilli and extra soy sauce, to serve

BROTH

- 1 litre (4 cups) chicken stock
- 1 litre (4 cups) water
- 300g (9½ ounces) daikon, chopped finely
- 2 green onions (scallions), cut into 5cm (2-inch) lengths
- 50g (1½-ounce) piece ginger, sliced

RICE

- 1 litre (4 cups) chicken stock
- 15g (½-ounce) piece ginger, sliced
- 2 cloves garlic, unpeeled, bruised
- 2 cups (400g) medium-grain brown rice

CHILLI GINGER SAUCE

- 2 fresh long red chillies, chopped coarsely
- 3 large cloves garlic, chopped
- 50g (1½-ounce) piece ginger, peeled, chopped
- 1 green onion (scallion), chopped
- 2 tablespoons dark soy sauce
- 1 teaspoon raw honey

1 Rub chicken all over with salt; rinse in cold water, pat dry with paper towel.
2 Fill chicken cavity with green onion and ginger; secure legs with kitchen string. Whisk honey, five spice, pepper, vinegar and soy sauce in a large bowl, add chicken; turn to coat. Leave, breast-side down, in marinade. Cover; refrigerate, overnight, turning occasionally.
3 Preheat oven to 240°C/475°F.
4 Place broth ingredients in a medium saucepan; season. Bring to the boil. Reduce heat; simmer for 30 minutes, skimming foam during cooking.
5 Meanwhile, remove chicken from marinade, place in a roasting pan; discard marinade. Roast chicken for 20 minutes. Reduce oven to 200°C/400°F; roast a further 50 minutes or until juices run clear when the thickest part of a thigh is pierced. Cover; keep warm.
6 Meanwhile, make rice.
7 Process chilli ginger sauce ingredients until smooth.
8 Using a spiraliser, cut cucumber into 'spaghetti'; combine with extra vinegar in a small bowl.
9 Cut chicken into six pieces. Place rice in serving bowls, top with chicken and cucumber 'spaghetti'. Spoon broth over rice and pan juices over chicken; top with coriander. Serve with chilli ginger sauce, sliced chilli and extra soy.
rice Bring stock, ginger and garlic to the boil in a medium saucepan; stir in rice. Reduce heat to low; cook, covered, for 45 minutes or liquid is absorbed.

prep + cook time 2 hours serves 4

Sweet potato gnocchi with ROAST CAPSICUM TOMATO SAUCE

» 580g (1¼ pounds) purple-skinned white-fleshed sweet potato
» 170g (5½ ounces) fresh firm ricotta
» ½ cup (40g) finely grated parmesan
» 1 teaspoon ground nutmeg
» 1 teaspoon sea salt
» 1 egg
» 1 cup (150g) white spelt flour, plus extra for dusting
» 2 tablespoons olive oil
» ¼ cup (20g) flaked parmesan
» ¼ cup loosely packed small fresh basil leaves

ROASTED TOMATO SAUCE
» 500g (1 pound) vine-ripened tomatoes, halved
» 6 cloves garlic, unpeeled
» 1 large red capsicum (bell pepper) (350g), chopped coarsely
» 1 medium red onion (170g), cut into wedges
» 1 tablespoon fresh oregano leaves
» 1 tablespoon fresh lemon thyme leaves
» 1 tablespoon fresh rosemary leaves
» ¼ cup (60ml) extra virgin olive oil
» 2 tablespoons sugar-free balsamic vinegar
» 1 teaspoon pure maple syrup
» ¼ cup loosely packed fresh basil leaves
» ¼ cup (20g) finely grated parmesan

1 Preheat oven to 200°C/400°F.
2 Wrap sweet potato in foil; bake for 1½ hours or until tender.
3 Meanwhile, make roasted tomato sauce.
4 Combine ricotta, grated parmesan, nutmeg, salt and egg in a large bowl until smooth. Cut sweet potato in half lengthways; spoon flesh into a small bowl, mash with a fork. Add hot sweet potato to ricotta mixture; combine well. Stir flour into sweet potato mixture to form a firm dough.
5 Bring a large saucepan of salted water to the boil. Divide dough into eight portions. Using floured hands, roll each portion on a floured surface into a 2cm (¾-inch) thick sausage shape; cut into 4cm (1½-inch) lengths. Squeeze gnocchi in the middle to form a bow shape. Place gnocchi, in a single layer, on an oven tray dusted with extra flour.
6 Cook gnocchi in boiling water, in three batches, for 2 minutes or until they float to the surface. Remove with a slotted spoon to an oiled tray. Reserve ½ cup gnocchi cooking water; stir reserved water into roasted tomato sauce.
7 Heat a large frying pan with olive oil over high heat; cook gnocchi, tossing occasionally, for 5 minutes or until lightly golden. Stir sauce into gnocchi to combine. Serve gnocchi topped with flaked parmesan and basil.
roasted tomato sauce Line a large roasting pan with baking paper. Add tomatoes, garlic, capsicum, onion, herbs and 2 tablespoons of the oil; season, toss to coat. Roast for 1 hour or until vegetables are very tender. Squeeze garlic from skins onto vegetables. Transfer mixture to a medium saucepan, add vinegar, syrup, remaining oil, basil and parmesan; season. Using a stick blender, blend sauce until smooth. Keep warm over a low heat.

Virtuous dressings

prep time 5 minutes makes ⅔ cup

MAPLE & DIJON DRESSING

Whisk ¼ cup macadamia oil, ¼ cup apple cider vinegar, 2 tablespoons pure maple syrup and 1 tablespoon dijon mustard in a small bowl until combined. Season to taste.

keeps Store in a sealed jar in the fridge for up to 1 month.

swap out You could substitute olive oil for macadamia oil.

serving suggestion Serve with a salad of mixed leaves, or beef and beetroot (beet), or chicken and haloumi, or lamb and roast sweet potato.

prep time 5 minutes makes 1 cup

HEALTHY CAESAR DRESSING

Blend or process 1 cup yoghurt, 2 tablespoons olive oil, 2 tablespoons finely grated parmesan, 4 finely chopped anchovies, ½ crushed clove garlic, 1 tablespoon lemon juice and 3 teaspoons dijon mustard until smooth. Season to taste.

keeps Store in a sealed jar in the fridge for up to 1 week.

serving suggestion Serve with a caesar salad of cos lettuce, hard-boiled egg, parmesan and crisp bacon or avocado.

prep time 10 minutes makes 1½ cups

LEMON, AVOCADO & DILL DRESSING

Blend or process 1 medium (250g) avocado, ¼ cup yoghurt, 2 tablespoons avocado oil, ⅓ cup water, ⅓ cup loosely packed fresh dill sprigs and ¼ cup of lemon juice until smooth. Season to taste. For a thinner consistency, add a little more water if necessary.

keeps Store in a sealed jar in the fridge for up to 1 week.

serving suggestion Serve with a salad of iceberg lettuce and soft-boiled egg, or poached chicken and pistachio, or smoked salmon.

prep time 5 minutes makes ½ cup

RASPBERRY & WHITE BALSAMIC VINAIGRETTE

Push ½ cup fresh or thawed frozen raspberries through a fine sieve into a small bowl, using the back of a spoon. Whisk in ¼ cup white balsamic vinegar, 2 tablespoons macadamia oil and 1 teaspoon norbu (monk fruit sugar) or stevia granules. Season to taste.

keeps Store in a sealed jar in the fridge for up to 1 week.

serving suggestion Serve with a salad of roast duck, slow cooked lamb or grilled chicken.

prep + cook time 2 hours (+ refrigeration) serves 4

Eastern mash-up RAMEN BOWLS

You will need to start this recipe a day ahead.

- 1 litre (4 cups) chicken stock
- 10g (½ ounce) dashino-moto stock powder
- 3 cups (750ml) water
- 3 cloves garlic, sliced thinly
- ¼ cup (60ml) soy sauce
- 2 tablespoons sake
- 1 teaspoon norbu (monk fruit sugar) or stevia granules
- 20g (¾-ounce) piece fresh ginger, sliced
- 1 long fresh red chilli, quartered lengthways
- 300g (9½ ounces) buckwheat soba noodles
- 2 green onions (scallions), cut into thin strips
- 3 sheets toasted nori (seaweed), quartered
- 1 teaspoon black sesame seeds

TEA EGGS

- 3 cups (750ml) water
- 1 cup (250ml) soy sauce
- ¼ cup (20g) black tea leaves
- 4 star anise
- rind of 1 mandarin
- 4 eggs, from the fridge

KIMCHI

- 250g (8 ounces) baby cucumbers (qukes)
- ¼ cup (50g) norbu (monk fruit sugar)
- 2 tablespoons salt
- ¼ cup (60ml) boiling water
- 2 green onions (scallions), chopped coarsely
- 1 teaspoon finely grated ginger
- 1 clove garlic
- 1 fresh long green chilli, sliced thinly
- 2 tablespoons rice vinegar
- 1 teaspoon fish sauce
- 1 tablespoon soy sauce
- 1½ tablespoons sesame seeds, toasted

1 Make tea eggs.

2 Place chicken stock, dashino-moto, the water, garlic, soy sauce, sake, norbu, ginger and chilli in a saucepan; bring to the boil. Reduce heat; simmer for 30 minutes.

3 Meanwhile, make kimchi.

4 Cook noodles in a saucepan of boiling water for 6 minutes or until just tender; drain.

5 Peel and halve tea eggs. Divide noodles and soup among bowls; top with eggs, kimchi, green onion and nori. Serve sprinkled with black sesame seeds.

tea eggs Bring the water, soy sauce, tea, star anise and rind to the boil in a medium saucepan. Reduce heat; simmer 1 hour. Cool. Cook eggs in a small saucepan of boiling water for 7 minutes. Run eggs under cold water to stop them continuing to cook. Crack shell all over, but do not peel. Place eggs in cooled tea mixture. Cover; refrigerate overnight.

kimchi Cut cucumbers in half lengthways; cut crossways into 5mm (¼-inch) slices. Stir norbu, salt and the water until dissolved. Place cucumber and salt mixture in a plastic zip-top bag, expel air; seal. Lie bag flat for 30 minutes. Meanwhile, process remaining ingredients until finely chopped; spoon into a bowl. Drain cucumbers; rinse, pat dry with paper towel. Add to bowl; toss to combine.

prep + cook time 40 minutes (+ standing) makes 4

Carrot taco shells WITH CHIPOTLE PORK

- 2 teaspoons olive oil
- 250g (8 ounces) minced (ground) pork
- 1 finely chopped chipotle chilli in adobo sauce, plus 2 teaspoons adobo sauce, optional
- ½ cup (140g) Greek-style yoghurt
- 40g (1½ ounces) gem lettuce leaves, shredded
- 1 medium avocado (250g), sliced thinly
- 2 tablespoons lime juice
- 1 small red onion (100g), sliced thinly
- 20g (¾ ounce) snow pea shoots
- 1 lime, cut into wedges
- extra gem lettuce leaves, to serve
- no-nasties chilli sauce (see page 129), to serve

CARROT TACO SHELLS

- 1½ cups (230g) coarsely grated carrot (see tips)
- ½ cup (60g) grated manchego cheese (see tips)
- 2 eggs, beaten lightly
- ¼ cup (35g) oat flour

1 Preheat oven to 200°C/400°F. Line two oven trays with baking paper.

2 Make carrot taco shells.

3 Meanwhile, heat oil in a large frying pan over high heat. Cook pork, breaking up any lumps with a spoon, for 5 minutes or until browned and cooked through. Add chilli; cook for a further 1 minute. Season to taste.

4 Swirl reserved adobo sauce, if using, through yoghurt. Divide shredded lettuce, pork mixture, avocado, combined lime juice and onion, yoghurt mixture and pea shoots evenly among taco shells. Serve with lime wedges, extra lettuce leaves and no-nasties chilli sauce.

carrot taco shells Steam or boil carrot for 3 minutes or until tender. Place in a tea towel (see tips) and squeeze to remove excess liquid. Place in a medium bowl with cheese, egg and flour; stir to combine. Season. Divide carrot mixture into quarters; spread out into four 14cm (5½-inch) rounds on trays. Bake taco shells for 20 minutes or until golden; stand on trays for 1 minute. Taking care as shells will still be warm, bend each round over a small bottle to form a taco shape. Leave to cool on bottle.

tips You will need approximately 3 medium (360g) carrots. Manchego is a semi-firm Spanish sheep's milk cheese available from major supermarkets and delis. Substitute with mature cheddar, if you like. Use an old yet clean tea towel for squeezing the grated carrot, as it may stain.

prep + cook time 2 hours serves 6

Beetroot & buckwheat risotto
WITH GOAT'S CURD

- 4 large beetroot (beets) (1.2kg), trimmed, leaves reserved
- ⅓ cup (80ml) extra virgin olive oil
- 2 tablespoons finely chopped fresh thyme
- ¾ cup (180ml) boiling water
- 1 teaspoon red wine vinegar
- 1 medium onion (150g), chopped finely
- 4 cloves garlic, chopped finely
- 1 bulb baby fennel (130g), trimmed, chopped finely
- 2 cups (400g) buckwheat
- ½ cup (125ml) dry white wine
- 1.25 litres (5 cups) vegetable stock, warmed
- ½ cup (40g) finely grated parmesan
- 40g (1½ ounces) butter
- 125g (4 ounces) goat's curd

1 Preheat oven to 200°C/400°F.

2 Place each beetroot on a square of foil; drizzle with 1 tablespoon of the oil, season and sprinkle with 1 tablespoon of the thyme. Wrap tightly to enclose; place on an oven tray. Bake for 1¼ hours or until tender. When cool enough to handle, remove skin from beetroot.

3 Blend 3 of the beetroot in a high-powered blender (or a food processor) with the boiling water until smooth. Cut remaining beetroot into thin wedges. Transfer to a small bowl, toss with 1 tablespoon of the olive oil and vinegar; season to taste.

4 Heat remaining 2 tablespoons of the olive oil in a large, deep cast iron or other heavy-based saucepan over medium heat. Add onion, garlic, fennel and remaining thyme; cook for 5 minutes or until onion softens. Add buckwheat; cook, stirring, for 1 minute or until coated. Add wine; cook, stirring, for 1 minute.

5 Add stock and beetroot puree; bring to the boil. Reduce heat to low; simmer for 25 minutes, stirring occasionally or until buckwheat is tender. Stir in parmesan and butter. Season to taste, cover; stand for 2 minutes.

6 Serve risotto topped with goat's curd, beetroot wedges and reserved beetroot leaves.

tips Choose a bunch of beetroot with beautiful small leaves, as they are also used in the recipe. Goat's curd is available from large supermarkets and delis; stir in a bowl before using for a smoother texture. You could also top the risotto with crumbled fresh goat's cheese or ricotta (see page 34).

swap out Barley can be substituted for buckwheat.

prep + cook time 1 hour 30 minutes (+ standing & cooling) serves 6

Eggplant & zucchini LASAGNE

THIS CLEVER VEGETARIAN LASAGNE STARS VEGETABLES IN DIFFERENT WAYS. EGGPLANT AND ZUCCHINI REPLACE THE PASTA, WHILE MUSHROOMS AND TOMATO COMBINE FOR A HEARTY TOMATO SAUCE, AND CAULIFLOWER AND RICOTTA ARE TRANSFORMED INTO A SILKY BÉCHAMEL.

- ⅓ cup (80ml) extra virgin olive oil
- 2 eggplants (600g)
- 3 large zucchini (450g)
- 200g (7 ounces) fresh shiitake mushrooms, stems discarded, chopped finely
- 2 tablespoons finely chopped sage
- 1 teaspoon smoked paprika
- 400g (12½ ounces) canned chopped tomatoes
- 125g (4 ounces) sun-dried tomatoes, chopped finely
- ¾ cup (90g) walnuts, chopped finely
- 1 cup (250ml) tomato passata
- 1 cup (250ml) vegetable stock
- ¼ cup (20g) finely grated parmesan

CAULIFLOWER BÉCHAMEL

- ¾ head cauliflower (750g), cut into florets
- 3 cloves garlic, bruised
- 1½ cups (375ml) vegetable stock
- 375g (12 ounces) fresh ricotta
- ¾ cup (60g) finely grated parmesan
- ¼ teaspoon ground nutmeg

1 Preheat oven grill to high. Line a large oven tray with foil; grease with oil.

2 Cut eggplant and zucchini lengthways into 4mm (⅛-inch) thick slices.

3 Working in batches, place eggplant in a single layer on oiled tray; brush with 1 tablespoon of the oil and season. Grill eggplant slices for 5 minutes each side or until golden. Repeat with zucchini slices and another 1 tablespoon of oil; grill for 3 minutes each side or until golden.

4 Preheat oven on 200°C/400°F.

5 Make cauliflower béchamel.

6 Meanwhile, heat 1 tablespoon of the oil in a frying pan over medium-high heat. Cook mushroom for 2 minutes, add sage and paprika; cook for a further 3 minutes or until golden. Stir in canned and dried tomatoes, walnuts, passata and stock to combine, bring to a simmer; simmer for 12 minutes or until thickened slightly. Season to taste.

7 Spread a quarter of the cauliflower béchamel in a 2.5 litre (10-cup) rectangular baking dish; arrange a layer of vegetables on top. Top with another quarter of the béchamel. Spoon over half of sun-dried tomato mixture, then repeat layering with vegetables, béchamel and tomato mixture, finishing with remaining béchamel. Top with parmesan; drizzle with remaining oil and season with salt and pepper.

8 Bake for 20 minutes or until top is golden and filling heated through. Stand for 10 minutes before serving. Top the lasagne with crisp sage leaves, if you like.

cauliflower béchamel Place cauliflower, garlic and stock in a medium saucepan over medium heat; bring to a simmer. Reduce heat to low; cook, covered, for 12 minutes or until cauliflower is tender. Cool for 10 minutes. Blend with cheeses and nutmeg until a smooth puree forms; season.

prep + cook time 25 minutes serves 4

Beetroot, coconut & seed SALAD WITH SNAPPER

EASY, FRESH AND VIBRANT, THIS RECIPE IS THE PERFECT WEEKNIGHT DINNER MEAL SOLUTION, PROVING THAT FISH REALLY IS FAST TO COOK. MAKE DOUBLE THE SALAD AND TAKE IT TO WORK THE NEXT DAY IN A SANDWICH. WE USED FOUR BABY GOLDEN BEETROOT AND FOUR TARGET BEETROOT, AND SLICED THE VEGETABLES THINLY WITH A MANDOLINE.

» ⅓ cup (50g) sunflower seeds
» ¼ cup (60ml) extra virgin olive oil
» 1 tablespoon lemon juice
» 1 teaspoon dijon mustard
» 1 teaspoon honey
» 4 x 200g (7-ounce) snapper fillets
» 1 teaspoon ground cumin
» 8 mixed baby beetroot (beets) (25g), sliced thinly
» 4 watermelon radishes (35g), sliced thinly
» ½ cup fresh small mint leaves
» ½ cup (40g) shaved coconut
» 1 lemon (140g), cut into wedges

1 Heat a small frying pan over medium heat; cook sunflower seeds, stirring continuously, for 2 minutes or until toasted; remove from pan.
2 Whisk 2 tablespoons of the olive oil, the juice, mustard and honey in a small bowl until well combined. Season to taste.
3 Heat a medium non-stick frying pan over medium-high heat. Brush snapper fillets with remaining olive oil; sprinkle with cumin and season. Cook fish, skin-side down, for 2 minutes; turn and cook for a further 2 minutes or until fish is cooked through.
4 Combine beetroot and radish with half each of the mint and sunflower seeds and the dressing in a medium bowl.
5 Divide salad among plates; scatter with remaining sunflower seeds and mint leaves. Top each with a snapper fillet; serve with shaved coconut and lemon wedges.

tips Whiting and john dory are good alternatives to snapper fillets. You could also serve the salad with pan-fried or grilled chicken or lamb.

swap out For a vegetarian option, swap the fish for crumbled goat's cheese.

prep + cook time 20 minutes serves 4

Pea fritters with AVOCADO CHEESE MASH

- 1 cup (150g) wholemeal self-raising flour
- 2 teaspoons finely grated lemon rind
- 2 small eggs
- 1 cup (250ml) skim milk
- 2 cups (240g) frozen peas, thawed
- 2 teaspoons rice bran oil
- 1 avocado (250g)
- 60g (2 ounces) fresh goat's cheese, crumbled
- ¼ cup chopped fresh mint leaves
- 60g (2 ounce) rocket leaves (arugula)
- 160g (5 ounces) chopped cherry tomatoes, quartered
- 4 lemon wedges

1 Combine sifted flour and rind in a medium bowl. Add egg and milk, whisk to combine. Fold through peas. Season with pepper.

2 Heat oil in a large, non-stick frying pan over medium heat; cook ⅓-cups of batter, in batches, for 3 minutes each side or until browned lightly and cooked through. Cover to keep warm.

3 Meanwhile, mash avocado in a small bowl with a fork. Stir through cheese and mint. Serve fritters with avocado mash, rocket, tomato and lemon wedges.

tips Thaw peas by running under boiling water. The mixture is quite loose, it will spread once in the pan.

prep + cook time 40 minutes (+ refrigeration) serves 4

Tofu 'BACON' BLT

WE'VE FLIPPED THE CLASSIC BACON, LETTUCE AND TOMATO COMBO ON ITS HEAD, DITCHING THE ANIMAL PROTEIN IN FAVOUR OF VEGAN-FRIENDLY TOFU, WHICH WE'VE TRANSFORMED WITH UMAMI-RICH FLAVOURS, SO IT'S EVERY BIT AS GOOD AS BACON.

You will need to start this recipe a day ahead.

- 8 large slices seeded sourdough rye bread (680g), toasted
- 1 large avocado (320g), mashed coarsely
- ½ cup (150g) purchased or homemade vegan mayonnaise (see page 118)
- 2 medium heirloom tomatoes (300g), sliced
- 8 butter lettuce leaves

TOFU BACON

- 375g (12 ounces) extra-firm tofu
- 1 tablespoon white (shiro) miso paste
- 1 tablespoon pure maple syrup
- 1 tablespoon tamari
- 1 teaspoon smoked paprika
- 1 tablespoon coconut oil, melted

1 Make tofu bacon.
2 Preheat oven to 220°C/425°F.
3 Bake one tray of the tofu bacon for 20 minutes, turning tofu over halfway through cooking, or until crisp and golden. Reserve remaining tofu bacon (see tips).
4 Spread half the toast evenly with avocado and mayonnaise. Top with tofu bacon, tomato and lettuce; season to taste. Sandwich with remaining toast.

tofu bacon Place tofu on a small wire rack over a deep-sided oven tray; cover tofu with a small piece of baking paper and another oven tray. Place cans of food on top to weight, then refrigerate for 1 hour to drain. Pat tofu dry with paper towel and slice thinly lengthways. Divide between two large oven trays lined with baking paper. Combine remaining ingredients in a small bowl; season with black pepper. Brush both sides of tofu with miso mixture. Cover and refrigerate overnight.

tips The tofu bacon recipe makes double the amount required for this recipe but it will keep uncooked in the fridge for up to 1 week; just bake as required. For other uses, see 'try this'.

try this

Use in wholegrain rolls with thinly shaved fennel and carrot, fresh coriander, mint and finely chopped chilli for a vegan tofu bánh mì.

Stirred into egg-based dishes: such as scrambled eggs, omelettes and frittatas.

Scattered over soups or stews for an added protein hit.

prep + cook time 1 hour 50 minutes serves 4

Olive chicken with MAPLE-ROASTED VEGETABLES

- » ¼ cup (60ml) olive oil
- » 1 whole chicken (1.6kg), cut into 10 pieces
- » 1 medium brown onion (150g), chopped coarsely
- » 2 cloves garlic, crushed
- » 3 sprigs fresh thyme
- » 18 sicilian green olives (90g)
- » 1 litre (4 cups) chicken stock
- » 1 tablespoon lemon juice

MAPLE-ROASTED VEGETABLES

- » 600g (1¼ pounds) kent pumpkin, cut into 2cm (¾-inch) wedges
- » 4 small parsnips (480g), unpeeled, quartered lengthways
- » 400g (12½ ounces) spring onions, trimmed to 10cm (4-inch) lengths, quartered lengthways
- » 2 tablespoons extra virgin olive oil
- » 2 tablespoons pure maple syrup
- » 1 cup (40g) loosely packed rocket (arugula) leaves
- » 1 tablespoon lemon juice

1 Heat oil in a large heavy-based saucepan over high heat; cook chicken, in batches, for 2 minutes each side or until browned. Remove from pan

2 Reduce heat of same pan to medium; cook onion, garlic, thyme and olives, stirring occasionally, for 5 minutes or until onion is softened. Increase heat to high; return chicken and any juices to pan. Add stock; bring to the boil. Reduce heat to low; simmer, covered, for 1 hour or until chicken is cooked through. Remove chicken from pan.

3 Meanwhile, preheat oven to 200°C/400°F; make maple roasted vegetables.

4 Increase saucepan heat to high; bring to the boil. Reduce heat slightly; cook, uncovered, for 20 minutes or until liquid has reduced to 1 cup (250ml). Add juice, season to taste.

5 Serve chicken with reduced mixture and vegetables.

maple-roasted vegetables Line two oven trays with baking paper. Divide pumpkin, parsnip and onion between trays; drizzle with oil and maple syrup, season, then toss to coat. Roast for 40 minutes, turning halfway through cooking or until tender. Combine rocket and juice in a medium bowl; season to taste. Just before serving, toss rocket through vegetables.

tip These olives contain pits, so warn your guests before eating. Alternatively use pitted olives.

prep + cook time 1 hour serves 6

Prawn chu chee curry
WITH ROTI BREAD

- 2 cups (400g) medium-grain brown rice
- 1 litre (4 cups) water
- ½ teaspoon salt
- ¼ cup (60g) ghee
- 2½ tablespoons thai red curry paste
- 1kg (2 pounds) uncooked prawns (shrimp), peeled, deveined, with tails intact
- 6 fresh kaffir lime leaves
- 270ml coconut milk
- 1 cup (250ml) fish stock
- 2 tablespoons coconut sugar
- 2 tablespoons fish sauce
- 1 tablespoon tamarind puree
- 225g (7 ounces) canned bamboo shoots, drained, rinsed
- ½ cup (85g) chopped fresh pineapple
- 1 fresh long red chilli, seeded, shredded finely

ROTI BREAD

- 1 teaspoon raw honey
- ¾ cup (180ml) warm water
- ¼ cup (60ml) milk
- ⅓ cup (80ml) rice bran oil
- 1 egg
- 3 cups (450g) white spelt flour
- 1 teaspoon salt
- 60g (2 ounces) ghee

1 Make roti bread.

2 Rinse rice in a sieve under cold water until water runs clear. Place rice in a medium saucepan with the water and salt; bring to the boil. Reduce heat to low; cook, covered, for 25 minutes or until water is absorbed. Remove from heat; stand, covered, for 5 minutes. Fluff with a fork and keep warm.

3 Meanwhile, heat a wok over medium-high heat. Add ghee and curry paste; cook, stirring, for 2 minutes. Add prawns and 3 crushed lime leaves; cook, stirring, for 2 minutes. Add coconut milk and stock; simmer for 5 minutes. Add sugar, sauce and tamarind. Stir in bamboo shoots and pineapple; cook for a further 2 minutes or until warmed though.

4 Finely shred remaining lime leaves; combine with chilli. Sprinkle lime leaf mixture on curry; serve with rice and warm roti bread.

roti bread Dissolve honey in a jug with the water, milk and 2 tablespoons of the oil; whisk in egg. Process flour and salt until combined. With the motor operating, gradually add milk mixture; process until it forms a sticky dough. Knead dough on a floured surface for 2 minutes or until smooth. Divide into six portions; roll into balls. Place balls in a medium bowl with remaining oil, turn to coat well. Pat a ball of dough out on a lightly oiled surface until 20cm (8-inch) round. Using oiled hands, carefully stretch dough out from the centre in a circular motion, until dough is translucent and forms a 40cm (16-inch) round (don't worry if the dough rips, this will add texture). Fold each side into the centre to form a 15cm (6-inch) square; do not press. Place on a baking-paper-lined oven tray. Repeat with remaining dough. Heat 2 teaspoons ghee in a large frying pan over medium heat; cook roti, in batches, for 2 minutes each side or until golden, adding remaining ghee with each batch.

prep + cook time 35 minutes (+ refrigeration) serves 8

Herb-crusted salmon
WITH PICKLED VEG

You will need to make the pickled veg a day ahead. You can also cook the salmon a day ahead, if you like.

- 2 tablespoons olive oil
- 1.3kg (2¾-pound) salmon fillet, skinned, pin-boned
- ¼ cup each finely chopped fresh dill, chervil, mint and chives
- 2 cups (50g) watercress sprigs

PICKLED VEG

- 2 cups (500ml) white wine vinegar
- 3 cups (750ml) water
- 2 tablespoons sea salt
- ¼ cup (50g) norbu (monk fruit sugar)
- 1 tablespoon pink peppercorns
- 4 bay leaves
- ½ cup fresh dill sprigs
- 3 fresh long red chillies, halved
- 170g (5½ ounces) asparagus, trimmed, halved
- 400g (12½ ounces) baby rainbow carrots, trimmed, scrubbed, halved lengthways
- 8 small radishes (120g), halved
- 250g (8 ounces) baby cucumbers, halved lengthways

HORSERADISH YOGHURT

- 1½ cups (420g) Greek-style yoghurt
- ⅓ cup (90g) horseradish cream
- 1½ tablespoons finely chopped fresh dill

1 Make pickled veg.
2 Preheat oven to 180°C/350°F. Line a large oven tray with baking paper; drizzle with half the oil, season with salt and pepper. Position salmon on tray to fit; rub with remaining oil, season.
3 Combine herbs in a small bowl; press onto salmon to thickly coat. Bake for 15 minutes for medium-rare or until cooked to your liking.
4 Meanwhile, make horseradish yoghurt.
5 Serve salmon with pickled veg, watercress and horseradish yoghurt.
pickled veg Place vinegar and the water in a deep glass or ceramic rectangular dish; stir in salt and norbu until dissolved. Add remaining ingredients, ensuring vegetables are completely covered (add extra water if necessary). Cover; refrigerate overnight.
horseradish yoghurt Whisk ingredients in a small bowl. Season. Refrigerate until required.

keeps The pickled veg can be made up to 1 week ahead. Store in an airtight container in the fridge.

swap out You can use black peppercorns instead of pink, ocean trout instead of salmon and any combination of soft-leaf herbs you prefer including flat-leaf parsley and tarragon.

Marinades

prep time 5 minutes makes ¾ cup

MISO & GINGER

Whisk ⅓ cup sake, ¼ cup orange juice, ¼ cup white (shiro) miso paste, 3 teaspoons finely grated ginger and 1 tablespoon raw honey in a small bowl until combined.

With salmon Combine salmon and marinade; refrigerate, covered, at least 2 hours. Pan-fry on each side until brown; finish cooking in the oven. Serve with brown rice, roasted eggplant and black sesame seeds.

With prawns Combine prawns and marinade; refrigerate, covered, at least 2 hours. Chargrill until cooked. Serve with vermicelli noodle salad.

With whole chicken Combine chicken and marinade. Roast in oven. Serve with roasted vegetables.

tip To prevent the marinade from sticking, line your frying, roasting or chargrill pan with baking paper.

prep time 5 minutes makes 1½ cups

STICKY BOURBON

Whisk ½ cup tamari, ¼ cup olive oil, ¼ cup apple cider vinegar, ⅓ cup bourbon, ¼ cup pure maple syrup, 2 cloves crushed garlic in a small bowl until combined.

With pork or beef ribs Combine ribs and marinade; refrigerate, covered, for 4 hours or overnight. Roast, basting with marinade during cooking.

With chicken thigh fillets Combine fillets and marinade; refrigerate, covered, for 4 hours or overnight. Chargrill until cooked. Serve with roasted vegetables and quinoa salad.

prep time 10 minutes makes 1½ cups

LEMON GRASS & COCONUT

Process 1 tablespoon coarsely chopped ginger, 1 thinly sliced stalk (white part only) lemon grass, 1 teaspoon ground turmeric, 1 teaspoon sea salt flakes, 2 chopped cloves garlic and 2 shallots until finely chopped. Add 270ml can coconut milk, 1 tablespoon fish sauce, 3 teaspoons finely grated lime rind and 1 tablespoon lime juice; process until combined.

With chicken thighs, drumsticks or tenderloins Combine chicken and marinade; refrigerate, covered, 4 hours or overnight. Chargrill or bake until cooked. Serve with asian greens, basmati rice and coriander.

With prawns Combine prawns and marinade; refrigerate, covered, for 1-2 hours. Chargrill until cooked. Serve with a sliced mango, mint and macadamia salad.

prep time 5 minutes makes 1¼ cups

CHILLI TERIYAKI

Whisk ½ cup soy sauce, ⅓ cup raw honey, ¼ cup apple cider vinegar, 2 teaspoons finely grated ginger, 1 seeded, finely chopped small red chilli and ½ teaspoon sesame oil in a small bowl until well combined.

With chicken breast or thigh fillets Combine chicken and marinade; refrigerate, covered, 2 hours or overnight. Thread onto skewers; chargrill or barbecue. Sprinkle with toasted sesame seeds. Serve with rice and asian greens.

With salmon Combine salmon and marinade; refrigerate, covered, for up to 4 hours. Pan-fry, grill or bake. Serve with an asian herb salad.

With beef stir-fry strips Combine beef with marinade; refrigerate, covered, for 2 hours or overnight. Stir-fry with green onions, broccolini and hokkien noodles.

prep + cook time 1 hour serves 4

Mandarin-glazed chicken ON UDON NOODLES

- 4 chicken breast supremes (720g) (see tip)
- 2 tablespoons rice bran oil
- 1 medium mandarin (200g), unpeeled, cut into four thick slices
- 4 cloves garlic, sliced thinly
- 2 long fresh red chillies, seeded, cut into matchsticks
- 300g (9½ ounces) leeks, trimmed, cut into matchsticks
- 270g (8½ ounces) dried udon noodles
- 2 green onions (scallions), sliced on the diagonal
- ¼ cup fresh coriander (cilantro) sprigs

GLAZE

- ⅓ cup (80ml) soy sauce
- ⅓ cup (80ml) chinese cooking wine (shao hsing)
- 2½ tablespoons raw honey
- 2 teaspoons finely grated mandarin rind
- ⅓ cup (80ml) mandarin juice
- 2 teaspoons finely grated ginger
- ½ teaspoon ground cinnamon
- ¼ teaspoon ground star anise

1 Preheat oven to 200°C/400°F. Line an oven tray with baking paper.
2 Make glaze.
3 Rub chicken with half the oil; season. Heat a large non-stick frying pan over medium heat; cook chicken for 5 minutes each side or until skin is golden. Transfer chicken to tray; brush glaze on both sides. Dip mandarin slices in glaze; place on chicken. Bake for 15 minutes, brushing with glaze halfway through cooking, or until chicken is cooked through. Cover; keep warm.
4 Heat remaining oil in same frying pan over medium heat; cook garlic and chilli for 1 minute. Add leek; cook for a further 5 minutes or until soft.
5 Meanwhile, cook noodles in a saucepan of boiling water for 10 minutes or until tender; drain, reserving ¼ cup cooking water.
6 Add noodles and reserved cooking water to pan with green onion and coriander; season, then toss to coat. Divide noodle mixture among shallow serving bowls; top with chicken and mandarin, drizzle with remaining glaze.
glaze Bring ingredients to a simmer in a small saucepan; cook for 5 minutes or until mixture thickens.

tip Toss the noodles with 1 teaspoon rice bran oil after cooking if you are not using immediately.

swap out Chicken breast supreme is a chicken breast with the skin and wing bone attached. Ask the butcher to prepare it for you or use skinless chicken breast fillets instead. You can use any Asian-style noodles you prefer.

prep + cook time 1 hour serves 4

Cauliflower & zucchini SOUP WITH CRISP PROSCIUTTO

» 1 slice prosciutto (14g), trimmed
» 1 tablespoon olive oil
» 1 leek (350g), trimmed, sliced thinly
» 1 clove garlic, crushed
» ¾ head cauliflower (750g), cut into florets
» 2 small potatoes (240g), chopped coarsely
» 2 litres (8 cups) water
» 1 teaspoon salt-reduced chicken stock powder
» 2 small zucchini (180g), sliced thickly
» ¼ cup thickened (heavy) cream
» 4 x 25g (¾-ounce) slices sourdough bread
» 1 tablespoon olive oil, extra
» 1 tablespoon torn fresh flat-leaf parsley leaves

1 Cook prosciutto in a medium non-stick saucepan over high heat, for 1 minute each side or until crisp; break into small shards.

2 Heat oil in the same pan over medium heat. Add leek and garlic; cook, stirring, for 5 minutes or until softened and lightly golden. Add cauliflower, potato, the water and stock powder. Bring to the boil. Reduce heat; simmer, uncovered, for 10 minutes. Add zucchini; cook, stirring occasionally, for 20 minutes or until vegetables are tender. Stir in cream. Using a stick blender, blend until smooth, adding a little more water if necessary.

3 Heat grill or grill plate. Brush both sides of bread with extra oil; grill until lightly toasted.

4 Divide soup into bowls, top with prosciutto and parsley; season with pepper and accompany each with a slice of toast.

keeps The soup can be made 2 days ahead and stored in the fridge, or freeze for up to 3 months.

prep + cook time 10 minutes serves 4

SMASHED TOAST

- 1 cup (240g) drained, rinsed canned chickpeas (garbanzo beans)
- 1 cup (120g) frozen peas, thawed
- 2 green onions (scallions), sliced thinly
- ½ cup loosely packed fresh mint leaves
- 2 tablespoons lemon juice
- 1 tablespoon tahini
- 1 small clove garlic, crushed
- 1 teaspoon ground cumin
- 1 teaspoon boiling water
- 4 x 40g (1½-ounce) slices soy and linseed bread, toasted
- 100g (3 ounces) yellow grape tomatoes, halved
- 50g (1½ ounces) fetta, crumbled
- 2 tablespoons seed and nut mix (see tips)
- ¼ cup micro cress (see tips)
- 1 tablespoon extra-virgin olive oil

1 Process chickpeas, peas, green onion, mint, juice, tahini, garlic and cumin with the boiling water until smooth. Season with pepper.

2 Spread pea mixture thickly over toast. Top with tomato, fetta, seed mix and cress. Drizzle with oil.

tips We used a seed and nut mix consisting of almonds, sunflower seeds and walnuts. Micro cress is cress harvested at seedling stage. It has small tender green leaves with a strong radish-like flavour. It is available year-round. You can replace it with finely chopped flat-leaf parsley, coriander or watercress.

prep + cook time 45 minutes serves 2

Roast salmon with SPICED LENTILS & DILL YOGHURT

FRESH HERBS AREN'T OFTEN THOUGHT OF AS A SOURCE OF NUTRIENTS, BUT SHOULD BE. FRESH CORIANDER LEAVES HAVE GOOD ANTIOXIDANT PROPERTIES AND ARE A RICH SOURCE OF VITAMIN K, A FAT-SOLUBLE VITAMIN BEST KNOWN FOR THE ROLE IT PLAYS IN BLOOD CLOTTING.

- » ⅓ cup (80g) French-style green lentils
- » 2 litres (8 cups) water
- » 400g (12½-ounce) piece boneless salmon fillet, skin on
- » ¼ cup (60ml) olive oil
- » 2 medium lemons (140g)
- » 1 teaspoon sea salt flakes
- » 1 teaspoon cracked black pepper
- » 1 medium onion (150g), chopped finely
- » 2 cloves garlic, crushed
- » 2 teaspoons ground cumin
- » 2 teaspoons ground coriander
- » 100g (3 ounces) baby spinach
- » ½ cup fresh coriander (cilantro) leaves
- » 2 tablespoons finely chopped dill
- » ½ cup (140g) Greek-style yoghurt
- » lemon cheeks and dill sprigs, to serve

1 Preheat oven to 200°C/400°F. Line an oven tray with baking paper.

2 Place lentils and the water in a large saucepan over medium-high heat. Bring to the boil. Reduce heat to medium; simmer lentils for 20 minutes or until tender. Drain.

3 Place salmon, skin-side down, on oven tray and rub with 1 tablespoon of the oil. Finely grate rind of 1 lemon over salmon; sprinkle with ½ teaspoon of the salt and ½ teaspoon of the pepper. Roast for 7 minutes or until almost cooked but slightly pink in the centre. Cut salmon in half lengthways.

4 Meanwhile, heat remaining oil in a medium frying pan over medium heat. Cook onion, garlic and spices, stirring for 3 minutes or until lightly golden. Add lentils to pan; cook, covered, for 1 minute. Remove pan from heat.

5 Juice 1 lemon into a medium bowl. Add lentil mixture, spinach, coriander and remaining salt and pepper; mix well.

6 Juice remaining lemon into a small bowl. Add dill and yoghurt; whisk to combine. Season to taste.

7 Divide lentil mixture between plates; top with salmon and drizzle with yoghurt mixture. Season to taste. Sprinkle with dill and serve with lemon cheeks.

swap out the salmon for a skinless, boneless ocean trout fillet and the spinach for rocket, if you like.

prep + cook time 45 minutes serves 4

'Spaghetti' & 'MEATBALLS'

THIS IS A VEGETARIAN PLAY ON THE CLASSIC PASTA AND MEATBALL THEME, EXCEPT IN OUR VERSION, THERE'S NEITHER MEAT NOR PASTA. BEANS, WALNUTS AND FETTA ALL COMBINE TO MAKE LUSCIOUS, HEARTY 'MEATBALLS', WHILE ZUCCHINI FILLS THE ROLE OF PASTA – TOGETHER THEY PROVIDE A GOOD DOSE OF YOUR DAILY VEGETABLE, PROTEIN AND CALCIUM NEEDS.

- 400g (12½ ounces) canned butter beans, drained, rinsed
- 100g (3 ounces) walnut pieces, chopped finely
- 1 egg
- ½ cup fresh basil leaves, chopped coarsely
- 2 cloves garlic, chopped finely
- ⅓ cup (50g) chickpea flour (besan)
- 120g (4 ounces) Greek fetta, crumbled
- ¼ cup (60ml) extra virgin olive oil
- 2 x 400g (12½ ounces) canned chopped tomatoes
- ½ cup (125ml) vegetable stock or water
- 4 large zucchini (600g), spiralised into spaghetti (see tip)

1 Place beans in a large bowl; mash lightly with a fork. Add walnuts, egg, half of the basil, garlic, flour and ½ cup of the fetta; stir until combined. Season generously to taste.
2 Using damp hands, roll bean mixture into 4cm (1½-inch) balls.
3 Heat 1 tablespoon of the oil in a large frying pan over medium heat. Cook 'meatballs', turning frequently, for 5 minutes or until browned.
4 Add tomatoes, stock and remaining oil to pan with 'meatballs'; season well. Cook for 15 minutes or until sauce thickens and reduces slightly and 'meatballs' are coated.
5 Meanwhile, place zucchini in a large sieve or colander over a large heatproof bowl. Pour over boiling water to soften. Drain and set aside.
6 Top zucchini 'spaghetti' with 'meatball' mixture; sprinkle with remaining fetta and basil. Season to taste.

tip Spiralisers are available from kitchen and homeware stores. Alternatively, you can cut the zucchini into julienne (matchsticks), using a mandoline or a very sharp knife.

prep + cook time 30 minutes (+ refrigeration & cooling) serves 2

Ginger chicken with RAW CITRUS RIBBON SALAD

- » 2 chicken breast fillets (500g)
- » 2 tablespoons vegetable oil
- » 1 large zucchini (150g)
- » 1 large carrot (180g)
- » 3 target beetroot (beets) (350g), sliced thinly
- » 1 cup (60g) bean sprouts
- » ¼ cup (40g) roasted cashews
- » 1 green onion (scallion), sliced thinly
- » ½ small red grapefruit (175g)
- » 1 lime (65g), halved

MARINADE

- » ¼ cup (60ml) soy sauce
- » 1 tablespoon pure maple syrup
- » 2 cloves garlic
- » 2 teaspoons finely grated fresh ginger
- » ½ teaspoon ground coriander
- » ¼ cup fresh coriander (cilantro) stalks
- » 2 tablespoons lime juice

DRESSING

- » 1 tablespoon pure maple syrup
- » ⅓ cup (50g) roasted cashews
- » 1 teaspoon finely grated fresh ginger
- » ½ fresh long red chilli, seeded
- » 2 tablespoons lime juice
- » 1 tablespoon soy sauce
- » ½ cup fresh coriander (cilantro) leaves

1 Make marinade.
2 Place chicken in a medium bowl; pour over marinade. Cover with plastic wrap; refrigerate for at least 2 hours or overnight. Drain; discard marinade.
3 Heat oil in a medium frying pan over medium heat. Cook chicken for 4 minutes each side or until golden and cooked through. Transfer to a plate; cool for 10 minutes. Slice thickly.
4 Make dressing.
5 Using a vegetable peeler, slice zucchini and carrot into long ribbons. Place vegetable ribbons, beetroot, bean sprouts, cashews and green onion on a large platter.
6 Using a small sharp knife, cut away rind and white pith from grapefruit and one lime half. Cut between citrus membranes to release segments; add to salad.
7 Top salad with sliced chicken, drizzle with dressing; season to taste. Slice remaining half lime in two; serve salad with lime and remaining dressing.
marinade Process all ingredients until smooth.
dressing Process all ingredients until as smooth as possible.

swap out If red grapefruit is unavailable, replace with navel orange or blood orange segments. Squeeze the citrus membranes to yield 2 tablespoons juice, then use in the dressing instead of lime juice.

prep time 25 minutes serves 2

No-fry stir-fry WITH COCONUT NAM JIM

- 2 small heads broccoli (500g)
- 200g (7 ounces) daikon, julienned
- 1 medium purple carrot (120g), julienned
- 1 green mango (350g), peeled, julienned
- 60g (2 ounces) asparagus, peeled lengthways into long ribbons
- ½ cup (75g) roasted cashews, chopped coarsely
- ¼ cup fresh thai basil leaves
- ¼ cup fresh coriander (cilantro) leaves

COCONUT NAM JIM

- 2 fresh long green chillies, seeded, chopped
- 2 shallots (50g), peeled, chopped coarsely
- 2 cloves garlic, chopped coarsely
- 2 tablespoons fresh coriander (cilantro) leaves
- ¼ cup (60ml) lime juice
- ¼ cup (60ml) coconut cream
- 1 tablespoon fish sauce
- 1 tablespoon raw honey

1 Make coconut nam jim.
2 Using a sharp knife; chop broccoli heads into very small pieces. Trim broccoli stems; using a julienne peeler, peel stems into long, thin matchsticks. (Alternatively, use a sharp knife.) Transfer all broccoli to a large bowl.
3 Add remaining ingredients to bowl, drizzle with coconut nam jim; toss to combine. Serve immediately.
coconut nam jim Blend or process ingredients until smooth. (Makes 1¼ cups)

tips A julienne peeler looks like a regular wide peeler, except it has wide serrations to make easy work of cutting vegetables into julienne. They are available from kitchen supply stores and Asian grocers. Use to cut the daikon, carrot and mango, as well as the broccoli into julienne.

swap out the purple carrot for a regular medium orange carrot, if that is what's in your fridge.

keeps Store coconut nam jim in an airtight jar in the fridge for up to 3 days; shake before using.

Sauces

prep + cook time 10 minutes makes 1½ cups

COCONUT SATAY SAUCE

Heat 1 tablespoon olive oil in a medium saucepan over medium heat; cook 1 teaspoon finely grated ginger, 1 finely chopped small fresh red chilli and 1 clove crushed garlic, for 2 minutes or until fragrant. Add ½ cup crunchy unsalted natural peanut butter, 3 teaspoons soy sauce, 1 teaspoon fish sauce and 1 teaspoon coconut sugar or stevia granules; stir over medium heat. Gradually whisk in 270ml canned coconut cream until combined; cook for 3 minutes or until combined. Stir in 1 tablespoon lime juice.

serving suggestion Serve with chicken or beef skewers or gado gado.

prep + cook time 35 minutes makes 1½ cups

SMOKEY BARBECUE SAUCE

Heat 1 tablespoon olive oil in a medium saucepan over medium-high heat; cook 1 finely chopped medium (150g) brown onion for 5 minutes or until softened. Add 2 coarsely chopped cloves garlic and 1 tablespoon smoked paprika; cook until fragrant. Add 2 teaspoons finely grated ginger, 1 tablespoon tomato paste, 1 tablespoon dijon mustard, ¼ cup pure maple syrup, ¼ cup apple cider vinegar and 400g (12½ ounces) canned crushed tomatoes. Simmer, uncovered, for 20 minutes or until thickened. Blend sauce until smooth; season to taste. Cool.

serving suggestion Serve with grilled lamb, chicken, beef or pork.

prep + cook time 45 minutes makes 1 cup

HONEY CHILLI SAUCE

Coarsely chop 4 fresh long red chillies. Remove seeds from 12 fresh long red chillies; coarsely chop. Process all chillies with 2 cloves garlic until finely chopped. Transfer to a medium saucepan; add 1¾ cups apple cider vinegar, ¾ cup raw honey and ¼ cup water; cook, stirring, for 5 minutes over low heat until honey melts. Increase heat, bring to a simmer; cook, stirring occasionally, for 20 minutes or until sauce thickens (sauce will thicken further on cooling). Cool.

keeps Store in an airtight container, in the fridge, for up to 1 month.

serving suggestion Serve with grilled chicken, prawns, fish, calamari or prawns.

prep + cook time 1 hour 15 minutes makes 2 cups

TOMATO KETCHUP

Heat 1 tablespoon olive oil in a medium saucepan; cook 1 coarsely chopped small (80g) brown onion for 5 minutes or until softened. Add 800g (1½ pounds) canned diced tomatoes and ½ cup apple cider vinegar; bring to a boil. Reduce heat to a simmer; stir in 2 tablespoons tomato paste, 2 tablespoons pure maple syrup, 1 teaspoon sea salt flakes, ½ teaspoon ground cloves, 1 teaspoon ground allspice, ¼ teaspoon cayenne pepper. Simmer over low heat 1 hour or until sauce reduces and thickens. For a smooth sauce, blend with a stick blender. Cool.

serving suggestion Serve with beef, chicken or lamb burgers and sweet potato fries.

prep + cook time 1 hour serves 6

Potato, spinach & chickpea CURRY WITH CORIANDER DOSA

- ¼ cup (60g) ghee
- 1 medium onion (150g), sliced thinly
- 1 clove garlic, crushed
- 1 fresh long red chilli, seeded, sliced thinly
- 2 teaspoons finely grated ginger
- 2 teaspoons black mustard seeds
- 2 teaspoons cumin seeds
- 1 teaspoon ground turmeric
- 3 medium tomatoes (450g), diced
- 1kg (2 pounds) potatoes, peeled, cut into 2cm (¾-inch) pieces
- ⅓ cup (80ml) water
- 1 bunch spinach (300g), chopped coarsely
- coriander sprigs, to serve

CORIANDER DOSA

- 1 cup (150g) chickpea flour (besan)
- 2 cups (500ml) room-temperature water
- 2 tablespoons lemon juice
- ¼ cup coarsely chopped fresh coriander (cilantro)

1 Heat 1½ tablespoons of the ghee in a medium saucepan over medium-high heat; cook onion, stirring, for 5 minutes or until soft. Add garlic, chilli, ginger and spices; cook, stirring, for 1 minute or until fragrant.

2 Add tomato to pan; cook, stirring, for 2 minutes or until softened. Add potato and the water; stir to coat in mixture. Cook, covered, over low-medium heat, stirring frequently, for 35 minutes or until potato is tender.

3 Meanwhile, make coriander dosa.

4 Just before serving, stir spinach into curry; cook for a further 3 minutes or until wilted. Season.

5 Top curry with coriander sprigs; serve with coriander dosa.

coriander dosa Whisk chickpea flour, the water and lemon juice in a medium bowl until a smooth, thin batter forms. Add a little extra water, if necessary to achieve the desired consistency. Stir in coriander. Heat 1 teaspoon ghee in a large 25cm (10-inch) wide, 22cm (9-inch) base non-stick frying pan or crêpe pan lined with a round of baking paper over high heat. Add ⅓ cup of batter to pan, swirling pan to cover base evenly; cook for 1½ minutes or until bubbles appear on the surface and dosa is golden underneath. Turn with a spatula; cook for a further 1 minute or until golden. Transfer to a plate. Repeat with remaining ghee and batter to make a total of 6 dosa.

prep + cook time 1 hour 30 minutes (+ refrigeration) serves 4

Creamy mushroom & KALE POT PIES

- 1 tablespoon olive oil
- 1 leek (350g), sliced thinly
- 200g (6½ ounces) swiss brown mushrooms, quartered
- 4 medium portobello mushrooms (200g), chopped coarsely
- 1 clove garlic, sliced thinly
- 60g (2 ounces) kale leaves, chopped coarsely
- ½ cup coarsely chopped fresh flat-leaf parsley
- 1 teaspoon finely grated lemon rind
- 2 teaspoons lemon juice
- 1 egg, beaten lightly
- 1 teaspoon sesame seeds
- ½ teaspoon fennel seeds, chopped coarsely
- ½ teaspoon sea salt flakes

SPELT PASTRY

- 1⅓ cups (200g) plain (all-purpose) spelt flour
- ¼ teaspoon fine sea salt
- ½ cup (120g) coconut oil, at room temperature
- 1 tablespoon iced water, approximately

WHITE SAUCE

- 1 cup (250ml) milk
- 1 small cauliflower (750g), chopped finely
- 1 cup (80g) grated parmesan

1 Make spelt pastry.

2 Meanwhile, make white sauce.

3 Preheat oven to 180C/350F. Place four 10cm (4¾-inch) round, 1¼-cup (310ml) ovenproof dishes on an oven tray.

4 Heat oil in a large frying pan over medium heat. Add leek; cook, stirring, for 5 minutes or until soft. Add mushroom and garlic; cook, stirring, for 10 minutes or until tender and liquid is evaporated. Stir through kale; cook for a further 1 minute or until just wilted. Remove from heat; stir in parsley, rind and juice; season to taste.

5 Combine mushroom mixture and white sauce in a large bowl; divide among dishes.

6 Roll out pastry between two sheets of baking paper until 3mm (⅛-inch) thick. Cut out four 12cm (4¾-inch) rounds from pastry. Cover dishes with pastry rounds, pressing around edges to seal. Brush tops with egg; sprinkle with combined seeds and sea salt.

7 Bake pot pies for 30 minutes or until pastry is golden.

spelt pastry Sift flour and salt into a large bowl. Using a teaspoon, scoop up spoonfuls of the coconut oil; scrape off with a second teaspoon into the bowl. Using your fingertips, rub into flour until mixture resembles wet sand. Add the iced water, a little at a time, stirring with a butter knife, until a dough forms. Gently knead on a lightly floured work surface for 30 seconds or until smooth. Enclose in plastic wrap; refrigerate for 10 minutes.

white sauce Place milk and cauliflower in a medium saucepan. Cover, bring to a simmer, reduce heat to low-medium; cook, covered, for 8 minutes or until cauliflower is just tender. Cool slightly. Blend cauliflower mixture and parmesan until smooth; season to taste.

prep + cook time 40 minutes serves 4

Spanish chicken & TOMATO STEW

- pinch saffron threads
- ¼ cup (60ml) hot water
- 4 x 150g (4½-ounce) skinless chicken thigh cutlets, fat trimmed
- 1 red onion (170g), sliced thinly
- 30g (1-ounce) piece salami, chopped coarsely
- 1 clove garlic, crushed
- 2 x 400g (12½ ounces) cans cherry tomatoes in tomato juice
- 1½ cups (400g) drained, rinsed canned cannellini beans
- ¼ cup chargrilled capsicum (bell pepper) strips
- 350g (11 ounces) broccolini, trimmed
- 2 tablespoons coarsely chopped fresh flat-leaf parsley
- 4 x 20g (¾-ounce) slices ciabatta

1 Combine saffron and the hot water in a jug.
2 Heat a medium, deep non-stick frying pan over medium heat. Add chicken; cook, turning, until browned all over. Remove from pan.
3 Add onion and salami to pan; cook, stirring, for 3 minutes or until soft. Add garlic; cook, stirring, for 1 minute or until fragrant.
4 Add tomatoes and saffron mixture to pan; bring to the boil. Return browned chicken to pan. Reduce heat; simmer, covered, for 25 minutes or until sauce thickens slightly.
5 Add beans and capsicum; simmer, uncovered, for 5 minutes or until chicken is cooked through.
6 Meanwhile, boil, steam or microwave broccolini until tender; drain.
7 Sprinkle stew with parsley; serve with broccolini and bread.

swap out You can replace the broccolini with any steamed green vegetable: asparagus, beans, brussels sprouts, broccoli, spinach and zucchini are all good choices.

prep + cook time 1 hour serves 4

Sweet potato & CELERIAC SOUP

- » 1 tablespoon rice bran oil
- » 1 brown onion (150g), chopped coarsely
- » 1 clove garlic, crushed
- » 2 teaspoons finely grated fresh ginger
- » 2 teaspoons ground cumin
- » 800g (1½ pounds) celeriac (celery root), peeled, chopped coarsely
- » 500g (1 pound) orange sweet potato, peeled, chopped coarsely
- » 1 cup (250ml) salt-reduced chicken stock
- » 1.25 litres (5 cups) water
- » ¼ cup Greek-style yoghurt
- » 1 tablespoon chopped fresh chives

1 Heat a medium saucepan over medium-low heat. Add oil and onion; cook, covered, stirring occasionally, for 5 minutes or until soft. Add garlic, ginger and cumin; cook, stirring, for 1 minute or until fragrant.

2 Add celeriac, sweet potato, stock and the water. Bring to the boil. Reduce heat; simmer, covered, for 20 minutes. Uncover; cook for a further 20 minutes or until vegetables are very soft. Cool for 10 minutes.

3 Blend or process sweet potato mixture until smooth; strain into same pan. Place soup over low heat; cook, stirring, until heated through.

4 Divide soup into four bowls; top with yoghurt, chives and freshly cracked black pepper.

tip You can process the soup using a stick blender.

prep + cook time 30 minutes serves 4

Corn & broccoli FRITTERS WITH TOMATO & BASIL

- 1 cup (95g) small broccoli florets, chopped
- ¾ cup (120g) wholemeal self-raising flour
- 1 egg
- ½ cup (125ml) skim milk
- 400g (12½ ounces) canned brown lentils, drained, rinsed
- 1 cup (160g) frozen corn kernels, thawed
- ⅓ cup (40g) grated cheddar
- 2 green onions (scallions), sliced thinly
- ¼ cup finely chopped fresh basil
- 1 tablespoon olive oil
- 2 medium tomatoes (300g), chopped
- ⅓ cup loosely packed fresh basil leaves, extra
- 2 teaspoons balsamic vinegar

1 Pour boiling water over broccoli in a medium heatproof bowl; stand for 1 minute, drain.
2 Place flour in a large bowl; make a well in the centre. Gradually whisk in the egg and milk until smooth. Stir in lentils, corn, broccoli, cheese, onion and basil. Season with pepper.
3 Heat oil in a large non-stick frying pan over medium-high heat. Drop heaped tablespoons of the batter into the pan in batches, allowing room for spreading. Cook for 2 minutes each side or until golden brown and cooked through. Repeat to make a total of 12 fritters.
4 Combine tomato, basil and vinegar in a small bowl.
5 Serve fritters with tomato mixture.

keeps Leftover fritters can be stored in the refrigerator for up to 3 days.

prep + cook time 45 minutes serves 4

Fish & fennel STEW

TOMATOES ARE ACIDIC, SO BALANCING OUT THEIR FLAVOUR WITH SOMETHING SWEET IS HELPFUL. WE'VE USED STEVIA, RATHER THAN TABLE SUGAR, TO BALANCE OUT THE FLAVOURS OF THE STEW.

- ¼ cup (60ml) extra virgin olive oil
- 1 medium onion (150g), chopped finely
- 2 medium fennel bulbs (600g), fronds reserved, sliced thinly
- 2 cloves garlic, crushed
- 1 fresh long red chilli, sliced thinly
- ½ cup (125ml) dry white wine
- 3 cups (750ml) fish stock or broth (see page 121)
- 800g (1½ pounds) canned diced tomatoes
- ¼ teaspoon liquid stevia or unrefined sugar, optional
- 750g (1½ pounds) boneless white fish fillets, cut into 3cm (1¼-inch) pieces
- 2 tablespoons coarsely chopped fresh flat-leaf parsley
- 4 slices seeded sourdough bread (280g)
- 2 teaspoons finely grated lemon rind
- 1 medium lemon (140g), cut into cheeks

1 Heat 1½ tablespoons of the olive oil in a large saucepan over medium heat. Add onion and fennel; cook, stirring, for 5 minutes or until soft. Add garlic and chilli; cook for 1 minute or until fragrant.

2 Add wine; bring to the boil. Add stock, tomatoes and stevia; bring to the boil. Reduce heat to low-medium; cook, covered, for 20 minutes. Season to taste. Add fish; cook, covered, stirring occasionally, for a further 5 minutes or until fish is cooked through. Stir in parsley.

3 Just before serving, preheat a chargrill pan over medium heat. Brush bread with remaining olive oil; cook for 1 minute each side or until golden and lightly charred.

4 Top stew with rind and reserved fennel fronds. Serve with grilled sourdough and lemon cheeks.

tips We used snapper fillets in this recipe. You could add extra seafood to the stew, such as uncooked prawns and mussels.

prep + cook time 40 minutes serves 4

Trout & radicchio GRAIN SALAD

- 1 cup (200g) brown rice and quinoa blend
- 500g (1 pound) fresh ocean trout fillets
- cooking-oil spray
- 340g (10 ounces) asparagus, trimmed, sliced very thinly lengthways (see tip)
- 2 lebanese cucumbers (260g), sliced thinly lengthways (see tip)
- 200g (6 ounces) baby cos (romaine) lettuce, leaves separated
- 100g (3 ounces) radicchio, torn
- 2 tablespoons lemon juice
- 1½ tablespoons olive oil
- ½ cup (140g) Greek-style yoghurt
- 2 teaspoons dijon mustard
- 1 teaspoon baby capers in vinegar, drained, rinsed, chopped finely
- 2 anchovy fillets, drained, chopped finely
- 1 medium lemon, cut into wedges

1 Cook rice blend in a medium saucepan of boiling water for 25 minutes or until tender; drain, rinse under cold water, drain.

2 Lightly spray trout with oil; season with black pepper. Cook, skin-side down, in a large non-stick frying pan over high heat for 3 minutes; turn over and cook for a further 2 minutes or until cooked. Remove skin, then flake flesh.

3 Combine rice blend, trout, asparagus, cucumber, lettuce and radicchio on a large platter. Add juice and oil; toss gently.

4 To make dressing, combine remaining ingredients, except the lemon wedges, in a jug. Serve the salad with dressing and lemon wedges.

tip Use a vegetable peeler, mandoline or V-slicer to thinly slice the asparagus and cucumber.

prep + cook time 1 hour (+ refrigeration) serves 4

Silver beet & MUSHROOM TART

- ¾ cup (110g) wholemeal plain spelt flour
- ¾ cup (110g) white plain spelt flour
- 1 teaspoon fennel seeds
- ¼ cup (60ml) olive oil
- 1 egg
- 1 tablespoon chilled water, approximately
- 20g (¾ ounce) reduced-fat spread
- 1 shallot, sliced thinly
- 3 large portobello mushrooms (300g), sliced thinly
- 750g (24 ounces) silver beet (swiss chard), trimmed, chopped
- 1 clove garlic, crushed
- 2 eggs, extra, beaten lightly
- 50g (1½ ounces) goat's cheese
- 2 tablespoons firmly packed fresh flat-leaf parsley leaves

1 Process flours and seeds until combined. Add oil, egg and the water; process until ingredients just come together. Shape into a disc, enclose in plastic wrap; refrigerate for 30 minutes.
2 Meanwhile, melt spread in a large frying pan over high heat; cook shallot and mushroom, stirring occasionally, for 8 minutes or until tender and excess liquid evaporates. Stir in silver beet and garlic; cook, stirring, for 2 minutes or until wilted; season, cool.
3 Preheat oven to 180°C/350°F.
4 Roll pastry between sheets of baking paper until 30cm (12 inches) round, and about 3mm (⅛-inch) thick. Remove top sheet of paper. Transfer pastry on base sheet of paper to an oven tray. Place mushroom mixture on pastry, leaving a 6cm (2½-inch) border. Gently fold pasty edges over filling, pleating at 5cm (2-inch) intervals.
5 Brush pastry border with a little of the extra egg; pour remaining egg over mushroom mixture. Bake for 40 minutes or until pastry is crisp and lightly golden.
6 Serve tart sprinkled with cheese and parsley.

tip The pastry is quite delicate; if cracks appear, use your fingers to rejoin the cracked edges.

keeps Leftover tart can be stored in the refrigerator for up to 2 days.

prep + cook time 30 minutes (+ cooling) serves 4

Lentil, asparagus & HEIRLOOM TOMATO SALAD

- » 250g (8 ounces) French-style green lentils
- » 1 teaspoon rice bran oil
- » 1 brown onion (150g), chopped finely
- » 1 clove garlic, crushed
- » 1 teaspoon finely grated fresh ginger
- » 1 teaspoon garam masala
- » 1 tablespoon lime juice
- » 170g (6 ounces) asparagus, trimmed, cut into 5cm (2-inch) lengths
- » 400g (13 ounces) heirloom cherry tomatoes, halved
- » 2 celery stalks (300g), trimmed, cut into matchsticks
- » ½ cup fresh mint leaves
- » ½ cup (40g) natural flaked almonds, roasted
- » 80g (3 ounces) fetta, crumbled

1 Cook lentils in a medium saucepan of boiling water for 15 minutes or until just tender; rinse, drain.

2 Heat oil in a medium non-stick frying pan over medium heat. Add onion; cook, stirring, for 5 minutes or until softened. Add garlic, ginger and garam masala; cook, stirring, for 1 minute or until fragrant. Transfer onion mixture to a large heatproof bowl. Add lentils and lime juice to onion mixture; stir to combine. Season, Cool.

3 Meanwhile, to blanch the asparagus, plunge into a large saucepan of boiling water for 1 minute; remove using tongs or a slotted spoon, and immediately plunge it into a bowl of iced water. Stand for a couple of minutes then drain.

4 Add asparagus, tomato, celery and mint to the lentil mixture; stir until just combined. Serve topped with almonds and fetta.

Drinks

prep time 10 minutes (+ refrigeration)
makes 1 litre (4 cups)

ICED GREEN TEA & CUCUMBER SIPPER

Brew 2 green tea bags in 3½ cups boiling water for 5 minutes. Stir in 1 tablespoon Natvia until dissolved. Cool in the fridge. Half fill a large jug with ice, then add ½ cup cucumber juice (see tip), 1 tablespoon lime juice, ½ cup lightly crushed fresh mint leaves, 1 thinly sliced (130g) lebanese cucumber, ½ thinly sliced (75g) pink lady apple and the chilled green tea; stir to combine.

tip You will need to juice 2 medium (260g) lebanese cucumbers for the amount of juice required here. If you don't have a juicer, use a blender; strain mixture through a fine sieve.

prep + cook time 25 minutes (+ refrigeration)
makes 1.25 litres (5 cups)

ICED ALMOND CHAI TEA

Place 3 cups water in a large saucepan with 2 teaspoons black tea leaves, 2 cinnamon sticks, 1 vanilla bean split lengthways, 1 tablespoon Natvia, 5 thick slices ginger, 6 cloves, 8 bruised cardamom pods, ½ teaspoon black peppercorns and 3 x 5cm (2in) strips orange rind; bring to the boil. Reduce heat; simmer for 20 minutes or until reduced to 1 cup. Remove from heat; refrigerate until chilled. Fill four tall glasses with ice cubes; pour ¼ cup of chai mix into each glass (or strain first if you prefer). Pour 1 cup almond milk into each glass.

tip Store chai mix in the fridge for up to 2 weeks.

prep + cook time 25 minutes (+ refrigeration)
makes 1 litre (4 cups)

CHAMOMILE & LEMON ICED TEA

Bring 1.25 litres (5 cups) of water to the boil in a medium saucepan; remove from heat. Add ⅓ cup dried chamomile flowers (or 3 tea bags), 2 tablespoons fresh lemon thyme sprigs and 4 slices lemon. Stir in 2 tablespoons Natvia until dissolved. Cover; steep for 20 minutes. Strain tea; refrigerate for at least 1 hour or until cooled. Serve tea mixture over ice with slices of lemon and extra sprigs fresh lemon thyme.

tip Chamomile tea is known for its soothing and calming effect, making this the perfect bedtime drink.

prep + cook time 10 minutes (+ refrigeration)
makes 1.25 litres (5 cups)

STRAWBERRY & BASIL SUNSHINE ICED TEA

Bring 1 litre (4 cups) water to the boil in a medium saucepan; remove from heat. Add 3 white tea bags and ½ cup fresh basil leaves; cover, steep for 5 minutes. Remove and discard basil and tea bags. Cool tea in the refrigerator. Blend 250g (8oz) ripe, hulled strawberries, ¼ cup of the cooled infused tea and 1 tablespoon Natvia until smooth; strain through a fine sieve to remove seeds. Stir strawberry puree into remaining cooled tea with 2 tablespoons lemon juice. Half fill a large jug with ice, top with 2 sprigs fresh basil and 10 halved strawberries; stir in tea mixture.

tip White tea is one of the least processed of all teas; buds and leaves are allowed to dry naturally before being processed to produce a delicate taste.

prep + cook time 50 minutes (+ standing) serves 4

Beetroot & lamb flatbreads
WITH TAHINI YOGHURT

- ½ cup (80g) wholemeal plain (all-purpose) flour
- 1 cup (150g) plain (all-purpose) flour
- ⅔ cup (160ml) water, approximately
- 1 tablespoon rice bran oil
- 1 red onion (170g), sliced thinly
- 200g (6 ounces) lean minced (ground) lamb
- 3 cloves garlic, crushed
- 2 teaspoons ground cumin
- ¼ teaspoon chilli flakes
- 200g (6 ounces) canned drained beetroot (beet) wedges
- 250g (8 ounces) cherry tomatoes, halved
- ¼ cup fresh mint leaves
- ¼ cup fresh coriander (cilantro) leaves

TAHINI YOGHURT

- ½ cup (140g) plain yoghurt
- 1 tablespoon tahini
- 1 clove garlic, crushed
- 1 tablespoon lemon juice
- 1 tablespoon coarsely chopped fresh coriander (cilantro)
- 1 tablespoon coarsely chopped fresh mint
- 1 teaspoon ground cumin
- 1 tablespoon water

1 Combine sifted flours in a large bowl. Add enough of the water to mix to a soft dough. Turn out onto a lightly floured surface. Knead gently for 1 minute or until smooth. Divide dough into four portions. Cover, stand for 30 minutes.

2 Heat oil in a large non-stick frying pan over medium-low heat; cook onion, stirring, for 5 minutes or until soft. Add mince; cook, stirring, over high heat, for 5 minutes or until browned. Add garlic, cumin and chilli; cook, stirring, for 1 minute or until fragrant. Season to taste.

3 Preheat oven to 220°C/425°F. Roll one piece of dough between two pieces of baking paper to make a 30cm (12-inch) oval. Discard top sheet of paper. Transfer bottom sheet of baking paper and dough onto a large baking tray. Top with one-quarter of the lamb mixture, one-quarter of the beetroot and one-quarter of the tomato. Repeat with remaining dough, lamb, beetroot and tomato to make four flatbreads. Arrange two flatbreads on two large baking trays (you may need to cut or fold the baking paper).

4 Bake for 15 minutes, swapping trays halfway through cooking time, or until bases are browned and crisp.

5 Meanwhile, make tahini yoghurt.

6 Serve flatbreads drizzled with tahini yoghurt and sprinkled with mint and coriander leaves.

tahini yoghurt Combine ingredients in a small bowl; season to taste.

prep + cook time 1 hour serves 4

PUMPKIN SALAD

- » 1.2kg (2½ pounds) jap pumpkin
- » ⅓ cup (80ml) extra virgin olive oil
- » 2 teaspoons finely grated lemon rind
- » 2 tablespoons lemon juice
- » 4 radishes (60g), sliced thinly
- » 2 green onions (scallions), sliced thinly
- » ¼ cup loosely packed fresh basil leaves
- » ¼ cup loosely packed fresh coriander (cilantro) leaves
- » ¼ cup loosely packed fresh mint leaves
- » ¼ cup fresh dill sprigs
- » 4 lebanese flatbread pockets (320g)
- » 1 cup (280g) store-bought labneh
- » 250g (8 ounces) baby roma (egg) tomatoes, sliced crossways (see tips)
- » ⅓ cup (45g) coarsely chopped pistachios

ADVIEH SPICE MIX

- » 2 teaspoons dried rose petals
- » 1 teaspoon caraway seeds
- » 1 teaspoon ground cinnamon
- » 1 teaspoon ground nutmeg
- » 1 teaspoon ground cardamom
- » ½ teaspoon ground cumin
- » ½ teaspoon ground cloves

1 Preheat oven to 220°C/425°F. Line two oven trays with baking paper.
2 Make advieh spice mix.
3 Wash, halve and remove seeds from pumpkin; cut into 12 wedges. Divide wedges between oven trays. Drizzle with 2 tablespoons of the oil, season on both sides with 2 teaspoons advieh spice mix and salt and pepper. Bake for 40 minutes or until pumpkin is golden and skin is crisp at the edges.
4 Whisk remaining oil with rind and juice in a small bowl; season to taste.
5 Soak radish and green onion in ice-cold water for 5 minutes; drain, dry on paper towel. Place radish and green onion in a medium bowl with herbs; toss gently to combine.
6 Toast flatbreads in the oven for 3 minutes. Place breads on plates; spread with labneh. Top with pumpkin, tomatoes and herb salad; sprinkle with pistachios, drizzle with dressing.
advieh spice mix Grind rose petals and caraway seeds using a mortar and pestle until a coarse powder. Stir in remaining spices.

tips Advieh is an aromatic Persian spice mix, that can be used to season vegetable, meat or fish dishes. You can make your own labneh using the recipe on page 78. We used a mix of tomato varieties for extra colour; halve, quarter and slice the tomatoes depending on their size.

prep + cook time 25 minutes serves 4

Miso broth WITH SALMON & SOBA

- 140g (5 ounces) soba noodles
- 2 teaspoons sesame oil
- 1½ teaspoons white (shiro) miso paste
- 4 cups (1 litre) water
- 100g (3 ounces) snow peas, sliced thinly
- 200g (6 ounces) baby spinach leaves
- 200g (6 ounces) enoki mushrooms, trimmed
- 240g (8 ounces) sashimi-grade salmon, sliced thinly across the grain
- 2 teaspoons sesame seeds, toasted
- 2 green onions (scallions), sliced thinly

1 Cook noodles in simmering water for 3 minutes; drain. Rinse under cold water; drain. Toss noodles with oil in a small bowl.

2 Combine miso and the water in a small saucepan; stir over high heat until mixture just comes to the boil. Remove from heat.

3 Divide noodles, snow peas, spinach, mushrooms and salmon evenly between four serving bowls; pour over the hot broth. Sprinkle with seeds and green onion; serve immediately.

tips You can sear the salmon on all sides and finely slice it before adding it to the soup. The salmon can be substituted with tuna or ocean trout.

prep + cook time 20 minutes (+ refrigeration) serves 4

Thai-flavoured PRAWN BURGERS

» 1 clove garlic
» 4 coriander roots (cilantro), with 1cm (½-inch) stem attached
» 1 tablespoon coarsely chopped fresh ginger
» 4 kaffir lime leaves, shredded
» 2 fresh long red chillies, sliced thinly
» 16 uncooked, peeled small king prawns (shrimp) (200g), chopped finely
» 2 small potatoes (240g), coarsely grated
» 2 tablespoons rice bran oil
» 1½ tablespoons lime juice
» 4 small (85g) wholemeal bread rolls, split in half crossways
» 8 medium butter lettuce leaves
» 1 small red onion (80g), sliced thinly
» 40g (1½ ounces) bean sprouts
» 1 lebanese cucumber (130g), cut into ribbons
» ⅔ cup fresh coriander leaves (cilantro)

1 Combine garlic, coriander root and stems, ginger, lime leaves and half the chilli. Using a mortar and pestle, pound until mixture forms a thick paste. Divide paste in half.

2 Combine half of the paste with the prawns and potato in a small bowl; using wet hands form mixture into four patties. Cover, refrigerate 2 hours or overnight.

3 Add half the oil and 2 teaspoons of juice to the remaining paste in a small bowl. Cover, refrigerate until required.

4 Heat remaining oil in a small non-stick frying pan over low heat; cook patties for 3 minutes each side or until cooked through. Transfer to a plate; drizzle patties with remaining juice.

5 Place bread rolls, cut-side down, in same pan for 1 minute or until warm.

6 Toss lettuce, onion, sprouts, cucumber, coriander leaves and remaining chilli through reserved paste mixture. Sandwich salad and patties between rolls.

tips Deseed the chillies if you prefer less heat. You can replace prawns with a 200g (6-ounce) firm white fish fillet, such as basa, if you like.

prep + cook time 45 minutes serves 4

Barbecued squid with LEMON-CRACKED WHEAT RISOTTO

- 400g (13 ounces) squid hoods, halved
- 1 clove garlic, crushed
- 1 tablespoon chopped fresh oregano
- 2 teaspoons finely grated lemon rind
- 2 tablespoons olive oil
- 1 brown onion (150g), chopped finely
- 2 cloves garlic, crushed, extra
- 1 tablespoon fresh lemon thyme leaves
- 1 cup (160g) coarse cracked wheat (see tip)
- 4 cups (1 litre) water
- 2 cups (240g) frozen peas
- 2 tablespoons lemon juice
- 1 tablespoon fresh oregano leaves, extra

1 Score the inside of the squid with a small sharp knife; cut into 4cm (1½-inch) strips. Combine in a bowl with garlic, chopped oregano, rind and 1 tablespoon oil.
2 Heat remaining oil in a medium non-stick frying pan over medium heat; cook onion, extra garlic and thyme, stirring, for 5 minutes or until softened.
3 Add cracked wheat and the water; cook, stirring occasionally, for 15 minutes or until cracked wheat is tender. Add peas and juice, stir for 2 minutes or until heated through.
4 Meanwhile, cook squid on a heated grill plate (or grill or barbecue) for 2 minutes, turning halfway through cooking time, or until just cooked through.
5 Slice squid. Serve cracked wheat with squid; sprinkle with extra oregano.

tip Cracked wheat can be bought from health food stores.

swap out You could also try this with thin strips of chicken or pork instead of the squid.

prep + cook time 20 minutes (+ refrigeration) serves 4

Crisp-skinned barramundi WITH MANDARIN SALSA

- 2 medium carrot (240g), cut into long thin matchsticks
- 1 celery stalk (150g), trimmed, cut into long thin matchsticks
- 4 green onions (scallions), sliced thinly diagonally
- 4 x 150g (4½ ounces) barramundi fillets, skin on
- 4 small mandarins (150g), segmented
- ½ cup (80g) pomegranate seeds
- 1 medium lemon, cut in wedges

LEMON VINAIGRETTE

- 1 teaspoon dijon mustard
- 2 tablespoons lemon juice
- 1 tablespoon olive oil
- 1 teaspoon black sesame seeds

1 Place carrot, celery and green onion in a medium bowl of iced water. Refrigerate for 1 hour or until curled; drain. Pat dry with paper towel.

2 Meanwhile, make lemon vinaigrette.

3 Heat a medium non-stick frying pan over medium-high heat. Cook fish, skin-side down, for 3 minutes. Turn; cook for 1 minute or until cooked through.

4 Combine carrot, celery, onion, mandarin, pomegranate and dressing in a large bowl.

5 Serve fish with salsa and lemon wedges.

lemon vinaigrette Place ingredients in a screw-top jar; shake well.

prep + cook time 2 hours (+ refrigeration) serves 6

Caramelised onion & SWEET POTATO TARTE TARTIN

- 20g (¾ ounce) butter
- 1 tablespoon olive oil
- 1 tablespoon pure maple syrup
- 3 cloves garlic, sliced thinly
- ½ teaspoon ground nutmeg
- 1 tablespoon fresh lemon thyme leaves
- 350g (11 ounces) baby orange sweet potato, cut into 1cm (½-inch) slices
- 1 cup (250ml) water
- 2 sheets puff pastry
- 1 egg yolk
- 1 tablespoon milk or water
- 100g (3 ounces) goat's curd

CARAMELISED ONIONS

- 20g (¾ ounce) butter
- 1 tablespoon olive oil
- 4 medium onions (800g), sliced finely
- ¼ cup (60ml) balsamic vinegar
- 2 tablespoons pure maple syrup
- 1 tablespoon dijon mustard

1 Make caramelised onions.

2 Heat butter, olive oil and maple syrup in a 30cm (12-inch) ovenproof frying pan over medium heat. Add garlic; cook, stirring, for 1 minute. Remove pan from heat. Sprinkle nutmeg and thyme over base of pan; pack sweet potato slices, in a single layer, on top; season. Pour half the water over the sweet potato. Return pan to heat; cook for 8 minutes or until the water evaporates. Add remaining water; cook a further 8 minutes or until sweet potato is browned underneath. Remove from heat; cool 5 minutes.

3 Spoon caramelised onions evenly over sweet potato slices with the back of a spoon. Set aside in the fridge to cool completely.

4 Preheat oven to 200°C/400°F.

5 Cut each pasty sheet on a diagonal into two triangles. Whisk egg yolk and milk together in a small bowl. Make a larger square with the four triangles, with the longest edges of the triangles forming the outside of the square; use a little egg wash to stick the pastry together. Place the pastry over the tart and trim overhang. Fold, nip and tuck the edges in to form the pastry around the tart. Brush with egg mixture and prick lightly with a fork. Bake for 20 minutes or until crisp and golden. Stand tart in pan for 5 minutes.

6 To serve, place pan over medium heat for 30 seconds to loosen the base then invert onto a wooden board, top with extra lemon thyme and spoonfuls of goat's curd.

caramelised onions Heat butter and oil in a large heavy-based frying pan over a medium heat; cook onion, stirring frequently for 30 minutes or until very soft and golden. Add vinegar, syrup and mustard; cook for 30 minutes over low heat or until caramelised and reduced. Season.

serving suggestion Sprinkle with baby rocket (arugula) leaves, if you like.

3pm Slump

SAVOURY

prep + cook time 10 minutes makes 9 cups

POPCORN

- » 1 teaspoon ground coriander
- » 1 teaspoon yellow mustard seeds
- » 1 teaspoon black peppercorns
- » 1 teaspoon garlic salt
- » 1 teaspoon sea salt flakes
- » ⅓ cup fresh dill sprigs, chopped finely
- » ¼ cup (60ml) olive oil
- » 2 tablespoons olive oil, extra
- » ¾ cup (180g) popping corn

1 Crush spices and salts using a mortar and pestle. Stir in dill and oil.
2 Heat extra oil in a large heavy-based saucepan over medium heat. Add popping corn; cover and cook for 3 minutes, shaking pan occasionally or until all corn has popped.
3 Place popcorn in a large bowl; discard any unpopped kernels. Add dill seasoning; stir well to combine. Serve immediately.

VARIATIONS

no-cheese cheesy popcorn Omit ingredients in step 1. Combine ¼ cup (60ml) olive oil, 1 teaspoon smoked paprika, ½ teaspoon garlic salt and ¼ cup nutritional yeast flakes. Toss with hot popcorn.

wasabi, nori & sesame popcorn Omit ingredients in step 1. Snip two nori (seaweed) sheets into thin strips, using kitchen scissors. Combine 2 teaspoons each wasabi paste, tamari, sesame oil and olive oil until smooth. Toss wasabi mixture with hot popcorn. Add nori and 2 tablespoons sesame seeds; toss well to coat.

prep + cook time 35 minutes makes 8

MINI FRITTATAS

- 2 teaspoons olive oil
- 1 small leek (200g), sliced thinly
- ½ clove garlic, crushed
- 3 cups (120g) firmly packed baby spinach leaves, chopped finely
- 5 eggs
- ½ cup (125ml) pouring cream
- 1 tablespoon finely chopped fresh mint
- 1 tablespoon finely chopped fresh basil
- 1 tablespoon finely chopped fresh dill
- 100g (3 ounces) goat's fetta, crumbled

1 Preheat oven to 180°C/350°F. Line 8 holes of a 12-hole (⅓ cup/80ml) muffin pan with paper cases.

2 Heat oil in a medium saucepan over medium heat; cook leek, stirring, for 3 minutes. Add garlic; cook for 2 minutes or until leek is soft. Add spinach; cook, stirring, 30 seconds or until wilted. Remove from heat. Set aside.

3 Whisk eggs, cream and herbs in a medium jug; season.

4 Divide spinach mixture into pan holes; pour in egg mixture, then top with fetta.

5 Bake frittatas for 20 minutes or until set. Leave in pan for 5 minutes before serving warm or at room temperature.

keeps Store in an airtight container in the fridge for up to 5 days or freeze for up to 1 month.

prep + cook time 1 hour serves 4

Healthy vegie fries WITH SUPER-FOOD GUACAMOLE

YOU MAY NEED TO TURN THE FAN ON IN YOUR OVEN FOR THE LAST 5-10 MINUTES OF COOKING, IF YOU FIND THAT THE VEGIE FRIES AREN'T BROWNING ENOUGH. SPIRULINA IS BY NO MEANS ESSENTIAL TO THE GUACAMOLE BUT IS A WAY OF BOOSTING YOUR GREEN VEGIE INTAKE IF YOU HAVE IT ON HAND.

» 1 large orange sweet potato (500g)
» 2 large parsnips (700g)
» ¼ cup (60ml) extra virgin olive oil

SUPER-FOOD GUACAMOLE
» 2 medium avocados (500g)
» 1 fresh small red chilli, chopped finely
» 1 small clove garlic, crushed
» 1 tablespoon lime juice
» ½ cup finely chopped fresh coriander (cilantro)
» ¼ teaspoon spirulina, optional (see tips)

1 Preheat oven to 220°C/440°F. Line two large oven trays with baking paper.
2 Scrub vegetables; pat dry with paper towel. Cut unpeeled vegetables into 1cm (½-inch) thick fries. Place vegetables in a medium bowl, drizzle with olive oil; toss to coat well.
3 Spread vegetables in a single layer evenly over oven trays. Season to taste with salt.
4 Bake vegetables, turning halfway through cooking, for 45 minutes or until golden and tender.
5 Meanwhile, make super-food guacamole.
6 Serve warm vegie fries with super-food guacamole.
super-food guacamole Mash avocado in a medium bowl. Add remaining ingredients, mix well; season to taste.

tips Spirulina is a nutrient-rich sea algae, packed with minerals, B-vitamins and iron. It is advisable to buy it in smallish quantities, as it is thought that the nutritional benefits can diminish after about 3 months of opening. It is available from major supermarkets and health food stores. You could also serve this recipe with a spinach and watercress salad to make it a more substantial meal.

prep + cook time 20 minutes serves 4

Creamy carrot & MISO DIP

- » 2 sheets original mountain bread (50g)
- » cooking oil spray
- » 2 medium carrots (260g), chopped coarsely
- » 1 small clove garlic, chopped
- » 1 medium shallot (25g), chopped coarsely
- » 2 tablespoons white (shiro) miso paste
- » ¼ cup (60ml) avocado or vegetable oil
- » 2 teaspoons sesame oil
- » 2 tablespoons rice wine vinegar
- » 1 tablespoon water
- » 1 teaspoon black sesame seeds
- » 1 tablespoon micro coriander (cilantro) leaves

1 Preheat oven to 200°C/400°F.

2 Place mountain bread on two oven trays, spray both sides with cooking oil; season with salt. Bake for 4 minutes or until golden and crisp. Break into large pieces.

3 Blend or process carrot, garlic, shallot, miso, oils, vinegar and the water for 30 seconds or until mixture is smooth; season to taste.

4 Serve dip sprinkled with sesame seeds and coriander, with mountain bread crisps.

keeps Mountain bread crisps will keep in an airtight container for up to 3 days. Dip will keep in an airtight container in the fridge for up to 3 days; stir before serving.

prep + cook time 15 minutes serves 6

15-minute herby pea & COCONUT SOUP

- 2 tablespoons coconut oil
- 200g (7 ounces) green onions (scallions), sliced
- 1kg (2 pounds) frozen peas
- 400ml can coconut cream
- 3 teaspoons sea salt flakes, or to taste
- 3 cups (750ml) boiling water
- ⅓ cup (80ml) lemon juice
- 2 cups fresh basil leaves
- 2 cups fresh coriander (cilantro) leaves
- ½ cup fresh dill sprigs
- ½ cup fresh mint sprigs
- Greek-style yoghurt or unsweetened coconut yoghurt, to serve, optional

1 Heat coconut oil in a large saucepan over medium-high heat. Cook onion, stirring for 3 minutes or until softened. Increase heat to high; add peas, coconut cream, salt and the water. Bring to the boil; cook, stirring occasionally, for 5 minutes or until peas are heated through.
2 Remove from heat, add lemon juice and all but ½ cup of the combined herbs. Cool for 5 minutes; process in batches until smooth. Return soup to pan; heat briefly until just warmed through.
3 Serve soup in bowls topped with remaining herbs and yoghurt, if you like; season to taste.

prep + cook time 30 minutes makes 10 rolls

Pea, miso & mint RICE PAPER ROLLS

- 2 cups (240g) frozen peas, thawed
- 1 medium avocado (250g), chopped coarsely
- 1 tablespoon white (shiro) miso paste
- 1 teaspoon finely grated lime rind
- 1 tablespoon lime juice
- ¼ cup coarsely chopped fresh mint leaves
- 10 x 22cm (9-inch) rice paper rounds
- 2 cups (160g) finely shredded purple cabbage
- 2 cups julienned daikon
- 1 teaspoon black sesame seeds
- pickled ginger, to serve

1 Process peas, avocado, miso, lime rind, juice and mint until well combined but not quite smooth. Season to taste.

2 Place one rice paper round in a medium bowl of lukewarm water for 15 seconds or until just soft. Place on a clean tea towel or paper towel.

3 Place 1 tablespoon of the cabbage on the centre of each rice paper round, top with 2 tablespoons pea mixture and 1 tablespoon of the daikon. Fold edges in and roll up firmly to enclose filling. Sprinkle with some black sesame seeds. Repeat with remaining rice paper rounds, filling and sesame seeds. Serve with pickled ginger.

keeps Best made on day of serving. Make a few hours ahead, then store, covered with damp paper towel in an airtight container in the fridge.

prep + cook time 20 minutes makes 3 cups

Spicy keep-on going TRAIL MIX

TRY THIS MIX AS A POST-WORK OUT SNACK, OR KEEP A JAR HANDY ON YOUR DESK AT WORK FOR TIMES WHEN YOU MIGHT CRAVE A SUGARY TREAT. A HANDFUL OF THE MIX WILL HELP STABILISE BLOOD SUGARS UNTIL A PROPER MEAL CAN BE HAD.

- 1½ tablespoons raw honey
- ½ teaspoon cayenne pepper
- ½ teaspoon smoked paprika
- 1½ teaspoons fine sea salt
- 1½ tablespoons coconut oil
- 1 cup (160g) natural almonds
- ½ cup (70g) skinless hazelnuts
- ½ cup (100g) pepitas (pumpkin seed kernels)
- ¼ cup (35g) sunflower seeds
- ½ cup (25g) flaked coconut

1 Preheat oven to 150°C/300°F. Line a large oven tray with baking paper.
2 Combine honey, spices, salt and coconut oil in a large bowl. Add nuts, seeds and coconut; mix until well coated.
3 Spread mixture in a single layer on tray.
4 Bake, stirring occasionally, for 15 minutes or until lightly browned. Cool on tray. Separate into small clusters.

keeps Store in an airtight container for up to 1 week.

KEEP ON GOING
KEEP ON

prep + cook time 1 hour serves 4 (makes 6 cups)

Kale chips with SESAME & CORIANDER

THINK OF THIS RECIPE AS MORE THAN JUST A SNACK.
TRY USING IT AS A TOPPER FOR SOUPS, SALADS AND EGG DISHES.

- » ¼ cup (70g) unhulled tahini
- » 2 teaspoons ground coriander
- » 1 tablespoon extra virgin olive oil
- » 2 tablespoons sesame seeds
- » 1 teaspoon sea salt flakes
- » 1 bunch green kale (250g), stems discarded

1 Preheat oven to 120°C/250°F fan-forced. Line two large oven trays with baking paper.
2 Combine tahini, coriander, oil, seeds and salt in a large bowl. Tear kale into bite-size pieces. Using your hands, rub tahini mixture onto kale leaves to coat.
3 Place in a single layer on trays. Bake, swapping trays halfway, for 50 minutes or until kale is dry and crisp.

tip The time it takes to dry the kale may differ depending on the size of the torn pieces.

keeps Store in an airtight container for up 2 weeks.

prep + cook time 20 minutes serves 4

Chia & tomato guacamole
WITH SUMAC CRISPS

- cooking oil spray
- 4 rye mountain breads (100g)
- 1½ teaspoons ground sumac
- 2 medium avocados (500g), chopped coarsely
- ⅓ cup (80ml) lime juice
- 1 small red onion (100g), chopped finely
- ⅓ cup (60g) semi-dried tomatoes, chopped finely
- ¼ cup fresh coriander (cilantro), chopped coarsely
- ½ teaspoon smoked paprika
- 1½ tablespoons black or white chia seeds
- 2 fresh long red chillies, sliced thinly

1 Preheat oven to 200°C/400°F. Line three oven trays with baking paper; spray with cooking oil.
2 Cut each sheet of mountain bread into 16 triangles. Place in a single layer on trays; spray with oil. Sprinkle with sumac; season with salt and pepper. Bake for 5 minutes or until golden and crisp.
3 Place avocado and juice in a medium bowl; mash lightly with a fork. Stir in red onion, tomato, coriander, paprika, 1 tablespoon chia seeds and three-quarters of the chilli. Season to taste.
4 Place guacamole in a serving bowl; top with remaining chilli and remaining chia seeds. Serve with sumac crisps.

keeps Guacamole can be stored, covered, in the fridge for up to 2 days. Sumac crisps will keep in an airtight container at room temperature for up to 1 week.

prep + cook time 1 hour (+ refrigeration) makes 12

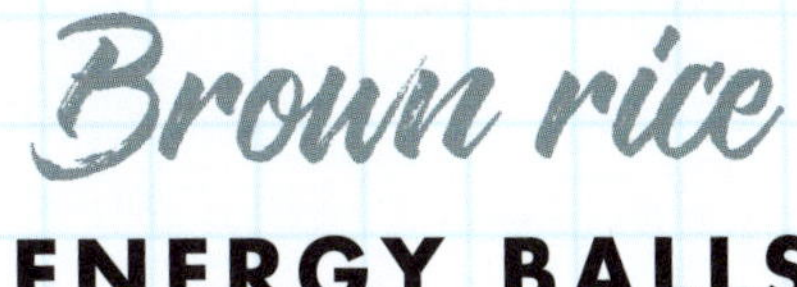

ENERGY BALLS

TURN THE ENERGY BALLS INTO LUNCH, BY STUFFING THEM INTO A PITTA POCKET OR WRAP WITH SALAD INGREDIENTS AND A LITTLE DRESSING MADE FROM GREEK-STYLE YOGHURT, A COUPLE OF TEASPOONS OF TAHINI AND LEMON JUICE.

» 1 cup (200g) medium-grain brown rice
» 2½ cups (625ml) chicken stock
» 2 tablespoons tahini
» 1 tablespoon tamari
» 1 tablespoon apple cider vinegar
» 2 tablespoons chia seeds
» 2 green onions (scallions), chopped finely
» 2 teaspoons finely grated fresh ginger
» 2 tablespoons black sesame seeds
» 2 tablespoons white sesame seeds

1 Rinse rice under running water until water runs clear. Place rice in a medium saucepan with stock; bring to the boil. Reduce heat to low; cook, covered, for 40 minutes or until stock is almost absorbed and rice is tender. Remove from heat; stand, covered, for 5 minutes.
2 Transfer hot rice to a medium bowl; immediately stir in tahini, tamari, vinegar, chia seeds, green onion and ginger, season to taste. Stand for 5 minutes or until cool enough to handle.
3 Roll 2 tablespoons of mixture into balls; roll in combined sesame seeds. Place balls on a baking-paper-lined tray. Refrigerate at least 30 minutes before eating.

tip As with meat, ingredients containing rice should always be kept refrigerated and never left at room temperature, otherwise food poisoning can occur.

keeps Rice balls will keep refrigerated for up to 5 days.

prep time 15 minutes serves 2

Raw slaw salad
WITH PUMPERNICKEL CRUMBS

SERVES TWO AS A VEGETARIAN MAIN OR SERVE AS A SIDE DISH FOR FOUR WITH GRILLED SALMON OR PORK.

» 125g (4 ounces) brussels sprouts
» 1 baby cauliflower (125g)
» 1 small fennel bulb (200g)
» ¼ cup (40g) sultanas
» 1½ teaspoons apple cider vinegar
» ⅓ cup (80ml) extra virgin olive oil
» ½ teaspoon sea salt flakes
» ½ teaspoon cracked black pepper
» ¼ cup (70g) Greek-style yoghurt
» 1 slice pumpernickel rye bread (50g), chopped coarsely
» 1 teaspoon capers
» ½ medium green apple (75g)

1 Trim base and outer leaves from sprouts. Using a sharp knife, thinly slice sprouts and cauliflower; place in a large bowl. Trim fennel; reserve half of the fronds. Thinly slice fennel; add to bowl.
2 Combine sultanas, vinegar, ¼ cup of the oil, salt, pepper and yoghurt in a small bowl.
3 Process pumpernickel until large breadcrumbs form. Heat a medium frying pan over high heat. Add crumbs to dry pan; cook, stirring continuously, for 4 minutes or until toasted.
4 Heat the remaining oil in a small frying pan over high heat; add capers. Cook, stirring for 2 minutes or until capers have burst their skins. (Be careful as the capers will pop in the hot oil and may splash.)
5 Cut apple lengthways into thin slices. Add to vegetable mixture. Pour over yoghurt dressing; mix gently to combine.
6 Serve salad sprinkled with toasted crumbs, capers and reserved fennel fronds.

prep time 15 minutes serves 4

Miso almond spread WITH AVOCADO

- 1½ tablespoons white (shiro) miso paste
- 2 tablespoons almond spread
- 2 tablespoons olive oil
- ½ teaspoon sesame oil
- 1 tablespoon mirin
- 1 tablespoon water
- 2 medium avocados (500g)
- ⅓ cup (50g) roasted cashews, chopped coarsely
- ½ teaspoon black sesame seeds

1 Stir miso, almond spread, oils, mirin and the water in a medium jug until smooth; season to taste.

2 Cut unpeeled avocados in half; discard stones. Spoon dressing into avocado hollow; sprinkle with cashews and sesame seeds. Serve immediately.

tips Use any of your favourite healthy dressings or dips for this quick and easy snack. The miso almond spread will keep in an airtight container and can also be used as a dressing for salads.

prep + cook time 45 minutes makes 24

Cauliflower PIZZA BITES

- 300g (9½ ounces) cauliflower florets, chopped
- ½ cup (60g) almond meal (ground almonds)
- ¼ cup (30g) finely grated vintage cheddar
- 1 teaspoon finely chopped fresh rosemary
- 1 teaspoon finely chopped fresh oregano
- 1 egg, beaten lightly
- 2 lebanese eggplants (160g)
- 2 medium zucchini (240g)
- 1 tablespoon olive oil
- 1 cup (150g) canned crushed tomatoes
- 1 clove garlic, crushed
- 20g (¾ ounce) fetta, crumbled
- ¼ cup (40g) pine nuts, toasted
- 2 tablespoons fresh oregano leaves, extra

1 Preheat oven to 220°C/425°F. Grease two flat-based 12-hole (2-tablespoon/40ml) patty pan trays; line bases with small rounds of baking paper.

2 Pulse cauliflower in a food processor until it resembles fine crumbs; transfer to a large bowl. Add almond meal, cheddar, herbs and egg; season and combine well. Spoon mixture into holes; press firmly on base and side to form a tart shell. Bake 10 minutes or until golden and crisp. Leave oven on.

3 Meanwhile, use a mandoline or V-slicer to cut eggplant and zucchini into 3mm (⅛-inch) thick slices. Cook vegetables on a heated oiled chargrill plate (or grill), on one side only, for 2 minutes or until lightly charred. Transfer to a medium bowl, add oil and season; toss to coat.

4 Combine tomatoes and garlic in a small bowl. Spoon 1 teaspoon tomato mixture into each pizza bite; top with grilled vegetables and fetta.

5 Bake bites for 5 minutes or until fetta is golden. Loosen each pizza bite from the pan using a butter knife. Serve topped with extra pine nuts and oregano.

tips You can use any leftover cheese you have in the fridge instead of cheddar. Make a double batch of bases; freeze half so you have them at the ready. Pizza bites can be made a day ahead and reheated in the microwave, on a plate lined with paper towel, on HIGH (100%) for 1 minute; stand for 2 minutes before serving.

prep + cook time 4 hours 10 minutes (+ cooling) makes 30

Seed & vegie PULP CRISPBREADS

HAVE YOU EVER WONDERED IF THERE WAS A USE FOR ALL THE LEFTOVER VEGETABLE PULP FROM JUICING? MAKE CRACKERS! THE DRY FIBROUS TEXTURE OF VEGETABLE PULP MAKES IT THE PERFECT INGREDIENT TO CREATE TASTY CRACKERS FOR SNACKING.

» ½ cup (80g) linseeds (flaxseeds)
» 2 tablespoons (20g) chia seeds
» ⅓ cup (80ml) water
» 1 tablespoon tamari
» 1 cup (150g) vegetable pulp, leftover from juicing (see tips)
» ¼ cup (35g) sunflower seeds
» 2 teaspoons sesame seeds
» ½ teaspoon cumin seeds
» 1 teaspoon caraway seeds
» 2 teaspoons raw honey

1 Preheat oven to 100°C/212°F. Lightly grease a 30cm x 40cm (12-inch x 16-inch) oven tray with baking paper.
2 Combine seeds, the water and tamari in a large bowl. Stand for 5 minutes. Add remaining ingredients; stir well to combine. Draw a 30cm x 40cm (12-inch x 16-inch) rectangle on a baking paper, turn it over. Spoon mixture onto centre of rectangle marked on baking paper; top with a second piece of paper. Roll mixture out to fill rectangle, remove top paper; transfer to oven tray on baking paper. If you prefer even-sized crackers, score mixture with a sharp knife into 5cm (2-inch) squares.
3 Bake for 2 hours, turn cracker over and bake for a further 2 hours or until dried and crisp. Turn oven off; leave cracker inside to cool completely.
4 Break cooled cracker into pieces; alternatively, using score lines, break into squares. Transfer to an airtight container.

tips You can use any leftover vegetable pulp from making fresh juice; we used carrot and beetroot. If you are making a fruit and vegetable juice, juice the vegetables first, then remove the pulp to use in the crackers before juicing the fruit. You can keep leftover vegetable pulp in the refrigerator for up to 2 days before making the crackers.

try this
With a bowl of loads-in-one goodness smash (see page 122), for dipping.
Spread with cashew cream 'cheese' (see page 106).
Dunked in 15-minute herby pea and coconut soup (see page 254).

keeps Store crackers in an airtight container for up to 4 days.

prep + cook time 1 hour serves 4 (makes 2½ cups)

Roasted sweet & sour CHICKPEAS & BEANS

- 2 x 400g (12½ ounces) canned chickpeas (garbanzo beans)
- 2 x 400g (12½ ounces) canned butter beans
- 1 tablespoon extra virgin olive oil
- 1 tablespoon finely grated lime rind
- 2 teaspoons ground cumin
- 2 teaspoons ground coriander
- 1 teaspoon chilli flakes
- 1 tablespoon coconut sugar

1 Preheat oven to 220°C/425°F. Line an oven tray with baking paper.
2 Drain then rinse chickpeas and beans; place in a medium heatproof bowl. Cover with boiling water; drain. Dry on paper towel. (This will ensure that the chickpeas and beans will dry and crisp during roasting.)
3 Place chickpeas and beans on tray. Bake for 50 minutes, stirring occasionally, or until golden and crisp.
4 Transfer roasted chickpeas and beans to a medium bowl. Add oil, rind, cumin, coriander, chilli flakes and coconut sugar. Season generously with salt and freshly ground black pepper; toss until well coated.

tips You can use dried legumes instead: soak them overnight first and cook for 1½ hours in boiling water. Experiment with different spices and herbs to flavour how you like it.

keeps Store the roasted mix in an airtight container or jar for up to 4 days.

prep + cook time 40 minutes serves 8

Roasted onion socca WITH CHILLI YOGHURT

SOCCA, ALSO KNOWN AS FARINATA, IS A TRADITIONAL ITALIAN AND PROVENÇAL PANCAKE MADE FROM CHICKPEA FLOUR.

You will need an ovenproof frying pan for this recipe.

- 1 medium brown onion (150g)
- ½ cup (125ml) olive oil
- 1½ cups (180g) chickpea flour (besan)
- 1 teaspoon salt flakes
- 1¼ cups (310ml) lukewarm water
- 2 teaspoons chopped fresh rosemary
- 1 tablespoon small fresh rosemary sprigs
- ¼ cup (20g) finely grated parmesan

CHILLI YOGHURT

- ½ cup (140g) Greek-style yoghurt
- 1 teaspoon raw honey
- 1 tablespoon coarsely chopped fresh flat-leaf parsley
- ¼ teaspoon chilli flakes

1 Preheat oven to 200°C/400°F. Line an oven tray with baking paper.
2 Cut onion into eight wedges; separate layers. Place onion in a medium bowl with 1 tablespoon of the olive oil; toss to coat. Season. Place onion on tray; bake for 20 minutes or until browned.
3 Place chickpea flour, salt, the water, chopped rosemary and ¼ cup of the olive oil in a medium bowl; whisk until smooth. Season with cracked black pepper. Set aside for 5 minutes.
4 Make chilli yoghurt.
5 Increase oven to 250°C/480°F. Heat a large heavy-based ovenproof frying pan over a medium-high heat. Add remaining oil, heat for a few seconds, pour in batter, top with onion and rosemary sprigs. Cook for 1 minute; transfer to oven, bake for 10 minutes or until golden and socca pulls away from the side of the pan.
6 Serve socca cut into wedges, topped with parmesan and chilli yoghurt.
chilli yoghurt Combine ingredients in a small bowl.

keeps Store socca in an airtight container in the fridge for up to 3 days or freeze for up to 1 month. Reheat socca between sheets of baking paper in a sandwich press.

prep + cook time 15 minutes makes 60

NORI CHIPS

- » 2 teaspoons sesame seeds
- » 1 teaspoon sea salt, crumbled
- » 10 nori (seaweed) sheets
- » 2 tablespoons sesame oil

NANAMI TOGARASHI

- » 1 tablespoon finely grated orange rind
- » 2 teaspoons cracked black pepper
- » 1 tablespoon chilli flakes
- » 2 teaspoons black sesame seeds

1 Make nanami togarashi.
2 Crush sesame seeds using a mortar and pestle; combine with 2 teaspoons of the nanami togarashi and the salt. (Store remaining nanami togarashi for another use.)
3 Using scissors, cut each nori sheet into triangles or squares. Place on a large baking-paper-lined oven tray; lightly brush nori with sesame oil.
4 Heat a large non-stick frying pan over medium-high heat; toast nori, in batches, for 2 minutes each side or until crisp. Return to paper-lined tray; sprinkle immediately with nanami togarashi mixture.
nanami togarashi Cook rind in a small dry frying pan over medium heat for 5 minutes or until rind is dry and crispy. Place in a screw-top jar with remaining ingredients; shake well to combine.

tips Nanami togarashi is a Japanese seven-spice mix, also called shichimi togarashi (both nana and shichi mean seven in Japanese). The blend contains red peppers, sansho pepper, orange rind, black and white sesame seeds, seaweed and ginger. It is available from Asian food stores if you don't want to make your own.

prep + cook time 25 minutes (+ cooling) makes 4½ cups

Powdered pecans & ALMONDS WITH ROSEMARY

- 2 cups (240g) pecans
- 2 cups (320g) natural almonds
- 1 tablespoon finely chopped fresh rosemary
- 1 teaspoon sea salt flakes
- ½ teaspoon freshly ground black pepper
- ¾ cup (180ml) rice malt syrup

1 Preheat oven to 180°C/350°F.
2 Place nuts on an oven tray; roast for 10 minutes or until light golden (see tips). Transfer immediately to a large heatproof bowl. Add rosemary, salt and pepper; toss to combine.
3 Meanwhile, place rice malt syrup in a small heavy-based saucepan over high heat. Cook without stirring, swirling pan occasionally, for 10 minutes or until syrup reaches 150°C/300°F (hard crack stage) on a sugar (candy) thermometer. (Alternatively, drop a spoonful of syrup into a glass of ice-cold water; syrup should form brittle threads that will break when bent.)
4 Working quickly, add syrup to warm nut mixture; stir vigorously (see tips) with a metal spoon until syrup hardens and nuts are cool enough to handle. Using your hands, roughly break up and toss nuts together, roughing up surface.
5 Leave nuts to cool completely; transfer to a large airtight jar.

tips While the nuts are roasting, start step 3, so that the nuts are warm when you toss them with the syrup. You will need to work rapidly, as the syrup sets quickly. Always take care around hot syrups as they can cause nasty burns.

keeps Store nuts in the pantry for up to 2 weeks.

prep + cook time 15 minutes serves 2

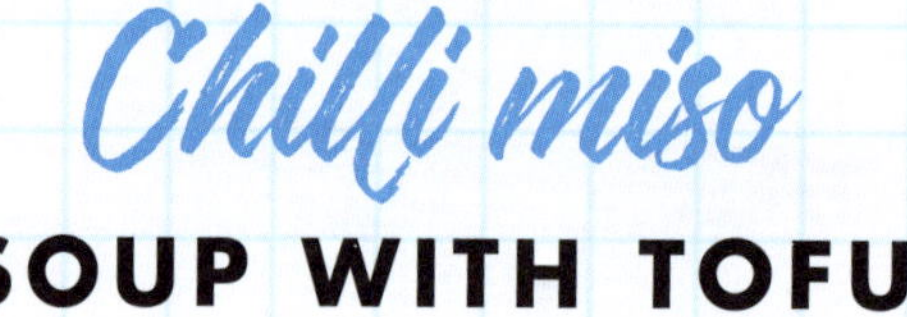

SOUP WITH TOFU

- ¼ cup (75g) dashi miso paste
- 3 cups (750ml) water
- 150g (4½ ounces) silken tofu, cut into 1cm (½-inch) cubes
- 3 green onions (scallions), sliced thinly on the diagonal
- 1 fresh long red chilli, sliced thinly on the diagonal
- 2 toasted nori (seaweed) sheets, each cut into eight pieces
- 2 teaspoons black sesame seeds

1 Whisk dashi miso paste and water in a small saucepan. Bring to a simmer over medium heat.
2 Meanwhile, divide tofu, green onion, chilli and nori between two bowls.
3 Pour miso soup into bowls; sprinkle with sesame seeds. Serve immediately.

prep + cook time 50 minutes (+ standing) serves 4

Cheat's teff flatbread WITH CASHEW CHEESE

You will need to start this recipe a day ahead.

- ⅔ cup (100g) teff flour (see tips)
- 1 teaspoon gluten-free baking powder
- ¼ teaspoon sea salt flakes
- 1 teaspoon nigella seeds
- ⅓ cup (80ml) water
- 3 eggs
- 1 teaspoon apple cider vinegar
- 1 teaspoon coconut oil or cooking oil spray

CASHEW CHEESE

- 1⅔ cups (250g) raw cashews
- 2 teaspoons sea salt flakes
- 2 teaspoons nutritional yeast flakes (see page 106)
- 3 teaspoons olive oil
- ⅓ cup (80ml) water
- 2 tablespoons lemon juice
- 1 clove garlic

1 Make cashew cream cheese.
2 Sift flour and baking powder into a medium bowl; stir in salt and seeds. Make a well in the centre; whisk in water, eggs and vinegar.
3 Heat a 20cm (8-inch) wide, 15cm (6-inch) base non-stick frying pan over medium heat. Brush pan with ¼ teaspoon of the coconut oil or coat lightly with oil spray. Pour ⅓ cup of the batter into hot pan; spread with an offset palette knife to cover pan. Cook for 2 minutes each side or until cooked through. Transfer flatbread to a plate; cover to keep warm.
4 Repeat with remaining batter to make a total of 4 flatbreads. Cut into wedges; serve topped with cashew cream cheese.
cashew cheese Place cashews in a small bowl; cover with cold water. Stand, covered, for 4 hours or overnight. Drain cashews; rinse under cold water, drain well. Blend cashews with remaining ingredients, using a high-powered blender if available; this type of blender will produce a very smooth consistency. (Makes 2 cups)

keeps Flatbreads are best made on day of serving or can be frozen for up to 1 month. Store cashew cream cheese in an airtight container in the fridge for up to 3 weeks.

try this topped with halved or quartered mixed heirloom cherry tomatoes and small basil leaves, seasoned with salt and pepper.

tips Teff flour is derived from the seeds of a hardy grass. It is a staple in Ethiopia, where it is used to make injera, a fermented flatbread. Teff is high in protein, calcium and resistant starch, a form of dietary fibre that can help with blood-sugar management. The pleasant nutty taste and its gluten-free status have contributed to its popularity in western countries. Teff flour is available from some supermarkets, delis and health food stores.

prep + cook time 45 minutes (+ refrigeration & freezing) serves 4

Instant flu-helper CHICKEN NOODLE SOUP

THIS RECIPE IS A PERFECT WORK LUNCH DURING COLD AND FLU SEASON; MAKE A BATCH OF THE SOUP CONCENTRATE AND KEEP IN THE FREEZER FOR WHEN THE COLD WEATHER HITS. YOU WILL NEED FOUR 2 CUP (500ML) HEATPROOF JARS WITH LIDS FOR THIS RECIPE.

» 3 litres (12 cups) chicken broth (see page 121)
» 5cm (2-inch) piece fresh ginger, sliced thinly
» 5cm (2-inch) piece fresh turmeric, grated finely
» 2 cloves garlic, bruised
» 200g (6½ ounces) kelp noodles
» 1 cup (180g) frozen corn kernels, thawed
» 3 baby buk choy (450g), quartered lengthways
» 1 fresh long red chilli, sliced thinly, optional
» 1½ cups (220g) cooked chicken, sliced or shredded
» 6 green onions (scallions), sliced thinly
» 2 tablespoons tamari
» 1.5 litres (6 cups) boiling water

1 Combine chicken broth, ginger, turmeric and garlic in a large saucepan. Bring to the boil; boil for 35 minutes or until reduced to 3 cups (750ml). Strain through a fine sieve into a medium heatproof bowl; discard solids. Cool slightly; refrigerate for 2 hours.
2 Discard any solidified fat from broth surface. Pour broth concentrate into two ice cube trays; freeze for up to 3 months.
3 To serve: Divide noodles, corn, buk choy, chilli, chicken and green onion among four 2 cup (500ml) heatproof jars with lids. Add four frozen broth cubes and 2 teaspoons tamari to each jar. Pour 1½ cups (375ml) of the boiling water into each jar; stir to dissolve broth cubes.

tip To cook chicken at the same time as stock, gently simmer a 250g (4-ounce) chicken breast in chicken stock (or water) in a saucepan over low heat for 10 minutes; cool in stock for 5 minutes. Cool and slice thinly. Place in a zip-top bag; freeze for up to 1 month.

prep time 10 minutes serves 8 (makes 3 cups)

Peanut butter & BEETROOT HUMMUS

- » 3 medium beetroot (beets) (500g)
- » ¼ cup (60ml) lemon juice
- » ½ cup (130g) natural crunchy peanut butter
- » 1 cup (200g) cannellini beans
- » 1 teaspoon sea salt flakes
- » 2 cloves garlic, peeled
- » ¼ teaspoon ground cumin
- » ½ cup fresh coriander (cilantro) leaves

PITTA BREAD CRISPS

- » 2 large wholemeal lebanese bread rounds (200g)
- » 2 tablespoons extra virgin olive oil
- » 1 teaspoon ground cumin
- » 1 teaspoon sumac
- » ¼ teaspoon sea salt flakes

1 Make pitta bread crisps.
2 Wearing kitchen gloves, peel beetroot, then chop coarsely.
3 Process beetroot with remaining ingredients until smooth.
4 Serve dip with pitta crisps.

pitta bread crisps Preheat oven to 200°C/400°F. Using scissors, snip around edge of bread rounds, then pull apart to separate. Place crumb-side up on two large oven trays. Brush with oil; sprinkle with spices. Bake, swapping trays from top to bottom, for 4 minutes or until golden. Cool; season lightly with salt. Break into large pieces.

keeps Store dip in the fridge for up to 3 days. The pitta bread crisps will keep in an airtight container in the pantry for up to 1 week.

swap out peanut butter with the same quantity of almond or macadamia spread, if preferred.

serving suggestion Serve with halved or quartered baby cucumbers, for dipping, if you like.

3pm Slump

SWEET

prep + cook time 25 minutes (+ refrigeration & freezing) makes 15

Cacao bombs
WITH PASSIONFRUIT

- 4 fresh dates (80g), pitted
- ¼ cup (60ml) boiling water
- 60g (2 ounces) cacao butter, chopped coarsely (see tips)
- ¼ cup (55g) coconut oil, solid (see tips)
- 2 tablespoons cacao powder
- 1 tablespoon pure maple syrup
- 2 pinches sea salt
- ¼ teaspoon pure vanilla extract
- 3 passionfruit, pulp removed

1 Place dates in a small bowl; cover with boiling water. Set aside for 15 minutes. Place 15 mini-patty paper cases on a large oven tray.

2 Place cacao butter, coconut oil, cacao powder, syrup and a pinch of salt in a small saucepan over medium heat; stir until melted and combined.

3 Divide half of the chocolate mixture evenly among paper cases, using 1½ teaspoons for each one. Reserve remaining chocolate mixture. Place in freezer for 10 minutes or until set.

4 Drain dates, reserving 1 tablespoon of the soaking water. Process dates, reserved water, vanilla and a pinch of salt until smooth. Spoon ½ teaspoon of the date caramel into centre of each patty case; top evenly with remaining chocolate mixture.

5 Refrigerate for at least 1 hour or until chocolate mixture is set; freeze. Serve topped with passionfruit pulp.

tips The coconut oil needs to be solid for this recipe. If you can't find cacao butter you can substitute cocoa butter.

keeps Store in an airtight container in the freezer for up to 2 weeks.

prep + cook time 15 minutes (+ freezing) makes 18

Frozen tahini, black sesame & COCONUT FUDGE

- 1 cup (250ml) coconut cream
- ⅓ cup (80ml) tahini
- 2 tablespoons pure maple syrup
- 1 teaspoon pure vanilla extract
- pinch sea salt
- 2 tablespoons coconut oil
- 1 teaspoon mesquite powder, optional (see tip)
- 1 teaspoon black sesame seeds

1 Grease a 10cm x 20cm (4-inch x 8-inch) loaf pan; line base and sides with baking paper.

2 Process coconut cream, tahini, syrup, vanilla, salt, coconut oil and mesquite powder, if using, until mixture is smooth.

3 Pour into tin; sprinkle with sesame seeds. Freeze for 2 hours or until set.

4 Using an oiled knife, cut into 18 pieces.

tip Mesquite powder is made from the extract of mesquite plant seeds indigenous to North and South America. Appreciated for its sweet, caramel-like flavour, it is rich in minerals and protein. It is available from health food stores.

keeps Store in an airtight container in the freezer for up to 2 weeks. Stand at room temperature for 10 minutes to soften before serving.

prep + cook time 20 minutes (+ standing & freezing) makes 16

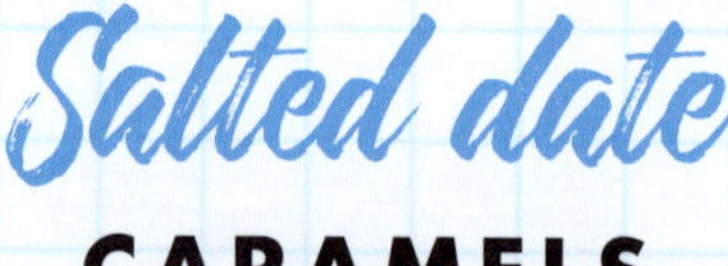

CARAMELS

- 2 cups (310g) fresh dates, pitted
- ¾ cup (150g) coconut oil
- ¼ cup (25g) cacao powder
- 1 teaspoon pure vanilla extract
- 2 tablespoons coconut oil, extra, at room temperature
- ½ teaspoon sea salt flakes
- ¼ cup (50g) coconut flour
- sea salt flakes, extra, for sprinkling

1 Place dates in a medium bowl, cover with boiling water; stand for 10 minutes to soften. Drain dates; discard water.

2 Meanwhile, melt coconut oil in a small saucepan; combine oil and sifted cacao in a small bowl. Stand until thickened slightly.

3 Process dates with vanilla, extra coconut oil and salt until smooth. Transfer mixture to a small bowl, cover; freeze for 30 minutes or until firm.

4 Line an oven tray with baking paper. Place coconut flour in a small bowl. Using damp hands, roll tablespoonfuls of date mixture into balls. Roll balls in coconut flour. Using a spoon, dip balls into cacao coating; place on tray. Sprinkle with extra salt. Freeze for 10 minutes or until set.

tips Don't worry if the coating on the caramels has a slight whitish look to it, this is simply the coconut fat and won't affect the taste. Store and eat the caramels straight from the freezer. Place the caramels in small paper cases to serve.

prep time 5 minutes serves 2 (makes 1 litre)

Spiced apple pie OAT SMOOTHIE

AS WELL AS BEING A GREAT AFTERNOON PICK-ME-UP, YOU CAN POUR THE SMOOTHIE INTO A LARGE GLASS BOTTLE AND TAKE TO WORK FOR A BREAKFAST ON THE GO.

- 1 cup (90g) rolled oats
- 2 tablespoons maca powder (see tips)
- 1 cup (250ml) almond milk
- 1 cup (250ml) pure apple juice
- 2 small red apples (260g), cored, chopped coarsely
- ¼ cup (70g) Greek-style yoghurt
- 4 fresh medjool dates (20g), pitted, chopped coarsely
- 1 teaspoon ground cinnamon
- ¼ teaspoon ground nutmeg
- 1 vanilla bean, split lengthways, seeds scraped
- 6 ice cubes

1 Place ingredients in a blender; blend until smooth.
2 Pour smoothie into tall glasses; sprinkle with a little extra ground cinnamon.

tips Maca powder is available from major supermarkets and health food stores. Maca is the root of a plant native to South America, where it has been consumed for several thousand years. It is a rich source of vitamin C, iron, copper and calcium, and a very good source of riboflavin, niacin, vitamin B6, potassium and manganese. It also contains about 14% protein and provides a good dose of fibre. Medjool dates are available from the fresh food section of major supermarkets.

swap out When pears are in season, use a juicy variety such as packham instead of the red apples and pear juice instead of apple juice.

prep + cook time 15 minutes serves 2

Papaya & macadamia salad WITH COCONUT YOGHURT

- 1 small papaya (650g)
- 1 cup (280g) coconut yoghurt
- ¼ cup (35g) roasted macadamia halves
- ⅓ cup (15g) coconut flakes, toasted
- 2 teaspoons finely grated lime rind (see tip)
- 2 limes (180g), cut into cheeks

1 Cut papaya in half lengthways; scoop out the seeds.
2 Spoon yoghurt into papaya hollow; sprinkle with macadamias, coconut and rind.
3 Serve immediately with lime cheeks.

tip If you have one, use a zester to cut the lime rind into long thin strips.

prep + cook time 10 minutes (+ freezing) makes 25

Frozen green POWER BITES

- 3 ripe medium bananas (600g)
- ¼ cup (30g) almond meal (ground almonds)
- ½ cup (70g) chopped pitted dates
- ½ cup (80g) currants
- ¾ cup (90g) coarsely chopped pecans
- ¼ cup (35g) sesame seeds
- ¼ cup (25g) cacao powder
- 2 tablespoons coconut butter, melted (see tips)
- ½ cup (40g) quinoa flakes
- 1 tablespoon spirulina powder (see tips)
- 2 tablespoons barley malt syrup
- 25 mini wooden popsicle sticks
- ¼ cup (20g) shredded coconut
- ¼ cup (30g) coarsely chopped pecans, extra

1 Mash banana in a large bowl with a fork. Add almond meal, dates, currants, pecans, sesame seeds, cacao, coconut butter, quinoa flakes, spirulina powder and syrup; stir until well combined.
2 Spoon mixture into 25 ice-cube tray holes (2-tablespoon capacity). Insert popsicle sticks; freeze for 5 hours or until set.
3 Stir shredded coconut in a small frying pan over medium heat for 5 minutes or until golden. Transfer immediately to a small bowl; cool. Stir in extra pecans until combined.
4 Carefully ease power bites from holes; dip in coconut mixture. Store in an airtight container in the freezer until ready to eat.

tips Coconut butter is the blended flesh of coconut. Spirulina is a cyanobacterium (sometimes referred to as blue-green algae although this is not technically correct) that grows in lakes. It is sold as a powder or as tablets. Spirulina powder is rich in protein – a tablespoon provides 4g of protein – and contains all of the essential amino acids. It is also a very good source of iron, making it a great supplement for vegans and vegetarians. It's rich in B group vitamins, copper and manganese, and is a source of the plant omega-3 fat, alpha-linolenic acid (ALA). Coconut butter and spirulina are both available from health food stores.

keeps Bites can be stored in the freezer for up to 1 month.

prep + cook time 15 minutes (+ refrigeration) makes 26

Ginger & sesame SEED LOGS

- 1 cup (100g) walnuts
- 1 cup (140g) macadamias
- 1 cup (90g) rolled oats
- 400g (12½ ounces) fresh medjool dates, pitted
- 1½ teaspoons ground ginger
- ½ teaspoon sea salt
- ½ cup (75g) sesame seeds

1 Process nuts and oats in a food processor until finely chopped. Add dates, ginger and salt; process until mixture forms a paste.

2 Shape level tablespoons of mixture into 5cm (2-inch) long logs; place on a baking-paper-lined oven tray. Refrigerate for 15 minutes.

3 Meanwhile, stir sesame seeds in a frying pan over medium heat for 2 minutes or until lightly toasted. Cool.

4 Roll logs in sesame seeds; place on a tray. Refrigerate for 2 hours or until firm.

tip Medjool dates are available from the fresh food section of major supermarkets.

keeps Store logs in an airtight container in the fridge for up to 2 weeks or freeze for up to 3 months.

prep + cook time 25 minutes (+ standing & freezing) makes 10

& BALSAMIC POPSICLES

You need a ten-hole ⅓-cup ice-block mould and ten ice-block sticks for this recipe.

- 6 trimmed stalks rhubarb (330g), cut into 8cm (3¼-inch) lengths
- 125g (4oz) fresh raspberries
- 1 vanilla bean, split lengthways, seeds scraped
- 1 tablespoon freshly squeezed orange juice
- 1 tablespoon Natvia
- 400ml can coconut cream
- ¼ cup (55g) Natvia, extra
- ½ cup (80g) natural sliced almonds, chopped coarsely

CHOCOLATE COATING

- 1 tablespoon Natvia
- ½ cup (100g) coconut oil
- ¼ cup (25g) cacao powder
- 1 teaspoon pure vanilla extract

1 Preheat oven to 200°C/400°F. Line an oven tray with baking paper.

2 Place rhubarb, raspberries, vanilla seeds and pod on oven tray; drizzle with combined orange juice and Natvia. Roast for 15 minutes or until tender; stand until cool. Discard vanilla pod.

3 Blend roasted rhubarb mixture with coconut cream and extra Natvia until smooth, using a high-powered blender, if available; this type of blender will produce a very smooth consistency. Pour into ice-block mould. Cover mould with a double layer of plastic wrap (this will help keep the ice-block sticks upright). Pierce plastic with a small knife, then push an ice-block stick into each hole. Freeze for 4 hours or until frozen.

4 When you're ready to coat the frozen popsicles, make chocolate coating.

5 Line a large oven tray with baking paper; place in the freezer. Pour chocolate coating into a small heatproof jug or mug; place jug over a bowl of boiling water to keep warm and prevent chocolate from thickening. Dip popsicle moulds very briefly in boiling water; remove popsicles. Dip the popsicles halfway into the chocolate coating, gently shake off excess chocolate, then sprinkle with almonds. Place on chilled tray. Freeze for 5 minutes or until coating is set.

chocolate coating Process Natvia in a spice grinder until consistency of icing sugar. Melt coconut oil in a small saucepan over a low heat. Add powdered Natvia, cacao and extract; whisk until combined and smooth.

keeps Store popsicles in the freezer for up to 1 month.

prep + cook time 50 minutes makes 8

Zucchini & blueberry LOAF CAKES

- » ⅓ cup (75g) Natvia
- » 3 medium zucchini (360g), grated coarsely
- » 2¾ cups (330g) almond meal (ground almonds)
- » 2 teaspoons ground cinnamon
- » ½ teaspoon sea salt
- » 2 teaspoons baking powder
- » ½ cup (110g) coconut oil, melted
- » 3 eggs, beaten lightly
- » 1 vanilla bean, split lengthways, seeds scraped
- » 3 teaspoons finely grated orange rind
- » ⅓ cup (80ml) freshly squeezed orange juice
- » 1 cup (150g) frozen blueberries
- » ½ cup (25g) coconut flakes, toasted

1 Preheat oven 180°C/350°F. Grease an 8-hole (½ cup/125ml) loaf pan tray; line base and long sides of holes with strips of baking paper, extending the paper 3cm (1¼ inches) over long sides.
2 Blend Natvia in a high-speed blender until consistency of icing sugar.
3 Squeeze liquid from zucchini; place zucchini in a large bowl. Add almond meal, powdered Natvia, cinnamon, salt and baking powder; stir to combine.
4 Whisk coconut oil, eggs, vanilla seeds, rind and juice in a small bowl. Add egg mixture to zucchini mixture; stir gently to combine. Fold in blueberries. Spoon mixture into pan holes.
5 Bake loaves for 35 minutes or until risen and slightly cracked on top. Leave loaves in pan for 5 minutes; transfer to a wire rack to cool.
6 Sprinkle loaves with toasted coconut.

swap out Swap the blueberries for raspberries for a more tart taste.

keeps These cakes will keep in an airtight container at room temperature for up to 2 days.

prep + cook time 45 minutes makes 16 pieces

Honey, macadamia & ROSEMARY SHORTBREAD

- 250g (8 ounces) unsalted butter, softened
- 2 tablespoons coconut sugar
- 2 tablespoons honey
- 2 cups (300g) white plain (all-purpose) spelt flour
- ⅓ cup (60g) rice flour
- 2 tablespoons finely chopped fresh rosemary
- ½ cup (75g) roasted macadamia halves, chopped coarsely

1 Preheat oven to 160°C/325°F. Line two oven trays with baking paper.

2 Beat butter and coconut sugar in a medium bowl with an electric mixer until light and fluffy. Beat in honey until well combined. Fold in sifted flours, rosemary and macadamias in two batches.

3 Divide dough in half, place each on a tray. Using lightly floured hands, press dough out to form 22cm (9-inch) rounds. Using fingertips, crimp edges to form a border. Using a sharp knife, score each shortbread into 8 wedges. Prick gently all over with a floured fork to create a pattern.

4 Bake, rotating trays halfway through, for 25 minutes or until golden. Cool on trays.

5 Using scored marks as a guide, cut into wedges.

swap out the macadamias for pine nuts or hazelnuts, if you like.

keeps Store in an airtight container for up to 2 weeks.

prep time 20 minutes (+ freezing & refrigeration) makes 16

Bountiful CHOC-COCONUT BARS

- » 200g (6½ ounces) shredded coconut
- » 2 tablespoons coconut oil, melted
- » ½ cup (125ml) coconut cream
- » ¼ teaspoon fine sea salt
- » ¼ cup (90g) rice malt syrup

CACAO COATING

- » ½ cup (100g) coconut oil
- » ½ cup (120g) cacao butter, chopped finely
- » ⅓ cup (80ml) pure maple syrup
- » 1 cup (100g) cacao powder

1 Grease an 11cm x 21cm (4½-inch x 8½-inch), 1 litre (4-cup) loaf pan; line with plastic wrap, allowing excess to overhang sides. Line an oven tray with baking paper.
2 Process shredded coconut, coconut oil, coconut cream, salt and rice malt syrup until just combined. Firmly and evenly press mixture into loaf pan; freeze for 30 minutes or until firm.
3 Meanwhile, make cacao coating.
4 Remove coconut filling from freezer. Cut into eight bars; cut each bar in half horizontally. Using two forks, dip coconut bars in cacao coating until well coated. Place on lined tray. Refrigerate for 30 minutes or until set. Trim off any excess chocolate.
cacao coating Combine coconut oil, cacao butter and maple syrup in a heatproof bowl over a pan of boiling water; stir until melted and combined. Whisk in cacao powder until well combined.

tip You could sprinkle the chocolate-coated bars with desiccated coconut before refrigerating, if you like.

keeps Store in an airtight container in the fridge for up to 2 weeks.

prep time 5 minutes (+ standing & refrigeration) serves 4

MOUSSE

IF PREFERRED, YOU CAN ENJOY THIS IMMEDIATELY AFTER MAKING AS A THICK-STYLE SMOOTHIE, RATHER THAN REFRIGERATING TO SET.

- 1½ cup (225g) fresh or frozen raspberries
- ¾ cup (115g) fresh or frozen blueberries
- 300g (9½ ounces) silken tofu
- ¼ cup (90g) raw honey
- ½ teaspoon maqui powder (see tips), optional
- 1 tablespoon fresh or frozen raspberries, extra
- 1 tablespoon fresh or frozen blueberries, extra

1 If using frozen berries, thaw in a medium bowl at room temperature for 1 hour; drain.
2 Blend thawed berries, tofu, honey and maqui, if using, until as smooth as possible, using a high-powered blender if available; this type of blender will produce a very smooth consistency. Pour mixture evenly among four ¾ cup (180ml) glasses or jars.
3 Refrigerate for 4 hours or until firm. Top with extra berries before serving.

tips Maqui powder is available from some health food stores. It has a slightly sweet, tart flavour. Maqui berries are considered one of the highest antioxidant-rich fruits available.

try this
Layered with the coconut meringue mixture (see lemon meringue pie, page 334) in glasses for a fruity parfait.
Topped with confetti (see confetti banana and tahini puddings, page 328).

keeps Cover with plastic wrap and store in the fridge for up to 4 days.

prep + cook time 1 hour (+ refrigeration) makes 12

Blackberry, apple & ALMOND BRAN MUFFINS

You will need to start the coconut whip recipe a day ahead.

- 2 tablespoons Natvia
- 1½ cups (225g) plain (all-purpose) flour
- 1 cup (120g) oat bran
- 2 teaspoons baking powder
- 1 teaspoon bicarbonate of soda (baking soda)
- 1 teaspoon ground cinnamon
- ½ teaspoon salt
- 1 cup (170g) coarsely grated apple (see tips)
- 1 cup (150g) frozen blackberries
- 2 eggs
- 1¼ cups (310ml) almond milk
- ⅓ cup (95g) almond spread
- 2 teaspoons pure vanilla extract
- 1 teaspoon oat bran, extra
- ¼ cup (20g) flaked almonds, roasted

COCONUT-BLACKBERRY WHIP

- 270ml can coconut cream, unopened
- 1 tablespoon Natvia
- ⅓ cup (50g) frozen blackberries, thawed, patted dry

1 Make coconut-blackberry whip.

2 Preheat oven 180°C/350°F. Grease two 6-hole (¾ cup/180ml) texas muffin pans; line with large squares of baking paper.

3 Process Natvia in a spice grinder until consistency of icing sugar.

4 Place flour, bran, powdered Natvia, baking powder, soda, cinnamon and salt in a large bowl; whisk to combine. Fold in apple and half the blackberries.

5 Whisk eggs, milk, almond spread and vanilla in a medium bowl. Pour over dry ingredients; fold until almost combined.

6 Spoon mixture into muffin holes, sprinkle with extra bran and push remaining blackberries into tops of muffins.

7 Bake for 30 minutes or until a skewer inserted into the centre comes out clean. Cool in pans.

8 Dollop coconut-blackberry whip on cooled muffins; top with almonds.

coconut-blackberry whip Chill coconut cream can overnight in the fridge, so that the cream separates and sets on top. Without shaking or tipping the can, carefully spoon out thick cream on top. Process Natvia in a spice grinder until consistency of icing sugar. Beat coconut cream, powdered Natvia and blackberries with an electric mixer on high speed for 5 minutes until thickened slightly. Refrigerate until required.

tips You will need 2 medium apples (300g) for the amount of grated apple in recipe. Best eaten on the day they are made.

swap out Use coconut yoghurt instead of coconut cream in the coconut-berry whip; blend ¾ cup coconut yoghurt, 2 teaspoons powdered Natvia and berries until smooth.

prep time 20 minutes makes 42 (14 each)

Bliss balls

APRICOT & TAHINI

» ½ cup (100g) dried apricots
» ¼ cup (30g) linseed (flaxseed) meal
» 1 cup (160g) almonds
» ¼ green apple (30g), unpeeled, grated coarsely
» 1 tablespoon raw honey, rice malt syrup or pure maple syrup
» 1 tablespoon tahini
» ¼ teaspoon orange blossom water, optional
» ½ cup (40g) shredded coconut

FIG & HAZELNUT

» 1 cup (140g) roasted skinned hazelnuts
» 100g (3 ounces) dried figs
» ¼ cup (30g) linseed (flaxseed) meal
» ¼ green apple (30g), grated coarsely
» ¼ teaspoon ground cinnamon
» 2 tablespoons white chia seeds

DATE & CACAO NIBS

» 100g (3 ounces) fresh dates, pitted
» 1 cup (160g) almonds
» ¼ cup (35g) cacao nibs
» ¼ green apple (30g), grated coarsely
» 2 teaspoons dutch-processed cocoa
» 2 teaspoons dutch-processed cocoa, extra

1 For apricot and tahini balls, process apricots, linseed meal, almonds and apple for 1 minute or until mixture is the consistency of breadcrumbs. Add honey, tahini and orange blossom water; process a further minute or until mixture clings together when pressed.

2 Roll tablespoons of the mixture into balls; wet your hands every third or fourth ball to stop the mixture from sticking. Coat balls in coconut.

3 Make fig and hazelnut balls, then date and cacao balls.

fig & hazelnut Process hazelnuts with figs, linseed meal, grated apple and cinnamon for 2 minutes or until mixture starts to clump together. Roll tablespoons of the mixture into balls then coat in chia seeds.

date & cacao nibs Process dates with almonds, cacao nibs, grated apple and cocoa for 2 minutes or until mixture starts to clump together. Roll tablespoons of the mixture into balls then dust with extra cocoa.

prep + cook time 10 minutes serves 4

Chai-spiced POPCORN

- 2 teaspoons Natvia
- ¼ cup (60ml) olive oil
- 2 teaspoons ground cinnamon
- 1 teaspoon ground ginger
- ½ teaspoon ground cardamom
- ½ teaspoon ground allspice
- ½ teaspoon sea salt flakes
- 2 tablespoons olive oil, extra
- ½ cup (120g) popping corn

1 Process Natvia in a spice grinder until consistency of icing sugar.
2 Combine oil, powdered Natvia, spices and salt in a small bowl.
3 Heat the extra oil in a large saucepan over medium heat. Add the popping corn, cover pan; cook, shaking the pan occasionally, for 5 minutes, or until popping stops.
4 Place popcorn in a large bowl; drizzle with spice mixture, stir until well coated.

tip If you have one, it's handy to use a saucepan with a glass lid so you can see if all the corn has popped.

keeps Popcorn can be made a day ahead; cool and store in an airtight container.

prep time 10 minutes makes 2 cups

Homemade chocolate HAZELNUT SPREAD

» 1 tablespoon Natvia
» 1½ cups (210g) hazelnuts
» ¼ cup (25g) cacao powder
» ¼ teaspoon sea salt flakes
» 1 teaspoon vanilla extract
» 1 tablespoon virgin coconut oil

1 Preheat oven 180°C/350°F.
2 Process Natvia in a spice grinder until consistency of icing sugar.
3 Spread hazelnuts on an oven tray and roast for 8 minutes or until golden. Rub warm hazelnuts in a clean tea towel to remove skins.
4 Process hazelnuts for 4 minutes, scraping down the sides occasionally, until smooth.
5 Add powdered Natvia, along with the remaining ingredients and process for a further 2 minutes, until smooth.
6 Spoon spread into a small airtight container.

try this Use this spread as a filling for cakes or cookies, or spread onto bread.

keeps Store in an airtight container at room temperature for up to 3 weeks.

prep time 10 minutes (+ refrigeration) serves 10

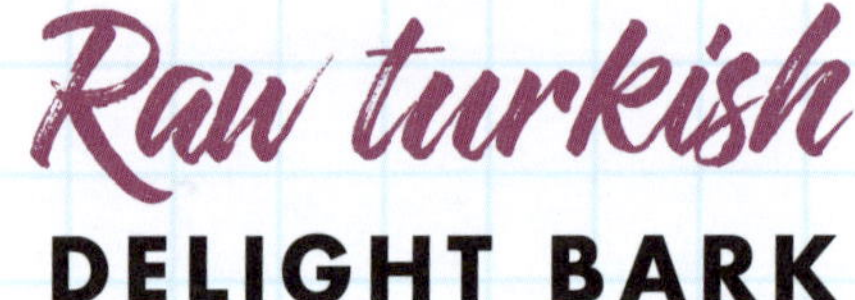

DELIGHT BARK

- » 1 cup (200g) coconut oil
- » ½ cup (50g) cacao powder
- » pinch sea salt
- » ⅓ cup (115g) rice malt syrup
- » ⅓ cup (50g) coarsely chopped raw almonds
- » ⅓ cup (50g) dried cherries
- » ¼ cup (4g) dried edible rose petals

1 Grease a 20cm x 30cm (8-inch x 12-inch) slice pan; line base with baking paper.
2 Whisk oil, sifted cacao and salt in a medium bowl until combined. Gradually add syrup, whisking to combine.
3 Spread mixture evenly into pan; sprinkle with almonds, cherries and rose petals. Refrigerate until set. Break into shards to serve.

tips Don't worry if the bark has a slight whitish look to it, this is simply the coconut fat and won't affect the taste. Because of the low melting point of the coconut oil, the bark should always be stored in the fridge otherwise it will be too soft to handle.

prep time 15 minutes (+ refrigeration) serves 8

Raw choc-chip COOKIE DOUGH

- 100g (3 ounces) brazil nuts
- 200g (6½ ounces) natural almonds
- 1 vanilla bean
- ¼ cup (60ml) pure maple syrup
- ¼ teaspoon ground cinnamon
- 2 tablespoons coconut oil, at room temperature
- 1 teaspoon sea salt flakes
- ¼ cup (30g) cacao nibs

1 Line an 18cm x 28cm (7¼-inch x 11¼-inch) oven tray with baking paper.

2 Process nuts until fine crumbs form. Split vanilla bean lengthways; scrape seeds from halves, using the tip of a knife. Add seeds to processor with maple syrup, cinnamon, coconut oil and salt. Pulse until a soft dough forms; it will be quite sticky.

3 Press dough into lined oven tray, using a spoon dipped in a little cold water. Sprinkle over 2 tablespoons of the cacao nibs; press into dough. Refrigerate for 25 minutes or until firm.

4 Lift baking paper and dough from tray. Using paper as an aid, roll dough into a sausage shape. Sprinkle over remaining cacao nibs, reroll in paper, then in foil. Twist ends of foil and paper to form a tight log. Refrigerate for a further 20 minutes or until firm.

5 Cut into thick slices; serve.

serving suggestion Serve with coconut and vanilla ice-cream (see page 102) and chopped sugar-free chocolate, if you like.

keeps Store raw cookie dough in a container in the fridge for up to 5 days.

prep time 5 minutes serves 4

Confetti banana & TAHINI PUDDING

- 3 medium ripe bananas (300g)
- 6 fresh dates (60g), pitted
- ⅓ cup (90g) tahini
- ⅓ cup (80g) coconut oil, melted
- 2 tablespoons coconut milk
- 1 tablespoon pure vanilla extract
- 2 medium fresh figs (60g), cut into wedges

CONFETTI

- 2 tablespoons activated buckwheat groats
- 2 tablespoons pistachios, chopped coarsely
- 2 tablespoons shredded coconut
- 2 tablespoons cacao nibs
- 2 teaspoons black chia seeds
- 2 tablespoons dried rose petals, optional
- 1 tablespoon bee pollen (see tip), optional

1 Make confetti.
2 Blend banana, dates, tahini, coconut oil, coconut milk and vanilla until as smooth as possible, using a high-powered blender if available; this type of blender will produce a very smooth consistency.
3 Spoon evenly into four ¾ cup (180ml) bowls. Top puddings with fig; sprinkle with confetti.
confetti Combine all ingredients in a small bowl. (Makes about 1 cup)

tip Bee pollen, available from health food stores, is not for everyone; care should be taken for people with a history of reactions to grass and other airborne allergens.

try this
Sprinkle confetti over fruit smoothie bowls.
Stirred through coconut and vanilla ice-cream (see page 102), for added crunch.

swap out dried rose petals for 2 tablespoons pomegranate seeds and the bee pollen for a little fennel pollen, if you like, especially if you are concerned about bee or honey allergies.

keeps Pudding is best made just before serving. Store confetti in an airtight jar in the pantry for up to 2 weeks.

prep+ cook time 1 hour (+ standing & freezing) makes 17

Raspberry chia jam LAMINGTONS

You will need to start this recipe a day ahead.

» 1⅓ cups (200g) raw cashews
» 150g (4½ ounces) cacao butter, chopped
» ⅔ cup (70g) cacao powder
» ½ cup (180g) raw honey
» ½ cup (40g) shredded coconut
» 1 cup (240g) coconut oil
» ¼ teaspoon pure vanilla extract
» 2 teaspoons rice malt syrup
» 1 cup (75g) shredded coconut, extra

RASPBERRY CHIA JAM

» 1½ cups (225g) frozen raspberries
» 2 tablespoons warm tap water
» 2 tablespoons raw honey
» 2 tablespoons white chia seeds

1 Place cashews in a medium bowl; cover with cold water. Stand, covered, for 4 hours or overnight. Drain cashews, rinse under cold water; drain well.
2 Make raspberry chia jam.
3 Grease a 20cm x 30cm (8-inch x 12-inch) slice pan; line with baking paper.
4 Place cacao butter in a small heavy-based saucepan over medium heat; stir until melted. Add cacao powder and half the honey; stir until smooth. Remove from heat; stir through shredded coconut. Spread mixture evenly into pan; freeze for 30 minutes or until set.
5 Place coconut oil, vanilla and remaining honey in a clean small heavy-based saucepan; stir over medium heat for 5 minutes or until melted and combined. Blend coconut oil mixture with soaked cashews, using a high-powered blender if available; this type of blender will produce a very smooth consistency. Cool and spread evenly over chilled cocoa layer, using a spatula. Cover with plastic wrap; freeze for 2 hours or until set.
6 Using a hot, dry knife, cut into 4cm (1½-inch) squares. Place 1 teaspoon jam on half of the squares; top with remaining squares to sandwich. Brush tops with rice malt syrup; sprinkle with extra shredded coconut. Transfer to an airtight container; freeze. Eat straight from the freezer.
raspberry chia jam Place raspberries in a food processor bowl or blender; stand until thawed. Stir warmed tap water (no hotter than 60°C/140°F) and honey in a small bowl to loosen; add to raspberries. Blend or process until pureed, transfer to a small bowl; stir in chia seeds. Cover and refrigerate for at least 3 hours or overnight until thickened to a jam-like consistency.

tips Spread leftover jam over toast or swirl through your favourite yoghurt. Try replacing raspberries with the same amount of fresh strawberries.

keeps Store leftover jam in a jar in the fridge for up to 3 days. Store raw lamingtons in an airtight container in the freezer for up 2 weeks.

Sweet Stuff

THE PERFECT FINISH

prep time 45 minutes (+ standing & freezing) serves 12

Lemon MERINGUE PIE

You will need to start this recipe a day ahead.

- 2 cups (300g) raw cashews
- 1½ cups (255g) activated buckwheat groats
- 1½ cups (180g) pecans
- 8 fresh dates (160g), pitted
- ⅓ cup (70g) coconut oil, melted
- ½ cup (125ml) coconut cream
- ¼ cup (90g) raw honey
- 2 tablespoons finely grated lemon rind
- ½ cup (125ml) lemon juice
- ¾ teaspoon ground turmeric
- ½ cup (100g) coconut oil, melted, extra

COCONUT MERINGUES

- 3 young drinking coconuts (3.6kg)
- ½ cup (125ml) coconut cream
- 1½ tablespoons raw honey
- ⅓ cup (70g) coconut oil, melted
- 1 teaspoon lemon juice

1 Place cashews in a medium bowl; cover with cold water. Stand, covered, for 4 hours or overnight. Drain cashews; rinse under cold water, drain well.

2 Grease a 25cm (10-inch), 3cm (1¼-inch) deep loose-based tart tin.

3 Process buckwheat, pecans, dates and coconut oil until mixture resembles coarse crumbs and holds together when pressed. Press mixture firmly and evenly over base and up side of tin to form a crust, using the back of a spoon. Freeze for 4 hours or overnight.

4 Blend drained cashews, coconut cream, honey, rind, juice and turmeric until smooth. Add extra coconut oil and blend until as smooth as possible, using a high-powered blender, if available; this type of blender will produce a very smooth consistency. Spread lemon filling over tart base; smooth top. Freeze for 4 hours or until firm.

5 Meanwhile, make coconut meringues.

6 Spoon meringue mixture into a piping bag fitted with a 1.5cm (¾-inch) plain tube; pipe rounds on top of pie, creating small peaks (teardrops). Freeze pie for 2 hours or until meringues are firm. (Meringues will not set as firmly as the filling.)

coconut meringues Place a coconut on its side on a chopping board; carefully cut off the dome-shaped top with a cleaver or large knife. You will need a large enough hole to be able to scoop out the flesh with a spoon – you will also need to use a bit of force. Drain coconut water into a large jug (reserve for another use). Spoon out the soft flesh. Repeat with remaining coconuts; you should have about 3 cups (270g) of the flesh. Blend flesh with remaining ingredients until as smooth as possible, using a high-powered blender, if available; this type of blender will produce a very smooth consistency. Pour meringue mixture into a small bowl. Cover; freeze for 2 hours or until thick. Whisk mixture vigorously to achieve an even consistency. Transfer to a medium bowl; refrigerate to firm while lemon filling sets.

keeps Store pie in an airtight container in the fridge for up to 5 days or freeze, without meringues, for up to 2 months.

prep + cook time 25 minutes (+ freezing) serves 4

Berry MOON ROCKS

- 250g (8 ounces) small fresh strawberries, hulled
- 175g (5½ ounces) fresh blackberries
- 125g (4 ounces) fresh raspberries
- 1 tablespoon Natvia
- 400g (12½ ounces) Greek-style yoghurt
- 1 vanilla bean, split lengthways, seeds scraped
- 1 cup (140g) finely chopped pistachios

1 Place all berries, separated in a single layer, on two baking-paper lined trays; freeze for 30 minutes.

2 Process Natvia in a spice grinder until consistency of icing sugar.

3 Combine yoghurt, powdered Natvia, vanilla seeds and ⅓ cup of the pistachios in a medium bowl. Add ½ cup of the frozen raspberries to the bowl, crush against the side of the bowl with a wooden spoon; mix well.

4 Using a toothpick, dip frozen berries, one at a time into the yoghurt mixture. Gently shake off excess yoghurt and place berries on lined trays, making sure they don't touch; remove toothpicks. Freeze coated berries for 3 hours until coating is set. Cover remaining yoghurt mixture; refrigerate.

5 Repeat dipping coated berries in remaining yoghurt mixture for a second coat; lightly sprinkle with remaining pistachios. Freeze for 4 hours or overnight until frozen. Store in an airtight container in the freezer.

tip Use any leftover yoghurt for breakfast or on its own as a delicious snack.

swap out mango or pineapple chunks for berries, if prefered.

keeps Store berry moon rocks in the freezer for up to 2 weeks.

prep + cook time 30 minutes (+ standing & freezing) makes 12

Tahini caramel CHOC CUPS

- » 1 cup (150g) raw cashews
- » 3 cups (750ml) water
- » 220g (7 ounces) dried dates, chopped coarsely
- » ⅓ cup (45g) coconut butter
- » ¼ cup (65g) unhulled tahini
- » ⅓ cup (80ml) pure maple syrup
- » 1 teaspoon salt flakes
- » ¼ cup (60ml) water, extra

BASE

- » 220g (7 ounces) dried dates, chopped coarsely
- » 1 cup (140g) macadamias, chopped coarsely
- » 2 tablespoons cacao nibs

CHOC LAYER

- » ½ cup (80g) coconut butter
- » ½ cup (125ml) pure maple syrup
- » ½ cup (50g) cacao powder
- » 1 vanilla bean, split lengthways, seeds scraped
- » 2 tablespoons hot water

1 Place cashews and the water in a medium bowl; stand for 2 hours. Drain well.

2 Grease a 12-hole (⅓-cup/80ml) muffin pan; line each hole with two strips of baking paper crossed over one another.

3 Make base; press rounded tablespoons of base mixture firmly into each pan hole. Refrigerate.

4 To make caramel, process the drained cashews, dates, coconut butter, tahini, maple syrup, salt and the extra water until smooth. Spoon rounded tablespoons of the caramel mixture equally among the bases; using wet fingers, level the surface.

5 Make choc layer. Spoon rounded teaspoons of choc layer over caramel; using a hot wet spoon, spread chocolate evenly. Freeze for 40 minutes or until firm.

6 Gently loosen cups from side of the pan holes with a hot palette knife; remove cups by lifting the baking paper strips.

base Process dates to a coarse paste. Add macadamias and cacao nibs; pulse until chopped.

choc layer Stir coconut butter and maple syrup in a small saucepan over medium heat until melted. Remove from heat. Add cacao powder, vanilla bean seeds and the hot water; whisk to combine.

tip Coconut butter is the processed flesh of coconut. It is available from health food stores.

prep time 20 minutes (+ freezing) serves 6

Watermelon & lemon TEA GRANITA

You will need to start this recipe a day ahead.

- 1 lemon herbal tea bag
- 1 cup (250ml) boiling water
- 1 tablespoon stevia granules or norbu (monk fruit sugar)
- 500g (1 pound) seedless watermelon, chopped
- 1½ tablespoons lemon juice
- 600g (1¼ pounds) seedless watermelon, extra, sliced thinly
- **FENNEL SALT**
- 1 tablespoon sea salt flakes
- 1 teaspoon fennel seeds
- 1 teaspoon finely grated lemon rind

1 Steep the tea bag in the boiling water for 10 minutes; discard tea bag. Stir stevia into tea until dissolved.
2 Blend or process chopped watermelon until smooth. Stir in tea and juice. Pour mixture into a 2.8-litre (11-cup) shallow dish.
3 Freeze granita for 1 hour. Using a fork, scrap to break up any ice crystals. Freeze for a further 6 hours, scraping with a fork every hour or until frozen.
4 Make fennel salt.
5 Divide extra sliced watermelon among tall serving glasses, top with granita; sprinkle with fennel salt before serving.
fennel salt Using a pestle and mortar, crush ingredients together.

serving suggestion Serve with extra strips of lemon rind and micro mint leaves.

prep time 35 minutes (+ refrigeration & standing) serves 12

Raw carrot cake with COCONUT 'CREAM CHEESE' FROSTING

You will need to start this recipe a day ahead.

- 225ml can coconut cream, unopened
- 1 cup (150g) raw cashews
- 1 cup (120g) almond meal (ground almonds)
- ½ teaspoon ground nutmeg
- 2 teaspoons ground cinnamon
- 1 teaspoon ground ginger
- 1⅓ cups (285g) coarsely chopped fresh pitted dates
- ¼ teaspoon fine sea salt
- 6 carrots (720g), peeled, grated finely
- 1 cup (80g) desiccated coconut
- ⅓ cup (55g) sultanas
- 1¼ cups (125g) walnuts, chopped coarsely
- ¼ cup (60ml) pure maple syrup
- 2 tablespoons coconut oil, melted
- 1 vanilla bean, split lengthways, seeds scraped

1 Chill coconut cream can overnight in the fridge, so that the cream separates and sets on top.

2 Place cashews in a small bowl; cover with cold water. Stand, covered for 4 hours or overnight. Drain cashews, rinse under cold water; drain well.

3 Grease a 20cm (8-inch) springform cake pan; line base and side with baking paper.

4 Process almond meal, ground spices, dates and half of the salt until dates are finely chopped and mixture sticks together.

5 Squeeze out all excess liquid from carrot. Add carrot and coconut to food processor; pulse until combined. Remove blade from processor; stir in sultanas and two-thirds of the walnuts until combined. Transfer mixture to lined cake pan; press down firmly on it to ensure it is packed in well. Refrigerate for at least 1 hour.

6 Meanwhile, to make coconut 'cream cheese' frosting, without shaking or tipping coconut cream can, carefully spoon out thickened coconut cream into a small bowl of an electric mixer (reserve thin liquid in an airtight container in the fridge for another use). Beat coconut cream with an electric mixer for 5 minutes or until soft peaks form.

7 Blend soaked cashews, syrup, coconut oil, vanilla seeds and remaining salt until very smooth, using a high-powered blender, if available; this type of blender will produce a very smooth consistency. Fold cashew mixture into whipped coconut cream in a bowl until combined. Cover bowl with plastic wrap; refrigerate for 20 minutes or until it is a spreadable consistency.

8 Release cake from pan, transfer to a serving plate; spread with frosting. Refrigerate for a further 30 minutes until firm. Top with remaining walnuts to serve.

swap out the walnuts for pecans and almond meal for hazelnut meal.

serving suggestion Serve topped with baby (dutch) carrots halved lengthways and drizzled with pure maple syrup, if you like.

prep time 25 minutes (+ standing & freezing) makes 16

CREAM SLICE

You will need to start this recipe a day ahead.

- ¾ cup (115g) raw cashews
- ¾ cup (130g) activated buckwheat groats
- ¾ cup (120g) natural almonds
- ⅔ cup (50g) desiccated coconut
- ½ cup (50g) cacao powder
- ⅓ cup (80ml) pure maple syrup
- ¾ cup (150g) coconut oil, melted
- ½ teaspoon pure vanilla extract
- 2 young drinking coconuts (2.4kg)
- 1 cup (250ml) coconut cream
- ⅓ cup (80ml) rice malt syrup
- 2 teaspoons pure vanilla extract, extra

1 Place cashews in a small bowl; cover with cold water. Stand, covered, for 4 hours or overnight. Drain cashews, rinse under cold water; drain well.

2 Grease a 20cm (8-inch) square cake pan; line base and sides with baking paper, extending the paper 5cm (2 inches) over sides. Line an oven tray with baking paper.

3 Process buckwheat, almonds, desiccated coconut, cacao powder, maple syrup, ¼ cup of the coconut oil and vanilla until mixture resembles coarse crumbs and starts to come together; be careful not to over-process. Press two-thirds of mixture firmly into lined pan, using a spatula. Press remaining mixture into a 1cm (½ inch) thick rectangle on lined tray. Freeze while preparing cream filling.

4 Place a coconut on its side on a chopping board. Carefully cut off the dome-shaped top with a cleaver or large knife; you will need to use a bit of force. Drain coconut water into a large jug. Spoon out the soft flesh. Repeat with remaining coconut; you should have approximately 2 cups (180g) coconut flesh (reserve coconut water for another use, see tip).

5 Blend coconut flesh, drained cashews, coconut cream, rice malt syrup and extra vanilla until smooth, using a high-powered blender, if available; this type of blender will produce a very smooth consistency. Add remaining coconut oil; blend until as smooth as possible. Pour cream filling over biscuit base in square pan.

6 Place the remaining biscuit rectangle from tray onto a cutting board, cut into 1cm (½-inch) pieces. Sprinkle pieces over cream filling in pan, pressing lightly into filling. Freeze for 5 hours or until set.

7 Remove slice from pan 10 minutes before serving to soften slightly. Cut into 16 squares.

tip Use the reserved coconut juice in your next smoothie.

keeps Store slice in an airtight container in the fridge for up to 5 days or freeze for up to 2 months.

prep time 20 minutes (+ refrigeration & freezing) serves 12

Rawtella pie

You will need to start this recipe a day ahead.

- 2 x 400ml cans coconut cream, unopened
- 2 cups (300g) raw cashews
- 1 cup (170g) activated buckwheat groats
- 1 cup (120g) pecans
- 5 fresh dates (100g), pitted
- ⅓ cup (35g) cacao powder
- 2 tablespoons pure maple syrup
- 2 tablespoons coconut oil, melted
- ½ cup (140g) raw chocolate hazelnut butter (see tips)
- ⅔ cup (160ml) coconut cream, extra
- ½ cup (125ml) pure maple syrup, extra
- ¼ cup (50g) coconut oil, melted, extra
- ¼ teaspoon natural hazelnut flavour (see tips)
- 1 teaspoon pure vanilla extract
- ¼ teaspoon sea salt flakes
- 60g (2 ounces) dark (semi-sweet) vegan chocolate, chopped coarsely
- ¼ cup (35g) roasted hazelnuts, chopped coarsely, optional (see swap out)

1 Chill coconut cream cans overnight in fridge, so that cream separates and sets on top.
2 Place cashews in a large bowl; cover with cold water. Stand, covered, for 4 hours or overnight. Drain cashews, rinse under cold water; drain well.
3 Grease a 22cm (9-inch) pie dish.
4 Process buckwheat, pecans, dates, ¼ cup of the cacao powder, syrup and coconut oil until mixture resembles coarse crumbs and starts to come together. Press mixture firmly and evenly over base of pan, using a spatula to smooth. Freeze while preparing filling.
5 Blend drained cashews with remaining cacao powder, chocolate hazelnut butter, extra coconut cream, extra syrup, extra oil, hazelnut flavour, vanilla and salt until as smooth as possible, using a high-powered blender if available; this type of blender will produce a very smooth consistency. Pour mixture over pie base; smooth top. Cover; freeze for 3 hours or until firm.
6 Without shaking or tipping the cans of coconut cream, carefully spoon out the thick coconut cream that has set on top. Beat cream in a small bowl with an electric mixer until soft peaks form; spoon on top of pie.
7 Place the chocolate in a small heatproof bowl over a saucepan of gently simmering water (don't allow bowl to touch water), stir until just melted; drizzle chocolate over pie. Serve pie sprinkled with chopped hazelnuts, if you like.

tips Natural hazelnut flavour is available from selected health food stores or can be purchased online. We used Medicine Flower's natural hazelnut flavour. Use only 2 or 4 drops of hazelnut 'oil' or 'essence' or 1 teaspoon hazelnut 'extract'. Raw chocolate hazelnut butter is made from cocoa, hazelnuts and coconut nectar. It is available from health food stores. As the hazelnuts sprinkled over are roasted, they are not in fact raw — you can omit these or use activated hazelnuts instead.

keeps Store pie in an airtight container in the fridge for up to 5 days, or freeze without whipped cream, for up to 2 months.

prep + cook time 15 minutes (+ freezing) makes 24

BANANA TREATS

You will need 24 mini popsicle sticks for this recipe.

» 6 medium bananas (1.2kg)
» ½ cup (55g) Natvia
» ¾ cup (150g) coconut oil
» 1 cup (100g) cacao powder
» 2 teaspoons vanilla extract
» ¾ cup (120g) roasted salted peanuts, chopped finely

1 Line a large tray with baking paper.
2 Peel and cut bananas into 4cm (1½-inch) pieces; place standing upright on tray. Push a popsicle stick into each banana piece; freeze for 1 hour.
3 Blend Natvia in a high-speed blender until consistency of icing sugar.
4 Melt coconut oil in a small saucepan over a low heat. Add powdered Natvia, cacao and vanilla; whisk until combined and smooth. Pour chocolate coating into a small heatproof jug or mug; place jug over a bowl of boiling water to keep warm and prevent chocolate from thickening.
5 Dip three-quarters of each banana into cacao mixture; sprinkle with chopped peanuts and stand upright on lined tray. Freeze for a further 30 minutes or until chocolate is set.

swap out You can replace the peanuts with any nut you like.

keeps Freeze these treats in an airtight container for up to 3 days.

prep + cook time 15 minutes serves 4

Blueberry & orange POPPY SEED CRÊPES

- » ½ cup (120g) mascarpone
- » 125g (4 ounces) blueberries
- » 2 teaspoons finely grated orange rind
- » ½ cup (75g) wholemeal spelt flour
- » 2 teaspoons poppy seeds
- » 1 egg
- » ⅔ cup (160ml) milk
- » 2 teaspoons rice malt syrup
- » 1 teaspoon pure vanilla extract
- » cooking oil spray
- » 2 tablespoons rice malt syrup, extra

1 Place mascarpone, ⅓ cup of the blueberries and rind in a bowl; mash with a fork to combine.
2 Whisk flour, poppy seeds, egg, milk, syrup and vanilla in a small bowl.
3 Lightly spray a crêpe pan or heavy-based small frying pan with oil. Heat pan over medium heat; pour a scant ¼ cup of the batter into pan; swirl pan to coat base evenly. Cook crêpe for 2 minutes or until browned underneath. Turn, cook for a further 1 minute or until browned. Repeat with remaining crêpe batter to make a total of four crêpes.
4 Spread each crêpe with a slightly rounded tablespoon of mascarpone mixture; fold into triangles to enclose. Serve crêpes topped with remaining blueberries and drizzled with extra syrup. Sprinkle with strips of orange rind, if you like.

prep + cook time 10 minutes (+ freezing) serves 4

Green chilli, mango & MELON SORBET

THIS REFRESHING SORBET USES RIPE SUMMER FRUIT AND TOOTH-FRIENDLY MONK FRUIT SUGAR FOR SWEETNESS. BEST OF ALL YOU DON'T NEED AN ICE-CREAM MACHINE TO MAKE IT!

- 2½ cups (520g) finely chopped mango (see tips)
- 2½ cups (450g) finely chopped honeydew melon (see tips)
- 1 fresh long green chilli, seeded, chopped finely
- 1½ tablespoons finely chopped fresh mint
- ½ cup fresh micro mint leaves

SUGAR SYRUP

- ½ cup (125ml) pure fresh apple juice
- 1 tablespoon finely grated lime rind
- 2 tablespoons lime juice
- ⅓ cup (65g) norbu (monk fruit sugar)

1 Place mango and melon in a single layer on a baking-paper-lined tray; sprinkle with chilli. Cover; freeze for 5 hours or overnight.

2 Make sugar syrup.

3 Place frozen fruit and chilli, and chopped mint in a food processor. With the motor running, slowly pour in sugar syrup until mixture is a smooth sorbet consistency. Tip mixture into a deep freezer-safe tray; freeze for 3½ hours, whisking half way through to break up ice crystals.

4 Serve scoops of sorbet in chilled glasses topped with micro mint leaves.

sugar syrup Bring apple juice to the boil in a small saucepan. Reduce heat to medium; simmer until reduced by half. Add rind; cool to room temperature. Whisk in lime juice and norbu until dissolved.

tips You will need about 3 medium mangoes (1.2kg) and ½ medium honeydew melon (750g) for the sorbet. You could use pineapple instead of mango.

keeps Freeze sorbet in an airtight container for up to 2 weeks. You may need to soften the sorbet for 5-10 minutes if it becomes too firm.

prep time 30 minutes (+ freezing & refrigeration) serves 6

Strawberry HALVA MOUSSE

- 2 cups (500ml) coconut cream (see tip)
- 250g (8 ounces) fresh strawberries, hulled
- 2 tablespoons Natvia
- 3 teaspoons vanilla extract
- 1 cup (280g) Greek-style yoghurt
- ¾ cup (210g) unhulled tahini
- 250g (8 ounces) fresh strawberries, extra, sliced
- ⅓ cup (65g) pomegranate seeds
- ¼ cup (35g) pistachios, chopped
- 1 tablespoon sesame seeds, toasted

1 Pour coconut cream into a medium metal bowl; place in the freezer for 30 minutes or until chilled.

2 Blend or process strawberries, 1 tablespoon of the Natvia and 1 teaspoon of the vanilla until smooth.

3 Blend remaining Natvia in a spice grinder until consistency of icing sugar.

4 Whisk chilled coconut cream with yoghurt, tahini, powdered Natvia and remaining vanilla until thickened slightly, then swirl through the strawberry mixture.

5 Spoon mixture into six 1-cup (250ml) serving glasses. Cover; refrigerate for 2 hours or until chilled and slightly thickened or eat immediately for a softer mousse.

6 Serve mousse topped with extra sliced strawberries, pomegranate seeds, pistachios and sesame seeds.

tip Use a brand of coconut cream that states it is 100% natural on the label. Coconut cream that has 'emulsifying agents' added (it will state this on the label) may cause the mousse to separate into creamy and watery layers.

keeps You can make the mousse a day ahead; store, covered, in the fridge.

prep time 25 minutes (+ standing & refrigeration) makes 12

TARTLETS

- 1½ cups (225g) cashews
- ⅔ cup (150g) fresh dates, pitted, chopped coarsely
- 1½ cups (115g) shredded coconut, toasted
- ½ teaspoon sea salt flakes
- ⅔ cup (150g) coconut oil, melted
- ½ cup (125ml) lime juice
- ¼ cup (60ml) lemon juice
- 2 avocados (500g), chopped coarsely
- ⅓ cup (80ml) pure maple syrup
- 8 drops stevia
- thinly sliced lime rind, to serve

1 Place cashews in a small bowl; cover with cold water. Stand, covered, for 2 hours. Drain cashews, rinse under cold water; drain well.

2 Process one-third of cashews until finely chopped. Add dates and process to form an almost smooth paste. Add shredded coconut, half of the salt and 2 tablespoons of the coconut oil; pulse to combine.

3 Line a 12-hole (⅓ cup/80ml) muffin tin with 2 strips of baking paper in a cross, over base and up sides of each muffin hole. Press slightly heaped tablespoons of the mixture into each hole, firmly pressing up against sides. Refrigerate until needed.

4 Blend remaining cashews with remaining ingredients, using a high-powered blender, if available; this type of blender will produce a very smooth consistency. Spoon mixture evenly into cases; refrigerate for at least 4 hours or until set. Serve topped with lime rind.

keeps Store in an airtight container in the fridge for up to 4 days.

prep time 25 minutes (+ standing & freezing) serves 2

Vietnamese-style COCONUT AFFOGATO

- ¼ cup (15g) fresh ground coffee
- ¾ cup (180ml) boiling water
- toasted shaved coconut flakes, to serve, optional

CHEAT'S COCONUT ICE-CREAM

- 2 tablespoons desiccated coconut
- 1 vanilla bean
- 400ml can coconut cream
- ½ cup (125ml) pure maple syrup
- 1 tablespoon coconut oil, at room temperature
- ½ teaspoon sea salt flakes

1 Make cheat's coconut ice-cream.
2 Place coffee in a plunger, pour over the boiling water. Stand for 4 minutes; press down on grounds. Pour into two espresso cups. (Alternatively, combine the boiling water and coffee in a heatproof jug, stand for 4 minutes; strain through a fine sieve.)
3 Meanwhile, remove ice-cream from freezer. Allow to soften slightly. Process in a small blender until a soft-serve consistency. (For a smoother result, process frozen coconut mixture until smooth, return to the zip-top bag; re-freeze until frozen.)
4 To serve, spoon coconut ice-cream evenly into two 1½ cup (375ml) glasses. Sprinkle with shaved coconut. Accompany with coffee for each person to pour over ice-cream before eating.
cheat's coconut ice-cream Place desiccated coconut in a small frying pan over high heat. Stir with a wooden spoon for 1 minute or until golden and toasted. Transfer to a plate; leave to cool completely. Split vanilla bean lengthways; scrape seeds from halves, using the tip of a knife. Process vanilla seeds, coconut cream, syrup, coconut oil and salt until smooth. Remove blade, stir in toasted coconut; transfer to a large zip-top bag. Close bag, place on a metal tray, spread coconut mixture flat; freeze for 3 hours.

prep time 45 minutes (+ standing, freezing & refrigeration) makes 20

Peppermint bites

You will need to start this recipe a day ahead.

- ¾ cup (115g) raw cashews
- ½ cup (80g) natural almonds
- ½ cup (60g) pecans
- ⅓ cup (65g) activated buckwheat groats (see tips)
- ⅔ cup (50g) desiccated coconut
- ½ cup (50g) cacao powder
- ¼ cup (40g) coconut sugar
- 4 fresh dates (80g), pitted
- ⅔ cup (140g) coconut oil, melted
- ¼ cup (60ml) coconut cream
- 2 tablespoons light agave syrup
- ½ teaspoon pure peppermint extract (see tips)

CHOCOLATE COATING

- ¼ cup (50g) coconut oil
- 60g (2 ounces) cacao butter, grated finely
- 2 tablespoons pure maple syrup
- ½ cup (50g) cacao powder

1 Place cashews in a medium bowl; cover with cold water. Stand, covered, for 4 hours or overnight. Drain cashews, rinse under cold water; drain well.

2 Lightly grease or oil a 20cm x 30cm (8-inch x 12-inch) slice pan; line with plastic wrap, extending plastic 5cm (2 inches) over sides.

3 Pulse almonds, pecans, buckwheat, desiccated coconut, cacao, coconut sugar, dates and ½ cup of the coconut oil until coarse crumbs form and mixture starts to come together; be careful not to over-process. Press nut mixture firmly and evenly over base of pan, using a spatula. Freeze for 15 minutes or until firm.

4 Lift biscuit base from pan; place on board. Cut base into 20 rounds using a 5cm (2-inch) cutter. Place rounds on a baking paper-lined tray; freeze while preparing peppermint cream.

5 To make peppermint cream, blend drained cashews with remaining coconut oil, coconut cream and agave syrup until as smooth as possible, using a high-powered blender, if available; this type of blender will produce a very smooth consistency. Add peppermint extract; blend until combined. Pour peppermint cream into a small bowl; cover, freeze for 1 hour or until thick but not set, stirring occasionally.

6 Spoon approximately 2 teaspoons of peppermint cream onto each biscuit round; using the back of the teaspoon, gently press down to flatten and smooth. Freeze for 3 hours or until set.

7 Make chocolate coating. Using a fork, lower biscuits, one at a time, into chocolate mixture. Allow excess to drain off, then place on tray. Refrigerate for 30 minutes or until chocolate is set.

chocolate coating Place coconut oil and cacao butter in a medium heatproof bowl over a smaller heatproof bowl of boiling water, whisk until combined and smooth; whisk in maple syrup. Whisk in cacao powder until combined and smooth.

tips Activated buckwheat groats are available from health food stores; they add a delicious crunch. Peppermint extract is available from health food stores. Buy peppermint extract rather than oil or essence, otherwise the flavour of the biscuits may be affected.

keeps Store biscuits in an airtight container in the fridge for up to 5 days.

Mylkshakes

prep time 10 minutes (+ standing)
makes 3 cups (750ml)

CLASSIC VANILLA MYLK

You will need to start this recipe a day ahead.

Place 1 cup (160g) natural almonds and a pinch fine sea salt in a large bowl; cover with cold water. Stand, covered, for 8 hours or overnight. Drain almonds; rinse under cold water, drain well. Blend almonds with 3 cups (750ml) filtered water until smooth. Pour mixture through a nut bag (or strainer lined with a fine cloth) into a large jug; squeeze nut bag to release all the mylk. Split 1 vanilla bean lengthways, scrape seeds into mylk; stir to combine.

keeps Store almond mylk in a sealed glass bottle in the fridge for up to 3 days.

prep time 15 minutes (+ standing)
serves 2 (makes 400ml)

STRAWBERRY MYLK

Make classic vanilla mylk (see left). Blend 1 cup of the chilled mylk with 1 cup fresh or frozen strawberries, 1 tablespoon cashew spread and 1 tablespoon raw honey.

tip Pair flavoured mylk with strawberry cream cookies (see page 406).

prep time 20 minutes (+ standing)
serves 2 (makes 400ml)

CHOC-PEANUT MYLKSHAKE

Make classic vanilla mylk (see opposite page). Make chocolate sauce. Blend 1 cup of the chilled mylk with 2 scoops coconut and vanilla ice-cream (see page 102) or ⅓ cup unsweetened coconut yoghurt, 3 pitted fresh dates, 2 tablespoons natural peanut butter and 1 tablespoon cacao powder until smooth. Drizzle 1½ tablespoons chocolate sauce around the inside of two ¾ cup glasses or bottles, before pouring in mylkshake.

chocolate sauce Combine 1 tablespoon cacao powder, 1 tablespoon melted coconut oil and 1 tablespoon pure maple syrup in a small bowl.

prep time 15 minutes (+ standing)
serves 2 (makes 400ml)

LATTE SHAKE

Make classic vanilla mylk (see opposite page). Blend 1 cup of the chilled mylk with ⅓ cup chilled espresso or strong coffee, 2 scoops coconut and vanilla ice-cream (see page 102) or ⅓ cup unsweetened coconut yoghurt and 1 pitted fresh date until smooth. Serve shake topped with an extra scoop of coconut and vanilla ice-cream or your favourite sugar-free ice-cream, if you like.

prep time 25 minutes (+ refrigeration & freezing) makes 16 pieces

Cacao & date CARAMEL SLICE

- ½ cup (115g) fresh dates, pitted
- 1 cup (130g) roasted almonds
- 1½ tablespoons coconut oil, melted
- ¼ teaspoon fine sea salt flakes

DATE CARAMEL

- 1 cup (230g) fresh dates, pitted
- ½ cup (125ml) pure maple syrup
- ⅓ cup (95g) natural crunchy peanut butter
- ¼ cup (60ml) melted coconut oil

CACAO TOPPING

- ¼ cup (20g) raw cacao powder
- ¼ cup (60ml) melted coconut oil
- 2 teaspoons pure maple syrup

1 Line a 19cm (7¾-inch) square pan with baking paper.
2 Process dates, almonds and coconut oil until smooth. Press mixture evenly onto the base of the pan. Refrigerate for 1 hour or until set.
3 Make date caramel; spread mixture evenly over base mixture in pan. Freeze for 1 hour or until firm.
4 Make cacao topping. Working quickly, pour topping over date caramel mixture; sprinkle with salt. Refrigerate for 1 hour or until set.
5 Use a hot sharp knife to cut slice into 16 pieces.
date caramel Process ingredients for 2 minutes or until very smooth.
cacao topping Whisk ingredients in a medium bowl until smooth.

tip Make cacao topping just before you are ready to use it or it may begin to set.

keeps The slice will keep in an airtight container in the fridge for up to 1 week.

prep + cook time 25 minutes (+ freezing) makes 8

Coconut & mango POPSICLES

» 1¾ cups (265g) frozen diced mango
» ½ cup (125ml) pure fresh apple juice
» 2 tablespoons norbu (monk fruit sugar)
» ¼ cup (60ml) water
» 270ml coconut cream
» ½ teaspoon sea salt flakes
» 8 popsicle sticks
» ¼ cup (10g) coconut flakes, toasted

1 Process mango and apple juice until smooth. Place 2 tablespoons mango puree into each of eight ½-cup (125ml) popsicle moulds; freeze for 30 minutes.
2 Meanwhile, stir norbu and the water in a small saucepan over low heat until sugar dissolves (do not allow to simmer or boil or the mixture will crystallise). Whisk sugar syrup, coconut cream and salt to combine. Spoon mixture into popsicle moulds to fill. Cover moulds with a double layer of plastic wrap; this will help to keep the popsicle sticks upright. Pierce plastic with a small knife, then push popsicle sticks into each hole. Freeze for at least 4 hours or overnight until set.
3 Dip popsicle moulds briefly in boiling water; remove popsicles. Place toasted coconut in a small bowl, dip each popsicle quickly in hot water then into the coconut. Freeze on a baking-paper-lined tray for 10 minutes or until ready to eat.

prep time 15 minutes (+ refrigeration) serves 6

Coconut & berry CHIA PUDDINGS

- 2½ cups (625ml) coconut milk
- ⅓ cup (55g) white chia seeds
- 1 teaspoon vanilla extract
- 1 medium banana (200g), chopped coarsely
- 1 tablespoon Natvia
- 2 teaspoons finely grated orange rind
- 3 cups (300g) mixed fresh berries (see tips)
- micro mint or small mint leaves, to serve

1 Place coconut milk, chia seeds and vanilla in a large bowl. Cover; refrigerate for 1 hour or overnight until thick.

2 Blend or process coconut milk mixture with banana, Natvia, rind and 2 cups of the berries. Transfer to a large jug and pour into six ¾-cup (180ml) serving glasses; refrigerate for 30 minutes or until pudding has thickened.

3 Serve puddings topped with remaining berries and mint.

tips Use whatever combination of berries you like, including cherries. If you have one, use a high-powered blender, such as a Thermomix or Vitamix to achieve a very smooth pudding consistency.

keeps Puddings can be made a day ahead; store, covered, in the fridge. Top with extra berries just before serving.

chia

prep + cook time 15 minutes (+ cooling) makes 20

Salted popcorn & NUT SLICE

- 3 cups (45g) salted natural popped popcorn
- 1 cup (150g) roasted salted macadamias, chopped
- 1 cup (160g) roasted salted peanuts, chopped
- 1 cup (80g) roasted coconut chips
- 1½ cups (450g) raw honey

1 Line an oven tray with baking paper.

2 Combine popcorn, nuts and coconut in a medium bowl. Place honey in a frying pan over medium-high heat; bring to the boil. Reduce heat; simmer for 5 minutes or until honey starts to caramelise. (Make sure you watch the mixture, once it starts to caramelise it can quickly burn.)

3 Immediately pour honey over popcorn mixture; stir quickly to combine. Using a spatula, scrape mixture out onto the tray; cover with a piece of baking paper. Using a rolling pin, roll out flat; remove top layer of paper, leave to cool and set. Serve cut into pieces.

tip You can use any kind of nuts in this recipe.

keeps This slice can be stored in an airtight container in the fridge for up to 2 weeks.

prep + cook time 1 hour 30 minutes (+ standing, cooling, refrigeration & freezing)
serves 4

Coconut sticky rice ice-cream WITH MANGO

You will need to start this recipe a day ahead.

- 75g (2½ ounces) black glutinous rice (see tips)
- 1 pandan leaf, tied in a knot, optional (see tips)
- 2 cups (500ml) water
- 2 x 400ml cans coconut cream
- ½ cup (110g) Natvia
- ¼ cup (60g) coconut oil
- ¾ teaspoon sea salt
- 1 tablespoon arrowroot
- 2 tablespoons black sesame seeds
- 2 small mangoes (600g), cheeks sliced thinly

1 Place rice in a small bowl, cover with water; stand for 8 hours or overnight.

2 Drain rice; place in a small saucepan with pandan leaf, if using, and the water. Bring to the boil, reduce heat to medium; simmer; for 20 minutes or until rice is tender and water is almost all absorbed.

3 Add half the coconut cream; cook for 10 minutes or until mixture thickens slightly. Add remaining coconut cream, Natvia, coconut oil and salt; stir to combine well. Whisk in arrowroot; cook mixture for 3 minutes or until thickened.

4 Remove pandan leaf; discard. Transfer mixture to a large bowl, cover surface with plastic wrap; cool for 45 minutes or until at room temperature. Using a mortar and pestle crush sesame seeds (see tip).

5 Transfer mixture to an ice-cream maker. Churn rice mixture in machine, following manufacturer's instructions, until almost firm and thick and creamy; add three-quarters of the crushed sesame seeds, ½ teaspoon at a time, until just mixed through. Transfer mixture to a 1 litre (4-cup) capacity airtight container and freeze for at least 4 hours or until firm.

6 Serve scoops of ice-cream with mango, sprinkled with remaining sesame seeds.

tips Remove the ice-cream from freezer 45 minutes before serving to soften slightly. Black glutinous rice and pandan leaves are available from Asian grocers. Pandan leaves are often sold frozen. To crush sesame seeds without a mortar and pestle, place the seeds on a chopping board, press down on the seeds with a small heavy-based saucepan, using a twisting action.

keeps Store in an airtight container in the freezer for up to 1 month.

prep + cook time 1 hour (+ cooling & freezing) serves 4

Apricot & pistachio FROZEN YOGHURT

- 1 cup (150g) dried apricots
- 2¼ cups (560ml) pure fresh apple juice
- 1 teaspoon ground cardamom
- 2¼ cups (630g) Greek-style yoghurt
- ¼ cup (90g) raw honey
- 2 tablespoons sesame seeds, toasted
- ½ cup (70g) pistachios, chopped coarsely

1 Place apricots and juice in a medium frying pan; bring to the boil. Reduce heat; simmer for 15 minutes or until apricots are tender and plump and the apple juice is syrupy. Cool.
2 Process cooled apricot mixture with cardamom until smooth. Transfer mixture to a large bowl. Cover; refrigerate until required.
3 Combine yoghurt, honey, sesame seeds and half the pistachios in a medium bowl. Place mixture in an ice-cream machine (see tips). Following manufacturer's directions, churn on the frozen yoghurt setting for 40 minutes until frozen. Spoon frozen yoghurt into the bowl with apricot mixture; fold the two mixtures together gently to create a marbled effect. Spoon into a 1.25-litre (5-cup) loaf pan, cover, freeze for 5 hours or overnight.
4 Serve yoghurt topped with remaining pistachios.

tip If you don't have an ice-cream machine, place yoghurt mixture only in the loaf pan, then cover with foil; freeze for 1 hour or until half frozen. Pulse mixture in a food processor to break-up ice crystals. Return mixture to pan, cover with foil; repeat freezing and processing. Fold through apricot mixture, return to pan and cover with foil; freeze for 5 hours or overnight until frozen.

keeps Store frozen yoghurt in the freezer for up to 2 weeks.

prep + cook time 30 minutes (+ standing & freezing) serves 6

FIZZED JELLY

THE TRICK TO CREATING THESE DELIGHTFUL FIZZY JELLIES IS TO CHILL THE GLASSES FIRST AND SET THE JELLIES QUICKLY IN THE FREEZER, PRESERVING ALL THE BUBBLES.

- 3 cups (750ml) blood orange juice
- ½ cup (110g) Natvia
- 2½ leaves (12.5g) titanium-strength gelatine (see tips)
- 1¼ cups (310ml) soda water, chilled
- 2 tablespoons micro basil or small basil leaves

BLOOD ORANGE SALAD

- 2 teaspoons Natvia
- 4 medium blood oranges (680g)
- 2 small pink grapefruits (700g)
- 100g (3oz) fresh strawberries, sliced thickly
- 1 teaspoon shredded fresh basil leaves

1 Chill six ½-cup (125ml) dessert glasses in the freezer.
2 Strain blood orange juice into a heavy-based medium saucepan. Add Natvia; stir over medium heat until dissolved. Bring to the boil. Reduce heat; simmer, for 15 minutes or until reduced to 1⅔ cups, skimming off any foam.
3 Soak gelatine leaves in cold water for 3 minutes or until softened. Squeeze out excess water, add gelatine to reduced juice; stir until dissolved. Cool to room temperature.
4 Transfer syrup to a large jug. Add soda water, pour into chilled glasses; freeze for 1½ hours or until set. (If you are not serving jellies immediately, cover, place in the fridge.)
5 Just before serving, make blood orange salad.
6 Serve jellies topped with blood orange salad and basil.
blood orange salad Process Natvia in a spice grinder until consistency of icing sugar. Using a small knife, cut rind with the white pith away from 1 orange. Hold the orange over a bowl to catch juices, then cut between the membrane on either side of segments to release the segment into the bowl. Using your hands, squeeze remaining juice from membrane over segments. Repeat with remaining oranges and grapefruit. Add strawberries, basil and powdered Natvia to the bowl; stir to combine. Cover; refrigerate until required.

tips You can use 1 tablespoon powdered gelatine instead of the leaf gelatine. Sprinkle over reduced blood orange juice in step 2; whisk to dissolve. Omit step 3.

keeps Jellies can be made the day before and will keep in the fridge for up to 4 days.

prep time 40 minutes (+ refrigeration) serves 10

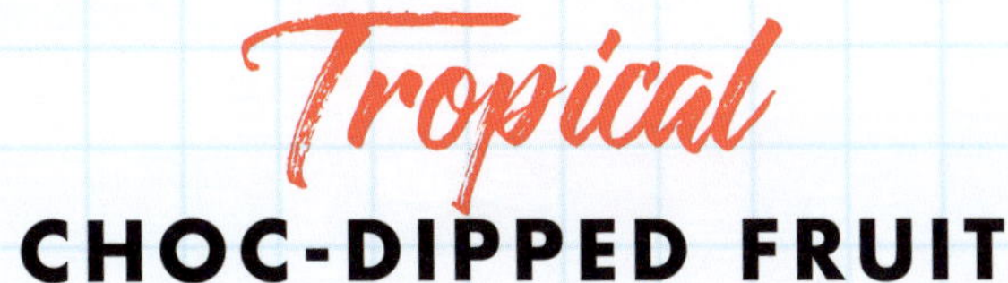

Tropical CHOC-DIPPED FRUIT

YOU WILL NEED TO VISIT A GOOD HEALTH OR GOURMET FOOD STORE TO GATHER THE EXOTIC INGREDIENTS FOR THIS RECIPE – THAT'S THE HARD PART. MAKING YOUR OWN CHOCOLATE, DIPPING THE FRUIT AND COATING IT ARE THE EASY BITS, RESULTING IN A SPECTACULAR DESSERT.

» 1kg (2-pound) piece watermelon, cut into small wedges
» 1 medium mandarin (200g), segmented
» 1 cup (150g) cherries
» 1 cup (130g) strawberries
» 1 medium kiwifruit (85g), sliced
» 8 purchased dehydrated orange slices (see tips)
» 8 purchased dehydrated pineapple slices (see tips)

CRUNCHY ADD-ONS

» 2 tablespoons freeze-dried raspberries, crushed
» 1 tablespoon desiccated coconut
» 1 tablespoon slivered pistachios, chopped
» 1 tablespoon unsprayed dried salad flowers (see tips)
» 1 tablespoon unsprayed freeze-dried rose petals
» 1 tablespoon activated buckwheat groats
» 2 teaspoons freeze-dried raspberry powder
» 1 teaspoon bee pollen, optional (see page 49)

CHOCOLATE COATING

» 2 tablespoons coconut oil
» ½ cup (120g) cacao butter, chopped finely
» 2 tablespoons pure maple syrup
» ½ teaspoon pure vanilla extract
» ¾ cup (100g) cacao powder

1 Place fruit on trays lined with baking paper. With a paper towel, pat watermelon dry to remove excess moisture.

2 Place crunchy add-ons in separate small bowls.

3 Make chocolate coating.

4 Working in batches, beginning with the smaller fruits, dip fruit into chocolate coating; allow excess chocolate to drain off. Sprinkle with a selection of crunchy add-ons; place on tray. If chocolate starts to thicken, reheat. Refrigerate choc-dipped fruit for 15 minutes or until chocolate is set.

5 Pour any leftover chocolate coating onto a plate lined with baking paper; sprinkle with leftover crunchy add-ons. Refrigerate for 15 minutes or until chocolate is set. Break into pieces and serve with the choc-dipped fruit.

chocolate coating Place coconut oil and cacao butter in a medium heatproof bowl over a smaller heatproof bowl of boiling water; whisk until combined and smooth. Whisk in syrup and vanilla; remove from heat. Whisk in cacao until combined and smooth.

tips You can use any combination of fresh, dried and dehydrated fruit. Dried salad flowers are available from The Essential Ingredient, labelled 'Salade de Fleur'.

prep time 55 minutes (+ standing, freezing & refrigeration) serves 16

Raw choc-peanut cake

You will need to start this recipe a day ahead.

- » ½ cup (80g) natural almonds
- » ¾ cup (90g) almond meal (ground almonds)
- » ¾ cup (60g) desiccated coconut
- » ¼ cup (60ml) pure maple syrup
- » 2 tablespoons almond spread
- » ⅓ cup (40g) cacao powder
- » ¼ teaspoon pure vanilla extract
- » 1 cup (140g) roasted unsalted peanuts, chopped coarsely

NOUGAT

- » 2½ cups (375g) raw cashews
- » 1 cup (250ml) coconut cream
- » ½ cup (125ml) pure maple syrup
- » ½ cup (130g) almond spread
- » 1 cup (80g) desiccated coconut
- » ½ cup (100g) coconut oil, melted
- » ½ teaspoon pure vanilla extract

CARAMEL

- » 1 cup (140g) fresh dates, pitted
- » ½ cup (140g) smooth peanut butter
- » ¼ cup (60ml) coconut cream
- » ¼ cup (50g) coconut oil, melted
- » 1 tablespoon pure maple syrup
- » ½ teaspoon fine sea salt

CHOCOLATE COATING

- » ¼ cup (50g) coconut oil
- » ¼ cup (60g) cacao butter, chopped finely
- » ¼ cup (60ml) pure maple syrup
- » ⅔ cup (70g) cacao powder

1 Make nougat.
2 Grease a 23cm (9¼-inch) springform cake pan. Line base and side with baking paper.
3 Process almonds until coarsely chopped. Add almond meal, coconut, maple syrup, almond spread, 2 tablespoons of the cacao powder and vanilla; process until combined and mixture starts to stick together. Press mixture over base of pan; smooth surface. Freeze until required.
4 Pour two-thirds of the nougat over base; freeze for 30 minutes.
5 Add remaining cacao powder to the remaining nougat mixture; blend until well combined. Spread over nougat layer; smooth top. Freeze for 3 hours or until firm.
6 Make caramel. Spread caramel over cake; sprinkle with chopped peanuts. Freeze for 30 minutes or until caramel firms up slightly.
7 Make chocolate coating.
8 Remove cake from pan; place on a plate. Drizzle chocolate coating over cake, allowing it to drip down the sides. Using a knife, smooth coating over cake. Refrigerate for 30 minutes or until set. Serve sprinkled with extra peanuts, if you like.

nougat Place cashews in a medium bowl; cover with cold water. Stand, covered, for 4 hours or overnight. Drain cashews, rinse under cold water; drain well. Blend drained cashews with coconut cream, maple syrup and almond spread until as smooth as possible, using a high-powered blender, if available; this type of blender will produce a very smooth consistency. Add remaining ingredients; blend until well combined.

caramel Place dates in a small bowl; add enough cold water to cover. Stand for 30 minutes, drain. Blend soaked dates with remaining ingredients until as smooth as possible, using a high-powered blender, if available; this type of blender will produce a very smooth consistency.

chocolate coating Place coconut oil and cacao butter in a large heatproof bowl over a medium heatproof bowl of boiling water, whisk until combined and smooth; whisk in syrup. Whisk in cacao powder until combined and smooth.

prep + cook time 40 minutes serves 4

Rosewater watermelon salad
WITH ROSEHIP SYRUP

- 4 rosehip and hibiscus tea bags
- ⅔ cup (160ml) hot water
- 1 tablespoon Natvia
- 2 tablespoons rosewater
- 800g (1½ pounds) piece seedless watermelon
- 4 medium nectarines (680g)
- 500g (1 pound) strawberries
- ⅓ cup (45g) pistachios, chopped coarsely
- ¼ cup loosely packed fresh mint leaves, chopped finely
- 1 tablespoon micro basil or small fresh mint leaves, extra

1 Place tea bags in a heatproof jug, cover with the hot water; steep for 30 minutes. Discard tea bags. Place tea with Natvia in a small heavy-based saucepan, bring to a simmer over medium-high heat; cook for 8 minutes or until reduced by half. Remove from heat; stir in rosewater, cool.

2 Meanwhile, remove rind from watermelon and cut flesh into small wedges. Halve and remove stones from nectarines; slice thinly. Halve strawberries.

3 Place chopped fruit in a large bowl with ¼ cup of the pistachios and the chopped mint; toss gently to combine. Drizzle with rosehip syrup; serve topped with remaining pistachios and extra mint.

serving suggestion Serve fruit salad in a hollowed out watermelon shell, if you like.

prep + cook time 1 hour (+ standing & freezing) serves 4

Coconut sundae WITH CARAMEL POPCORN

- 8 large scoops coconut and vanilla ice-cream (see page 102)
- 2 raw twicker bars (see page 400), broken in half, optional

CARAMEL POPCORN

- 1 tablespoon coconut oil
- ¼ cup (60g) popping corn
- ⅔ cup (160ml) coconut nectar
- ¼ cup (70g) cashew spread
- ½ teaspoon pure vanilla extract
- ½ teaspoon sea salt flakes

1 Preheat oven to 160°C/325°F. Line an oven tray with baking paper.

2 Make caramel popcorn.

3 Spoon popcorn mixture in an even layer onto oven tray; bake for 8 minutes or until golden brown, stirring occasionally to prevent popcorn from burning. Cool popcorn mixture on tray. (Makes 6 cups caramel popcorn)

4 Divide ice-cream among four ¾ cup (180ml) glasses; drizzle with remaining cashew caramel sauce. Top evenly with caramel popcorn and raw twicker bars, if using.

caramel popcorn Heat coconut oil in a large saucepan over medium-high heat. Add popping corn, cover with a lid; shake pan lightly when kernels start to pop. Cook for 3 minutes or until kernels have popped, shaking pan regularly. Transfer to a large heatproof bowl; discard any uncooked kernels. Combine coconut nectar, cashew spread, vanilla and salt in a medium bowl. Pour half the cashew caramel over popcorn; stir well to coat. Transfer the remaining cashew caramel to a jar with a lid until ready to serve sundaes.

tip If you don't have time to make your own ice-cream or raw twicker bars, simply make the caramel popcorn and serve with your favourite sugar-free ice-cream.

keeps Store caramel popcorn in an airtight container in the pantry for up to 2 days. Store cashew caramel in a jar in the fridge for up to 1 week.

prep + cook time 15 minutes serves 4

Buckwheat waffles WITH GRILLED PEACHES

- ⅓ cup (60g) coconut oil
- 2 tablespoons norbu (monk fruit sugar)
- 3 eggs, separated
- 1 cup (150g) self-raising flour
- ⅓ cup (50g) plain (all-purpose) flour
- ⅓ cup (50g) buckwheat flour
- ⅓ cup (50g) cornflour (cornstarch)
- 1 teaspoon baking powder
- 1 teaspoon bicarbonate of soda (baking soda)
- ½ teaspoon salt
- ½ teaspoon ground ginger
- 1½ cups (375ml) milk
- 1½ teaspoons white vinegar
- cooking oil spray
- 4 medium yellow peaches (600g), halved, stones removed
- 1 cup (280g) Greek-style yoghurt
- ⅓ cup small fresh mint leaves
- ⅓ cup (90g) raw honey

1 Beat coconut oil and norbu in a medium bowl with an electric mixer until combined. Beat in egg yolks one at a time.

2 Beat egg whites in a small bowl with an electric mixer until soft peaks form. Gently fold egg whites into egg-yolk mixture.

3 Fold sifted dry ingredients, milk and vinegar into egg mixture until mixture just comes together (do not over mix; it may look quite lumpy at this stage).

4 Spray a heated waffle iron with cooking oil; pour a level ½-cup of batter on the bottom element of waffle iron. Close iron; cook waffle 2 minutes or until browned on both sides and crisp. Transfer to a plate; cover to keep warm. Repeat to make a total of 8 waffles.

5 Meanwhile, heat an oiled chargrill pan over high heat; cook peaches for 3 minutes each side or until grill marks show.

6 Serve waffles with yoghurt, peach halves and mint; drizzle with honey.

prep + cook time 35 minutes (+ standing, refrigeration & freezing) serves 4

Kombucha berry jellies WITH CINNAMON-CASHEW ICE-CREAM

You will need to start this recipe a day ahead.

- 1 cup (250ml) apple juice
- 2cm (¾-inch) piece ginger (10g), sliced thinly
- 4 teaspoons (14g) powdered gelatine
- 2 cups (500ml) hibiscus-flavoured kombucha
- 125g (4 ounces) fresh raspberries
- 125g (4 ounces) fresh blueberries, halved if large

CINNAMON-CASHEW ICE-CREAM

- 1½ cups (225g) raw cashews
- 1¼ cups (310ml) water
- 2 tablespoons pure maple syrup
- 1 teaspoon vanilla bean paste
- ½ teaspoon ground cinnamon
- ¼ teaspoon fine sea salt

1 Heat juice and ginger in a small saucepan over medium heat until mixture is just simmering. Remove from heat; quickly sprinkle over gelatine; whisk to dissolve. Pour into a large bowl; cool to room temperature.

2 Discard ginger slices. Add kombucha to juice mixture (see tips); whisk to combine. Stand for 5 minutes to allow any bubbles to settle.

3 Divide three-quarters of the berries among four 1-cup (250ml) bundt or jelly moulds. Pour in jelly mixture; refrigerate for 4 hours or overnight until set.

4 Make cinnamon-cashew ice-cream.

5 Dip moulds in boiling water briefly to release jellies. Turn out onto serving plates. Serve topped with scoops of cinnamon-cashew ice-cream and remaining berries.

cinnamon-cashew ice-cream Place cashews in a large bowl; cover with cold water. Stand, covered, for at least 2 hours or overnight. Drain cashews, rinse under cold water; drain well. Blend cashews with remaining ingredients until as smooth as possible, using a high-powered blender, if available; this type of blender will produce a very smooth consistency. Churn mixture in an ice-cream maker, following manufacturer's instructions, until the consistency of soft-serve ice-cream. Spoon into a 3-cup (750ml) loaf pan; cover and freeze for 2 hours. Remove from freezer 15 minutes before serving.

tips Ensure that the gelatine mixture has cooled before combining it with the kombucha or the excess heat will destroy the probiotics in the kombucha. To make this ice-cream without an ice-cream machine, pour the cashew mixture into a large zip-top plastic bag; seal. Freeze, flat-side down, on a large tray for 1 hour or until partially frozen. Process mixture until smooth. Repeat freezing and processing mixture once more. Spoon into the loaf pan and freeze for 2 hours or until the consistency of soft-serve ice-cream.

prep time 25 minutes (+ standing & freezing) makes 14 slices

Raw citrus CHEESECAKE SLICE

You will need to start this recipe a day ahead.

- 3 cups (450g) raw cashews
- 1 cup (140g) raw macadamias
- ¾ cup (120g) natural almonds
- ½ cup (40g) desiccated coconut
- 6 fresh dates (120g), pitted
- ¼ teaspoon sea salt flakes
- ⅔ cup (160ml) rice malt syrup
- ⅓ cup (80ml) coconut cream
- ½ teaspoon pure vanilla extract
- 2 tablespoons finely grated lemon rind
- ⅓ cup (80ml) lemon juice
- 1 cup (200g) coconut oil, melted
- ½ teaspoon ground turmeric
- 2 tablespoons finely grated orange rind
- 2 tablespoons orange juice
- 2 tablespoons raw macadamias, extra, chopped finely
- 7 dehydrated orange slices, cut into quarters, optional (see tips)

1 Place cashews in a large bowl; cover with cold water. Stand, covered, for 4 hours or overnight. Drain cashews; rinse under cold water, drain well.

2 Grease an 18cm x 28cm (7¼-inch x 11¼-inch) slice pan; line base and sides with baking paper, extending paper 5cm (2 inches) over sides.

3 Process macadamias, almonds, desiccated coconut, dates and salt until mixture resembles coarse crumbs and starts to stick together; be careful not to over-process. Press nut mixture firmly and evenly over base of pan, using a spatula. Freeze until required.

4 To make lemon filling, blend drained cashews, syrup, coconut cream, vanilla, lemon rind and juice until well combined. Add ¾ cup of the coconut oil; blend until as smooth as possible, using a high-powered blender, if available; this type of blender will produce a very smooth consistency. Pour two-thirds of the lemon filling over base; smooth top. Freeze slice for 1 hour to firm slightly.

5 Add turmeric, orange rind and juice to the remaining lemon filling and blend until combined. Add remaining oil; blend until well combined. Pour orange filling over lemon layer; tilt pan to spread evenly. Freeze slice for 4 hours or until set.

6 Cut slice into 14 rectangles. Serve slice topped with extra chopped macadamias and quartered dehydrated orange pieces, if you like.

tips Dehydrated orange slices are available from some health food stores or, to make your own, see raw jaffa cake, page 425.

keeps Store slice in an airtight container in the fridge for up to 5 days, or freeze for up to 2 months.

prep + cook time 30 minutes (+ freezing) serves 10

Salted coconut & PASSIONFRUIT SEMIFREDDO

- » 2 cups (500ml) coconut cream (see tips)
- » 6 eggs, separated
- » ⅓ cup (115g) raw honey or pure maple syrup
- » 2 teaspoons pure vanilla extract
- » ½ cup (50g) coconut milk powder
- » 1 teaspoon sea salt flakes
- » ⅓ cup (80ml) fresh passionfruit pulp (see tips)
- » ½ cup (25g) unsweetened coconut flakes
- » ¼ cup (60ml) fresh passionfruit pulp, extra
- » 1 tablespoon micro mint or small mint leaves

1 Pour coconut cream into a medium metal bowl; place in the freezer for 30 minutes or until chilled.
2 Grease a 9cm (3¾-inch) deep, 11.5cm x 20cm (4¾-inch x 8-inch) loaf pan. Line with baking paper, extending the paper 5cm (2 inches) over sides of pan.
3 Beat egg yolks, 2 tablespoons of the honey and the vanilla in a small bowl with an electric mixer on high for 5 minutes or until thick and pale. Transfer to a large bowl.
4 Beat egg whites in a clean small bowl with an electric mixer until soft peaks form. Gradually add the remaining honey; beat until thick and glossy.
5 Whisk chilled coconut cream, coconut milk powder and salt in a medium bowl until slightly thickened. Gently fold egg whites and coconut cream mixture into egg yolk mixture.
6 Pour mixture into lined pan; freeze for 1 hour or until mixture has thickened slightly. Swirl through passionfruit pulp; freeze for at least another 3 hours or overnight.
7 Stand semifreddo at room temperature for 5 minutes before inverting onto a platter. Top with coconut flakes, extra passionfruit and mint to serve.

tips Use a brand of coconut cream that states it is 100% natural on the label. Coconut cream that has 'emulsifying agents' added (it will state this on the label) may cause the semifreddo to separate into creamy and watery layers. You will need about 9 passionfruit to get the amount of pulp required. You could also peel the flesh of a fresh coconut with a vegetable peeler, if you prefer, and substitute it for the coconut flakes.

prep time 50 minutes (+ standing, freezing & refrigeration) makes 16

Chocolate HAZELNUT SLICE

OUR GENEROUS, DREAMILY RICH SLICE WITH CRUNCHY LITTLE POCKETS OF NUTS AND BUCKWHEAT IS INSPIRED BY BELOVED FERRERO ROCHER CHOCOLATES.

You will need to start this recipe a day ahead.

» 2 cups (300g) raw cashews
» 2 cups (280g) hazelnuts
» ½ cup (60g) almond meal (ground almonds)
» ⅓ cup (35g) cacao powder
» 2 teaspoons pure vanilla extract
» ¾ cup (150g) activated buckwheat groats
» ⅓ cup (80ml) coconut nectar
» ⅔ cup (140g) coconut oil, melted
» ½ cup (140g) chocolate hazelnut spread
» ½ cup (125ml) pure maple syrup
» ¼ cup (60ml) coconut cream
» ⅛ teaspoon natural hazelnut flavour
» ¼ teaspoon fine sea salt

CHOCOLATE GANACHE

» ¾ cup (75g) cacao powder
» ⅓ cup (70g) coconut oil, melted
» ¾ cup (180ml) pure maple syrup
» ½ teaspoon pure vanilla extract

1 Place cashews in a large bowl; cover with cold water. Stand, covered, for 4 hours or overnight. Drain cashews, rinse under cold water; drain well.
2 Lightly grease or oil an 18cm x 28cm (7¼-inch x 11¼-inch) slice pan; line base and sides with baking paper, extending the paper 5cm (2 inches) over sides.
3 Process 1 cup of the hazelnuts, the almond meal, cacao powder and half the vanilla until mixture resembles coarse crumbs. Add buckwheat groats, nectar and 2 tablespoons of the coconut oil; process until just combined. Press nut mixture firmly and evenly over base of pan, using a plastic spatula. Freeze while preparing filling.
4 Blend drained cashews with remaining coconut oil, chocolate hazelnut spread, syrup, coconut cream, remaining vanilla, hazelnut flavour and salt until as smooth as possible, using a high-powered blender, if available; this type of blender will produce a very smooth consistency. Pour half the mixture over base; smooth top.
5 Finely chop ⅔ cup of the remaining hazelnuts; sprinkle over filling. Pour over remaining cashew mixture; smooth top. Cover; freeze for 3 hours or until firm.
6 Make chocolate ganache.
7 Pour chocolate ganache over slice; smooth top. Refrigerate for 20 minutes.
8 Coarsely chop remaining hazelnuts. Sprinkle over slice.
9 Cut slice into rectangles.
chocolate ganache Blend ingredients until as smooth as possible, using a high-powered blender, if available; this type of blender will produce a very smooth consistency.

keeps Store in an airtight container in the fridge for up to 6 days or freezer for up to 2 months.

prep + cook time 20 minutes (+ standing) makes 36

Chocolate POWER PUFFS

- 1¼ cups (25g) puffed rice
- 1¼ cups (40g) puffed millet
- ½ cup (75g) sunflower seeds
- ¾ cup (90g) goji berries or unsweetened dried cranberries
- ¼ cup (35g) chia seeds
- ½ cup (100g) coconut oil, melted
- ½ cup (180g) raw honey
- 1¼ cups (125g) cacao powder

1 Combine puffed rice, puffed millet, sunflower seeds, goji berries and chia seeds in a large bowl.

2 Stir coconut oil and honey in a small saucepan over low heat until almost melted; remove from heat. Add cacao powder; whisk to combine. Pour cacao mixture over dry ingredients in bowl; stir well to combine.

3 Line an oven tray with baking paper. Using wet hands, roll heaped tablespoons of mixture into balls, place on tray; refrigerate for 30 minutes. Store in an airtight container.

prep + cook time 20 minutes (+ standing & refrigeration) serves 10

Earl grey & chocolate VEGAN CHEESECAKE

THIS VEGAN CHEESECAKE IS BASED ON NUTS, WHICH PROVIDES A WONDERFUL, NATURAL RICHNESS AND FLAVOUR. WHEN FIGS ARE NOT IN SEASON, SERVE THIS CHEESECAKE TOPPED WITH FRESH RASPBERRIES AND FLAKED ALMONDS.

You will need to start this recipe a day ahead.

» 4 cups (600g) raw unsalted cashews
» 8 earl grey tea bags
» ¼ cup (25g) cacao powder
» 1 cup (230g) fresh dates, pitted
» 1 cup (200g) coconut oil
» 2 teaspoons pure vanilla extract
» 8 small figs (400g), torn in half
» 2 teaspoons cacao powder, extra

CHEESECAKE BASE

» 1 cup (170g) activated buckwheat groats (see tips)
» ½ cup (80g) natural almonds
» ⅓ cup (35g) cacao powder
» 1 cup (230g) fresh dates, pitted
» ¼ cup (50g) coconut oil
» 2 tablespoons warm water
» 1 teaspoon pure vanilla extract

1 Place cashews and tea bags in a large bowl, cover with cold water; stand for 24 hours.
2 Grease a 22cm (9-inch) (base measure) springform pan; line with baking paper.
3 Make cheesecake base. Using the back of a spoon, spread mixture evenly onto base of pan. Refrigerate for 15 minutes or until firm.
4 Drain cashews and tea bags, reserving ½ cup of the soaking liquid. Place cashews in the bowl of a food processor; empty tea leaves from tea bags onto cashews. Add reserved soaking liquid, cacao, dates, oil and vanilla; process until mixture is as smooth as possible. Spread filling mixture over chilled base. Refrigerate for at least 4 hours or until firm.
5 Before serving, top cheesecake with figs and dust with extra cacao.
cheesecake base Process buckwheat, almonds and cacao powder until finely ground. With the motor operating, add dates, oil, the water and vanilla; process until well combined and the mixture sticks together when pressed.

tips Activated buckwheat groats have been soaked, washed, rinsed and dehydrated; the process is said to aid digestion. If you have one, use a high-speed blender such as a Vitamix when making the filling, to make the mixture very smooth. Use a hot, dry knife to slice the cheesecake cleanly.

prep time 35 minutes (+ standing & freezing) makes 20

CHOC-CARAMEL BARS

» 1 cup (140g) raw macadamias
» ½ cup (60g) pecans
» ¾ cup (60g) desiccated coconut
» ⅓ cup (70g) coconut oil, melted
» 1 tablespoon pure maple syrup
» ¼ teaspoon sea salt flakes

CARAMEL

» 9 fresh dates (180g), pitted
» ⅓ cup (95g) smooth natural peanut butter (see tip)
» ¼ cup (50g) coconut oil, melted
» ¼ cup (60ml) coconut cream
» ½ teaspoon sea salt flakes

CHOCOLATE COATING

» ¼ cup (50g) coconut oil
» ¼ cup (60g) cacao butter, chopped finely
» 2 tablespoons pure maple syrup
» ½ cup (50g) cacao powder

1 Make caramel.
2 Grease a 20cm (8-inch) square cake pan; line base and sides with baking paper, extending the paper 5cm (2 inches) over sides.
3 For raw shortbread layer, process nuts, desiccated coconut, oil, maple syrup and salt until mixture resembles coarse crumbs and starts to come together. Press firmly and evenly over base of pan using a spatula. Freeze for 20 minutes or until set.
4 Spread caramel over shortbread; smooth top. Freeze for 1 hour or until set.
5 Remove caramel-topped shortbread from pan; cut into 20 bars, 10cm (4 inches) long and slightly less than 2cm (¾ inch) wide. Place on a baking-paper-lined tray; return to freezer until ready to coat.
6 Make chocolate coating.
7 Working one at a time, using tongs, dip bars in chocolate coating, turning to coat. Gently shake off excess chocolate; return to tray. Freeze for 10 minutes or until set.
8 Trim off any excess chocolate from bars. Using a spoon, drizzle remaining chocolate over bars. (If chocolate coating has thickened too much, reheat.) Freeze for 5 minutes or until chocolate is set.

caramel Place dates in a small bowl, cover with cold water. Stand for 30 minutes; drain. Blend drained dates with remaining ingredients until as smooth as possible, using a high-powered blender, if available; this type of blender will produce a very smooth consistency.

chocolate coating Place coconut oil and cacao butter in a medium heatproof bowl over a smaller heatproof bowl of boiling water, whisk until combined and smooth; whisk in syrup. Remove from heat; whisk in cacao powder until combined and smooth.

tip Use a good-quality natural peanut butter, made from 100% peanuts.

keeps Store in an airtight container in the fridge for up to 5 days or freeze for up to 2 months.

Hot drinks

prep + cook time 15 minutes
serves 2 (makes 2 cups)

TURMERIC & HONEY TONIC

Place 2 cups unsweetened almond milk, 1 tablespoon raw honey, 2 teaspoons grated fresh turmeric, 1 cinnamon stick and 4 slices fresh ginger in a small saucepan over low-medium heat; bring almost to the boil. Remove from heat; set aside for 10 minutes to allow flavours to infuse. Strain mixture through a fine sieve into heatproof glasses; dust with a pinch of ground cinnamon.

prep + cook time 10 minutes
serves 2 (makes 1½ cups)

TURKISH DELIGHT NIGHT CAP

Stir 2 cups whole milk, 1 tablespoon raw honey and 2 cinnamon sticks in a small saucepan over low-medium heat; simmer, without boiling, for 10 minutes. Remove from heat; stand for 10 minutes. Discard cinnamon. Return pan to low heat; simmer 5 minutes or until heated through. Stir in 1 teaspoon rosewater, or to taste (see tip). Pour into heatproof glasses; dust with ground cinnamon.

tip The strength of rosewater varies from brand to brand, start with a little less, then taste and adjust to your liking.

prep + cook time 20 minutes
serves 2 (makes 3 cups)

HOT! HOT! HOT! CHOCOLATE

Split a vanilla bean lengthways, scrape seeds, using the tip of a knife; add seeds and pod to a saucepan. Cut 1 fresh long red chilli into four. Add three pieces to the pan; thinly slice remaining chilli, reserve to serve. Add 3 cups coconut milk blend (see tip) to the pan; bring to the boil. Remove from heat; stand for 5 minutes to infuse. Discard chilli and bean. Stir 2 tablespoons raw cacao powder and 1 tablespoon rice malt syrup into infused milk; simmer, stirring, 2 minutes or until cacao is dissolved and milk heated through. Serve topped with remaining chilli.

tip We used Pureharvest Coco Quench a blend of coconut and rice milks; it has a thinner consistency than canned coconut milk, but still has a great coconut milk taste.

prep + cook time 10 minutes
serves 2 (makes 3 cups)

HOT SALTED CAROB LATTE

Split a vanilla bean lengthways, scrape seeds from one pod half using the tip of a knife; add seeds and pod half to a small saucepan. Add 3 cups soy milk, 1½ tablespoons carob powder, pinch of salt flakes and 1 tablespoon raw honey to pan. Place pan over low-medium heat; simmer, stirring continuously, for 5 minutes or until carob powder dissolves and mixture is heated. Discard pod. Transfer to a blender; blend until frothy. Pour into heatproof glasses; dust with ¼ teaspoon carob powder.

prep + cook time 15 minutes serves 4

Squashed plum & RICOTTA SANDWICHES

- 2 tablespoons melted coconut oil
- 2 teaspoons sugar-free icing mix (see tip)
- 1 teaspoon ground ginger
- 4 medium blood plums (340g), halved, stones removed
- 1 tablespoon pure maple syrup
- 8 x 2cm (¾-inch) slices sourdough bread
- 1 cup (240g) firm ricotta

1 Preheat a sandwich press. Brush press with half the coconut oil.
2 Combine icing mix and ginger in a small bowl.
3 Place plums, cut-side down, in the sandwich press. Cook, pressing down on the lid occasionally, for 6 minutes or until plums are tender and browned. Remove plums; wipe sandwich press clean.
4 Meanwhile, combine maple syrup and remaining coconut oil in a small bowl. Brush oil mixture over one side of each piece of bread.
5 Place four slices of bread, oiled-side down, on a board; spread with ricotta and top with plums. Top with remaining bread slices, oiled-side up. Cook in sandwich press, in two batches, for 3 minutes or until golden and heated through. Serve sandwiches dusted with ginger mixture.

tip We used Natvia icing mix made from stevia. It is available in the baking aisle of most supermarkets.

prep time 40 minutes (+ standing & freezing) makes 20

Raw strawberry CREAM COOKIES

You will need to start this recipe a day ahead.

- 1 cup (140g) raw macadamias
- ¾ cup (90g) pecans
- ¾ cup (65g) desiccated coconut
- ⅓ cup (70g) coconut oil, melted
- 1 tablespoon raw honey
- ½ teaspoon pure vanilla extract

STRAWBERRY CREAM

- 1 cup (150g) raw cashews
- 250g (8 ounces) strawberries
- ½ cup (100g) coconut oil, melted
- ¼ cup (90g) raw honey
- 1 tablespoon freeze-dried strawberry powder, optional

CHOCOLATE COATING

- ¼ cup (50g) coconut oil
- ¾ cup (180g) cacao butter, chopped finely
- ⅓ cup (80ml) pure maple syrup
- ½ teaspoon pure vanilla extract
- 1 cup (100g) cacao powder

1 Place cashews for strawberry cream in a small bowl; cover with cold water. Stand, covered, for 4 hours or overnight. Drain cashews; rinse under cold water, drain well.

2 Make strawberry cream.

3 Grease a 20cm x 30cm (8-inch x 12-inch) slice pan; line with plastic wrap, extending plastic 5cm (2 inches) over sides.

4 Process macadamias, pecans, desiccated coconut, coconut oil, honey and vanilla until mixture resembles coarse crumbs and holds together when pressed; be careful not to over-process. Press nut mixture firmly and evenly over base of pan. Freeze for 15 minutes or until firm.

5 Lift cookie base from pan; place on a chopping board. Cut 20 rounds using a 5cm (2-inch) cutter, pushing scraps together as necessary. Place rounds on baking paper-lined tray.

6 Spoon strawberry cream into piping bag fitted with a 1cm (½-inch) plain tube; pipe 5cm (2-inch) rounds on top of cookies, creating small peaks. Return cookies to freezer while you prepare chocolate coating.

7 Make chocolate coating.

8 Using a fork, lower cookies, one at a time, into chocolate coating. Spoon chocolate over; allow excess chocolate to drain off. Place cookies on tray; freeze for 10 minutes or until chocolate is set. Repeat process to coat cookies twice in chocolate coating, if necessary. If chocolate has thickened too much, reheat briefly. Return cookies to freezer for 10 minutes or until set. Trim off any excess chocolate.

strawberry cream Blend drained cashews with remaining ingredients until as smooth as possible, using a high-powered blender, if available; this type of blender will achieve a very smooth consistency. Pour into a medium bowl; freeze for 1¼ hours or until very thick. Whisk vigorously until smooth.

chocolate coating Place coconut oil and cacao butter in a large heatproof bowl over a medium heatproof bowl of boiling water; whisk until combined and smooth. Whisk in syrup and vanilla; remove from heat. Whisk in cacao powder until combined and smooth.

prep + cook time 1 hour 30 minutes (+ freezing) serves 8

Roasted berry FROZEN YOGHURT LAYER LOAF

- 2 cups (300g) fresh blueberries
- 2 cups (260g) fresh strawberries
- 1 cup (220g) Natvia
- 2 cups (500ml) water
- 1 vanilla bean, cut into thirds
- 1½ tablespoons powdered gelatine
- 3 cups (840g) Greek-style yoghurt
- ½ cup (120g) mashed ripe banana (see tips)
- ⅓ cup (55g) roasted almonds, chopped coarsely
- frozen or fresh cherries, strawberries and blueberries, to serve, optional

1 Preheat oven to 190°C/375°F. Line two large oven trays with baking paper. Line a 14cm x 24cm x 7cm (5½-inch x 9½-inch x 2¾-inch) loaf pan (1.5 litre/6 cups) with plastic wrap, extending the plastic 3cm (1¼ inches) over the side.
2 Place blueberries on one tray. Hull and quarter strawberries; place on other tray. Roast both berries for 15 minutes or until soft; cool on trays.
3 Combine ⅓ cup (75g) of the Natvia, ⅔ cup (160ml) of the water and one-third of the vanilla bean in a small saucepan; stir over low heat for 4 minutes or until Natvia dissolves. Bring to the boil, without stirring; reduce heat, simmer for 15 minutes or until reduced to ⅓ cup (80ml). Remove vanilla bean. Sprinkle 2 teaspoons of the gelatine over hot syrup and whisk until gelatine melts.
4 Working quickly so the gelatine doesn't set, process gelatine mixture with 1 cup (280g) of the yoghurt. Pulse through blueberries until just combined. Pour into loaf tin; freeze for 30 minutes or until just frozen.
5 Repeat step 3.
6 Working quickly, stir gelatine mixture and mashed banana together in a medium bowl until smooth. Stir through 1 cup (280g) of remaining yoghurt and almonds. Pour over blueberry layer; freeze for 30 minutes or until just frozen.
7 Repeat step 3.
8 Working quickly, process gelatine mixture and strawberries in cleaned food processor. Add remaining yoghurt; pulse until just combined. Pour over banana layer; freeze for 3 hours or overnight.
9 Remove loaf from freezer 15 minutes before serving. Invert onto a chopping board, remove plastic wrap; cut into slices. Serve topped with cherries and extra berries.

tips You will need about 1 medium banana (200g) to make ½ cup mashed banana. Store loaf in an airtight container in the freezer for up to 1 month.

swap out the almonds in the banana layer and replace with the same amount of toasted coconut flakes or coarsely chopped unsalted peanuts, if you like.

prep + cook time 15 minutes (+ freezing) makes 10

Matcha CHOC POP

You will need 10 x ½-cup (125ml) popsicle moulds and 10 paddle pop sticks for this recipe. The higher the percentage of cocoa solids a chocolate contains, the less room there is for additives, such as sugar, and the more intense the chocolate flavour.

- 1 litre (4 cups) coconut milk
- ⅔ cup (240g) honey
- 1 tablespoon matcha (green tea) powder (see tip)
- 80g (2½ ounces) raw, organic dark chocolate (85% cocoa)

1 Whisk coconut milk, honey and matcha powder in a large jug until combined. Pour among 10 x ½ cup (125ml) popsicle moulds. Freeze for 2 hours or until starting to firm. Insert sticks two-thirds into the centre of each pop; freeze for 4 hours or overnight until firm.
2 Place moulds in a bowl of room temperature water; pull sticks quickly to remove pops from moulds. Transfer pops to a baking-paper-lined tray; return to freezer.
3 Place chocolate in a small heatproof bowl. Place bowl over a small saucepan of simmering water (don't let water touch base of bowl); stir until smooth and melted. Cool for 5 minutes. Working quickly, dip a spoon in chocolate; drizzle widthways across pops. Freeze for 5 minutes or until chocolate is set.

tip Matcha is a type of green tea that has been blended into a fine powder. You can find it at specialty tea stores or Asian supermarkets.

prep time 20 minutes (+ standing & freezing) serves 12

Purple berry CRUSH PIE

You will need to start this recipe a day ahead.

- » 2 cups (300g) raw cashews
- » 150g (4½ ounces) frozen raspberries
- » 150g (4½ ounces) frozen blueberries
- » ½ cup (125ml) rice malt syrup
- » ¼ cup (60ml) coconut cream
- » 1 tablespoon finely grated lemon rind
- » ¼ cup (60ml) lemon juice
- » ⅔ cup (140g) coconut oil, melted
- » 1 cup (150g) fresh or frozen mixed berries, to serve

ALMOND BASE

- » ½ cup (80g) natural almonds
- » ½ cup (85g) activated buckwheat groats
- » ⅓ cup (40g) almond meal (ground almonds)
- » ¼ cup (25g) cacao powder
- » 2 tablespoons yacon syrup or rice malt syrup (see tips)
- » 1 tablespoon coconut oil, melted
- » 1 teaspoon pure vanilla extract

1 Place cashews in a medium bowl; cover with cold water. Stand, covered, for 4 hours or overnight. Drain cashews, rinse under cold water; drain well.
2 Meanwhile, thaw raspberries and blueberries in a medium bowl at room temperature for 1 hour; do not drain.
3 Grease a 20cm (8-inch) round sandwich or shallow cake pan.
4 Make almond base.
5 Blend drained cashews, thawed berries, rice malt syrup, coconut cream, rind and juice until well combined. Add coconut oil and blend until as smooth as possible, using a high-powered blender, if available; this type of blender will produce a very smooth consistency.
6 Pour two-thirds of filling mixture over base, smooth top; freeze for 4 hours or until set. Meanwhile, transfer remaining filling to a small bowl; refrigerate to firm while base sets.
7 Using a palette knife, spread remaining filling over pie, creating soft swirls.
8 Top with mixed berries just before serving.
almond base Process all ingredients until mixture resembles coarse crumbs and starts to come together. Press mixture firmly and evenly over base of pan, using a spatula. Freeze while preparing filling.

tips Yacon syrup is available from some health food stores. It has a consistency very similar to rice malt syrup, with a distinct treacle-like flavour and a mild level of sweetness. It is considered by many to be one of the healthiest sweeteners available.

keeps Store pie in an airtight container in the fridge for up to 5 days or freeze the undecorated pie for up to 2 months.

prep + cook time 30 minutes (+ standing & freezing) makes 12

Chocolate caramel GOOD TIMES

You will need to start this recipe 2 days ahead.

- 2 cups (300g) raw cashews
- 1 cup (250ml) coconut cream
- 2 tablespoons coconut oil, melted
- ¼ cup (60ml) pure maple syrup
- 1 cup (140g) slivered almonds, roasted, chopped coarsely

CARAMEL SAUCE

- 1 cup (250ml) coconut cream
- ⅓ cup (80ml) pure maple syrup
- 1 vanilla bean, split lengthways, seeds scraped

CHOCOLATE COATING

- 75g (2½ ounces) cacao butter, chopped finely
- 2 tablespoons pure maple syrup
- ½ cup (50g) cacao powder

1 Place cashews in a small bowl; cover with cold water. Stand, covered, for 4 hours or overnight.

2 Meanwhile, make caramel sauce.

3 Drain cashews, rinse under cold water; drain well. Blend cashews with coconut cream, coconut oil and maple syrup, using a high-powered blender if available; this type of blender will produce a very smooth consistency.

4 Dollop cashew and caramel mixtures alternately in each hole of two 6-hole (⅓ cup/80ml) popsicle moulds. Push a popsicle stick into each mould; freeze overnight or until firm.

5 When ready to coat the frozen popsicles, make chocolate coating.

6 Line an oven tray with baking paper; place in the freezer. Pour chocolate coating into a small jug. Place almonds in a small bowl. Dip popsicle mould briefly in hot water; remove popsicles from moulds. Dip popsicles into chocolate coating; dip in almonds to coat evenly.

7 Place on chilled tray. Freeze for 5 minutes or until coating is set.

caramel sauce Place all ingredients in a small saucepan. Bring to the boil over medium heat, reduce heat to low; simmer, stirring occasionally, for 25 minutes or until thickened. Remove vanilla. Transfer to a small bowl, cover with plastic wrap; refrigerate until chilled. (Makes about ¾ cup)

chocolate coating Place cacao butter in a medium heatproof bowl over a smaller heatproof bowl of boiling water, whisk until combined and smooth; whisk in maple syrup. Whisk in cacao powder until combined and smooth. Cool to room temperature.

prep time 30 minutes (+ standing & freezing) serves 12

Raw blueberry LEMON CHEESECAKE

You will need to start this recipe a day ahead.

- 3 cups (450g) raw cashews
- 1 cup (140g) macadamias
- ½ cup (40g) desiccated coconut
- 5 fresh dates (100g), pitted
- ½ cup (60g) pecans
- ¼ teaspoon fine sea salt
- ⅓ cup (80ml) coconut cream
- ⅔ cup (160ml) pure maple syrup or ½ cup (125ml) light agave syrup
- 1½ tablespoons finely grated lemon rind
- ⅓ cup (80ml) lemon juice
- ½ teaspoon pure vanilla extract
- ⅔ cup (140g) coconut oil, melted
- 40g (1½ ounces) cacao butter, melted
- 1½ cups (225g) frozen blueberries
- 125g (4 ounces) fresh blueberries
- 1 large lemon, sliced thinly crossways

1 Place cashews in a medium bowl; cover with cold water. Stand, covered, for 4 hours or overnight. Drain cashews, rinse under cold water; drain well.

2 Grease a 20cm (8-inch) springform cake pan. Line base and side with baking paper.

3 Process macadamias, desiccated coconut and dates until mixture resembles coarse crumbs. Add pecans and salt; process until combined and mixture starts to stick together. Press nut mixture firmly and evenly over base of pan, using a spatula. Freeze until required.

4 Blend drained cashews, coconut cream, maple syrup, rind, juice and vanilla until as smooth as possible, using a high-powered blender, if available; this type of blender will produce a very smooth consistency. Add oil and cacao butter; process until well combined and completely smooth.

5 Pour two-thirds of the lemon filling over base; smooth top. Sprinkle with ½ cup frozen blueberries; press berries lightly into filling. Freeze for 1 hour to firm slightly.

6 Meanwhile, thaw remaining frozen blueberries. Add thawed blueberries and any juice to remaining lemon filling; blend until as smooth as possible, using a clean and dry high-powered blender, if available; this type of blender will produce a very smooth consistency. Spread the blueberry filling over lemon filling; smooth top. Freeze cake for 4 hours or until firm.

7 Remove cake from pan; place on a plate. Serve topped with fresh blueberries and lemon slices.

swap out the frozen and fresh blueberries in the recipe with the same quantities of mixed berries, if you like.

keeps Store cake in an airtight container in the fridge for up to 5 days. The undecorated cake can be frozen in a container for up to 2 months.

prep time 15 minutes (+ refrigeration) makes 12

Raw gingerbread APPLE CUPCAKES

You will need to start the labneh recipe a day ahead. These cupcakes are gluten-free; to make them dairy-free, follow the tips in 'swap out'.

- 1½ cups (130g) dried apple slices
- 3 cups (330g) coarsely chopped walnuts
- 12 fresh dates (240g), pitted
- 60g (2 ounces) butter, melted
- 1 tablespoon finely grated fresh ginger
- 1½ teaspoons pure vanilla extract
- ½ teaspoon sea salt flakes
- ½ teaspoon mixed spice
- 2 tablespoons coarsely chopped dried apple slices, extra
- 2 tablespoons freeze-dried rose petals, optional

SPICED HONEY LABNEH

- 2 cups (560g) Greek-style yoghurt
- 1½ tablespoons raw honey
- 1½ teaspoons finely grated fresh ginger

1 Make spiced honey labneh.
2 Line a 12-hole (⅓ cup/80ml) muffin tin with paper cases.
3 Place apple slices in a medium bowl; cover with boiling water. Stand for 5 minutes; drain, reserving 1½ tablespoons of the soaking water.
4 Process apple, reserved water, walnuts, dates, butter, ginger, vanilla, salt and ¼ teaspoon of the mixed spice until well combined. Press evenly into paper cases; cover with plastic wrap and refrigerate for at least 4 hours or overnight until firm.
5 Top cupcakes with spiced honey labneh. Sprinkle with remaining mixed spice, extra chopped dried apple and rose petals, if you like.
spiced honey labneh Line a small sieve with muslin (or a clean loosely-woven cotton cloth); place sieve over a medium bowl. Spoon yoghurt into lined sieve; cover and refrigerate overnight. Transfer to a bowl. Stir in honey and ginger. Cover with plastic wrap; refrigerate until required.

swap out apple and replace with dried pears. To make a dairy-free version, substitute coconut oil for butter and unsweetened coconut yoghurt for the spiced honey labneh.

keeps Store cupcakes in an airtight container in the fridge for up to 1 week.

prep + cook time 1 hour 15 minutes (+ standing & freezing) serves 16

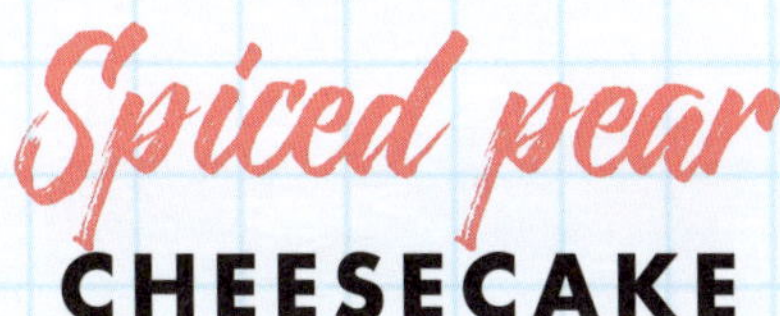

Spiced pear CHEESECAKE

You will need to start this recipe a day ahead.

- 2 cups (300g) raw cashews
- 1 cup (140g) raw macadamias
- 5 medium brown pears (1.2kg), such as beurre bosc
- ½ cup (125ml) coconut nectar
- 1½ cups (180g) pecans
- ½ cup (50g) walnuts
- ½ cup dried figs (100g), chopped finely
- ⅛ teaspoon sea salt flakes
- 130g (4½-ounce) piece fresh ginger, grated finely
- 1 cup (250ml) coconut cream
- ⅓ cup (80ml) coconut nectar, extra
- 2 teaspoons pure vanilla extract
- 2½ teaspoons ground cinnamon
- ¾ cup (150g) coconut oil, melted
- 1 tablespoon freeze-dried rose petals, optional
- 2 teaspoons cacao nibs, optional

1 Place cashews and macadamias in a large bowl; cover with cold water. Stand, covered, for 4 hours or overnight. Drain nuts; rinse under cold water; drain well.

2 Preheat oven to 160°C/325°F. Grease a 22cm (9-inch) springform cake pan. Line three oven trays with baking paper.

3 Peel and cut three of the pears into 1cm (½-inch) cubes; place on one oven tray. Drizzle with ⅓ cup of the nectar; toss to coat evenly. Bake for 40 minutes or until tender. Transfer to a wire rack to cool.

4 Thinly slice remaining pears lengthways with a mandoline or sharp knife. Place slices in a single layer on remaining oven trays. Drizzle with remaining nectar; turn to evenly coat. Bake for 20 minutes. Turn slices; bake for a further 15 minutes or until dark golden brown; (check frequently to ensure they do not burn). Transfer to a wire rack to cool completely. Store in an airtight container until ready to serve.

5 Process pecans, walnuts, fig and salt until fine crumbs form. Press mixture over base of cake pan; use the back of a spoon to press down firmly and smooth surface. Freeze while preparing filling.

6 Press grated ginger through a fine sieve over a small bowl; you will need ¼ cup (60ml) ginger juice. Discard pulp. Blend ginger juice with drained cashews and macadamias, coconut cream, extra nectar, vanilla and 2 teaspoons of the cinnamon until well combined. Add coconut oil; blend until as smooth as possible, using a high-powered blender, if available; this type of blender will produce a very smooth consistency.

7 Pour half the filling mixture over base. Scatter with diced pear; press a few of the pear pieces lightly into filling. Pour remaining filling over to cover pear; smooth top. Freeze cake for 5 hours or until set.

8 Sift remaining cinnamon over top of cake, arrange pear slices on top; serve scattered with rose petals and cacao nibs.

prep time 25 minutes (+ cooling & freezing) serves 6

Orange-pomegranate & CHOCOLATE GRANITAS

- » 2 large pomegranates (860g)
- » 2 cups (450ml) fresh strained orange juice
- » 1 cup (360g) rice malt syrup
- » 1 vanilla bean
- » 3 cups (750ml) water
- » 1 cup (100g) cacao powder
- » ½ cup (125ml) pouring cream

1 For the orange-pomegranate granita, cut or tear pomegranates in half crossways; scoop seeds out and place in a food processor bowl. Pulse for 10 seconds or until juice from seeds is released. Strain juice through a fine sieve over a medium bowl; you will need ⅔ cup (160ml) juice for the recipe.

2 Pour measured pomegranate juice, orange juice and ½ cup (180g) of the rice malt syrup into a medium saucepan. Bring to the boil over high heat, stirring until syrup dissolves. Pour mixture into a 4cm (1½-inch) deep, 22cm (9-inch) square cake pan. Cool for 15 minutes; freeze for 4 hours or until frozen.

3 For the chocolate granita, split vanilla bean lengthways, scrape seeds from halves, using the tip of a knife. Add to a medium saucepan along with the water, cacao and the remaining syrup. Bring to the boil, reduce heat to low; simmer, whisking, for 2 minutes or until cacao is dissolved. Stir in cream. Pour into a 4cm (1½-inch) deep, 22cm (9-inch) square cake pan. Cool for 15 minutes; freeze for 4 hours or until frozen.

4 Remove both granitas from freezer. Using a fork, break up the ice crystals; return to freezer until ready to serve.

5 Remove granitas from freezer 10 minutes before serving. Layer granitas in small glasses or bowls; top with extra pomegranate seeds, if you like.

tip Try replacing pomegranate juice with ¾ cup (180ml) freshly squeezed blood orange juice, when in season; strain the juice to remove any pulp, which may affect the granita texture.

prep time 30 minutes (+ standing, refrigeration, freezing & dehydration) serves 16

Raw jaffa cake

You will need to start this recipe a day ahead.

- ¾ cup (120g) natural almonds
- ⅓ cup (40g) almond meal (ground almonds)
- ¼ cup (25g) cacao powder
- ½ cup (100g) activated buckwheat groats
- ¼ cup (60ml) coconut nectar
- 20g (¾ ounce) coconut oil, melted
- ¾ teaspoon pure vanilla extract

CHOC-DIPPED ORANGE SLICES

- 1 medium orange (240g)
- 100g (3 ounces) vegan dark chocolate (70% cocoa), grated coarsely

FILLING

- 2 cups (300g) raw cashews
- ½ cup (125ml) pure maple syrup
- ½ cup (100g) coconut oil, melted
- ⅓ cup (35g) cacao powder
- 1½ tablespoons finely grated orange rind
- ¾ cup (180ml) fresh orange juice
- 40g (1½ ounces) cacao butter, melted
- ½ teaspoon pure vanilla extract

CHOCOLATE GANACHE

- ½ cup (50g) cacao powder
- ½ cup (125ml) pure maple syrup
- ¼ cup (50g) coconut oil, melted
- 1 teaspoon pure vanilla extract

1 Make choc-dipped orange slices and filling.
2 Grease a 23cm (9¼-inch) springform cake pan. Line base and side with baking paper.
3 Process almond, almond meal and cacao powder until mixture resembles coarse crumbs. Add buckwheat groats, coconut nectar, oil and vanilla; process until just combined. Press nut mixture firmly and evenly over base of pan, using a spatula. Freeze for 15 minutes.
4 Pour filling over base; freeze for 2½ hours or until firm.
5 Make chocolate ganache. Pour over cake; smooth top. Refrigerate for 15 minutes or until set.
6 Remove cake from pan; place on a plate. Top with choc-dipped orange slices; serve.

choc-dipped orange slices Preheat dehydrator to 46°C/115°F. Cut orange into 3mm (⅛-inch) thick slices; remove any seeds. Arrange slices on mesh dehydrator trays. Dehydrate for 12-24 hours, turning slices halfway, or until slices are dry and brittle; the time will depend on the quality of dehydrator and juiciness of the orange. (Alternatively, preheat oven to its lowest temperature, ideally 50°C/122°F. Line an oven tray with baking paper; place a greased wire rack on top. Arrange orange slices on rack. Place tray in oven; leave door slightly ajar so air can circulate and moisture can escape. Bake for 12 hours or until dry and brittle, turning slices occasionally.) Melt chocolate in a small heatproof bowl over a bowl of hot water. Dip orange slices halfway into chocolate; gently shake away excess chocolate. Place slices on a tray lined with baking paper; refrigerate for 15 minutes or until set. Leave some slices uncoated, if you prefer.

filling Place cashews in a medium bowl; cover with cold water. Stand, covered, for 4 hours or overnight. Drain cashews, rinse under cold water; drain well. Blend cashews with remaining ingredients until as smooth as possible, using a high-powered blender, if available; this type of blender will produce a very smooth consistency.

chocolate ganache Blend all the ingredients until smooth and silky.

keeps Store cake in an airtight container in the fridge for up to 5 days or freeze the undecorated cake for up to 2 months.

Baking
HOMEMADE TREATS

prep + cook time 45 minutes makes 8

Raspberry, polenta & PINK PEPPERCORN SCROLLS

- 2 cups (300g) white spelt flour, plus extra, for dusting
- ½ cup (85g) fine polenta
- 1½ teaspoons baking powder
- pinch salt
- ½ cup (125ml) buttermilk
- ¼ cup (85g) rice malt syrup
- 1 teaspoon pink peppercorns
- 1 teaspoon pure vanilla extract
- 1 tablespoon finely grated orange rind
- 2 tablespoons rice malt syrup, extra
- 75g (2½ ounces) fresh raspberries

1 Preheat oven to 180°C/350°F. Grease an oven tray; line with baking paper.

2 Combine flour, polenta, baking powder and salt in a large bowl. Make a well in the centre. Add buttermilk and syrup. Using a butter knife, 'cut' through mixture until a rough dough forms.

3 Using a mortar and pestle, crush pink peppercorns. Stir in vanilla, rind and 1 tablespoon of the extra syrup.

4 Turn dough onto a lightly floured surface; knead lightly. Press out into a 18cm x 28cm (7¼-inch x 11¼-inch) rectangle; spread with peppercorn mixture. Using your hands, tear raspberries into small pieces, place on dough.

5 Starting from one long side, roll up dough to form a log. Cut log into 8 even slices. Place slices 5cm (2-inches) apart, cut-side up, on tray.

6 Bake scrolls for 25 minutes or until risen and light golden. Brush with remaining extra syrup. Serve warm with extra fresh raspberries, if you like.

tips Pink peppercorns are unrelated to black peppercorns, they carry no heat and have a pine-like taste slightly similar to juniper berries. If unavailable don't worry, the recipe will still have plenty of flavour without them. The scrolls are best eaten warm on the day of making. If made ahead on the day, reheat in the oven before serving.

prep + cook time 1 hour 30 minutes serves 6

Ginger, pear & PISTACHIO CRUMBLES

- 6 medium firm pears (1.4kg), peeled, chopped coarsely
- 125g (4 ounces) fresh or frozen raspberries
- 2 tablespoons cornflour (cornstarch) or arrowroot
- 1 tablespoon finely grated fresh ginger
- ¼ cup (60ml) pure maple syrup
- 1 tablespoon lemon juice
- 1 teaspoon pure vanilla extract
- 1 cup (140g) pistachios
- 1 cup (120g) pecans
- 1 cup (90g) rolled oats
- ¼ cup (60ml) olive oil
- ¼ cup (60ml) pure maple syrup, extra
- 1 teaspoon pure vanilla extract, extra
- 2 tablespoons freeze-dried or fresh pomegranate seeds
- 2 cups (560g) thick no-sugar-added vanilla yoghurt (see swap out)

1 Preheat oven to 160°C/325°F.

2 Place pears, raspberries, cornflour, ginger, maple syrup, juice and vanilla in a large bowl; toss to coat fruit in mixture. Spoon mixture into six 1-cup (250ml) ovenproof dishes.

3 Process pistachios and pecans until chopped roughly. Transfer to a medium bowl; stir in oats, oil and extra maple syrup and vanilla; spoon over fruit mixture.

4 Bake crumbles, uncovered, for 1 hour. Cover with foil; bake a further 15 minutes or until crumble topping is golden and pears are soft.

5 Just before serving, sprinkle pomegranate seeds on crumbles. Serve with yoghurt.

swap out If you can't find sugar-free vanilla yoghurt you can stir vanilla bean seeds or extract through plain Greek-style yoghurt. Freeze-dried pomegranate seeds are available from health food stores or use unsweetened dried cranberries instead.

prep + cook time 30 minutes (+ standing) makes 6

Peaches & cream DOUGHNUTS

THESE DAIRY- AND GLUTEN-FREE DOUGHNUTS ARE SUPERFAST TO MAKE, HOWEVER, YOU WILL NEED A SPECIAL DOUGHNUT-SHAPED PAN, AVAILABLE FROM KITCHENWARE STORES, FOR THIS RECIPE.

- ½ cup (120g) drained canned peach slices in natural juice, reserve juice (see tips)
- ¼ cup (60ml) coconut cream
- 1 egg
- 1 teaspoon pure vanilla extract
- 1½ cups (180g) almond meal (ground almonds)
- 2 tablespoons stevia powder
- 1 teaspoon baking powder
- ⅓ cup (50g) dried peaches, chopped finely
- 2 tablespoons finely chopped pecans
- 1 tablespoon dried cornflower petals, optional

PEACH GLAZE

- ½ cup (125ml) canned peach juice (see tips)
- ½ cup (50g) coconut milk powder
- 1 teaspoon cornflour (cornstarch)
- ½ teaspoon pure vanilla extract

1 Preheat oven to 180°C/350°F. Grease a 6-hole (⅓ cup/80ml) non-stick doughnut pan.

2 Blend or process peaches, coconut cream, egg and vanilla until smooth. Add almond meal, stevia and baking powder; blend or process to combine. Spoon evenly into pan.

3 Bake for 20 minutes or until a skewer inserted into the centre of a doughnut comes out clean. Stand doughnuts in pan for 5 minutes. Turn, top-side up, onto a wire rack over a tray.

4 Make peach glaze.

5 Dip doughnuts in warm glaze; sprinkle with dried peach, pecans and cornflower petals, if using. Cool on a wire rack.

peach glaze Place all ingredients in a small heavy-based saucepan; whisk well until smooth. Bring to a simmer over high heat, whisking continuously until thick.

tips You will need a 400g (12½-ounce) can of peach slices in natural juices; reserve ½ cup drained fruit for the doughnuts and ¼ cup of the drained syrup for the glaze. Some brands of vanilla extract contain a negligible amount of added sucrose. Edible dried cornflower petals are available from some gourmet food stores and online.

swap out peach slices in natural juice for plum slices and juice and almond meal for hazelnut meal. Omit dried peaches and sprinkle with freeze-dried rose petals and chopped pistachios.

prep + cook time 50 minutes (+ standing & cooling) makes 20

Milky tea COOKIE SANDWICH

- 2¼ cups (200g) traditional rolled oats
- ½ cup (40g) desiccated coconut
- ⅓ cup (40g) coarsely chopped pecans
- ¼ cup (55g) Natvia
- 1½ teaspoons ground ginger
- ½ cup (100g) coconut oil, melted
- 1 tablespoon almond spread
- ½ teaspoon sea salt flakes

MILKY TEA CREAM

- 4 english breakfast tea bags
- 1 cup (150g) raw cashews
- 2 cups (500ml) boiling water
- 1 tablespoon Natvia

1 Preheat oven to 180°C/350°F. Grease two large oven trays; line with baking paper.
2 Make milky tea cream.
3 Process oats, coconut, pecans, Natvia, ginger, coconut oil, almond spread and salt for 45 seconds or until thoroughly combined and mixture starts to come together. Working in two batches roll mixture out between two sheets of baking paper until 5mm (¼-inch) thick. (The mixture will be moist and sticky but will dry during cooking. If it's too moist to roll out, chill in freezer for 15 minutes or until firm.) Using a 5cm (2-inch) round cutter, cut out 40 rounds, re-rolling as necessary. Using a palette knife, carefully transfer cookies to trays 1cm (½ inch) apart.
4 Bake for 15 minutes or until lightly browned and a cookie can be pushed gently without breaking. Stand on trays for 10 minutes; before transferring to a wire rack to cool.
5 Pipe approximately 2 teaspoons of milky tea cream onto half of the cookies; sandwich with remaining cookies.
milky tea cream Place 3 of the tea bags and cashews in a medium bowl. Cover with the boiling water; stand for 20 minutes. Strain over a bowl; reserve ⅓ cup (80ml) of the tea liquid. Discard soaked tea bags. Open remaining tea bag, measure ½ teaspoon tea leaves; discard remainder. In a small food processor, blend measured tea, soaked cashews, ¼ cup reserved tea liquid and the Natvia until a smooth icing consistency; if too thick, blend with remaining 1 tablespoon reserved liquid. Spoon mixture into a piping bag fitted with a 1cm (½ inch) straight nozzle. Refrigerate 1 hour.

keeps Store filled cookies in an airtight container in the fridge for up to 1 week.

prep + cook time 40 minutes (+ standing) makes 16

Chewies

- 2 cups (180g) rolled oats
- 1 cup (100g) desiccated coconut
- ½ cup (80g) wholemeal plain (all-purpose) flour
- ¼ cup (50g) pepitas (pumpkin seed kernels)
- ¼ cup (30g) natural flaked almonds
- ¼ cup (40g) sultanas
- ¼ cup (30g) goji berries
- ¼ cup (35g) dried cranberries
- 1 teaspoon bicarbonate of soda (baking soda)
- ¼ teaspoon sea salt flakes
- ⅓ cup (75g) coconut oil
- ¾ cup (180ml) rice malt syrup
- ½ teaspoon pure vanilla extract (see tip)
- 2 tablespoons desiccated coconut, extra
- 2 tablespoons pepitas (pumpkin seed kernels), extra

1 Preheat oven to 170°C/340°F. Grease a 20cm x 30cm (8-inch x 12-inch) slice pan; line base with baking paper, extending the paper 5cm (2 inches) over short sides of pan.

2 Combine dry ingredients in a large bowl.

3 Place coconut oil and rice malt syrup in a small saucepan; bring to the boil. Boil until oil is melted. Remove from heat; stir in vanilla.

4 Add oil mixture to dry mixture; stir thoroughly to combine (the mixture will be quite stiff, use clean hands to combine well, if necessary). Spoon mixture into pan, pressing down firmly with a spatula or damp hands to level. Sprinkle with extra coconut and extra pepitas.

5 Bake for 25 minutes or until golden. Turn off oven; leave slice in oven for a further 5 minutes to dry out slightly. Remove from oven; leave slice in pan for 15 minutes.

6 Use the baking paper to help lift the whole slice onto a wire rack to cool. Cool completely. Remove paper, then cut into 16 pieces.

tip Vanilla extract contains a tiny amount of refined sugar, if you prefer, either use the scraped seeds of a vanilla bean or vanilla bean powder available from health food stores.

keeps Chewies will keep in an airtight container for up to 1 week. If they become sticky, place in the oven at 150°C/300°F for 5 minutes; turn the oven off and leave for 5 minutes.

prep + cook time 1 hour 20 minutes (+ refrigeration) makes 6

Apple & spice FREE-FORM TARTS

- 4 large green apples (800g), peeled, cored, sliced thickly
- ⅔ cup (90g) coconut sugar, plus extra to dust
- ¼ cup (40g) white spelt flour
- 1 teaspoon ground cinnamon
- ½ teaspoon ground ginger
- 1 teaspoon ground cardamom
- ½ teaspoon sea salt flakes
- 30g (1 ounce) butter, chopped finely
- 2 tablespoons apple cider vinegar
- 1 cup (280g) Greek-style yoghurt
- 1 teaspoon finely grated orange rind

SPELT PASTRY

- 3 cups (450g) white spelt flour
- 1 vanilla bean, split lengthways, seeds scraped
- ¼ cup (40g) coconut sugar
- ½ teaspoon ground nutmeg
- ½ teaspoon sea salt flakes
- 200g (6½ ounces) butter, cut into small cubes
- 2 tablespoons ice-cold water, approximately

1 Make spelt pastry.
2 Place apples, sugar, flour, spices, salt, butter and vinegar in a large bowl; toss to coat.
3 Preheat oven 180°C/350°F. Line two oven trays with baking paper.
4 Cut pastry in half; roll out each piece between two sheets of lightly floured baking paper until 3mm (⅛-inch) thick. Remove top layer of paper. Using a 17cm (6¾-inch) bowl (or plate) as a guide, cut out 3 rounds from each pastry half. Place apple mixture in the centre, leaving a 3cm (1¼-inch) border. Reserve liquid from apple in the bowl. Fold pastry in, pleating it as you go to partially overlap the filling and create an open topped pie.
5 Transfer the pies to oven tray, brush with liquid from apple mixture; bake for 50 minutes or until golden and apples are tender.
6 Meanwhile, combine yoghurt and rind in a small bowl.
7 Using a large metal lifter, carefully transfer pies to plates. Serve with orange yoghurt.
spelt pastry Process flour, vanilla seeds, sugar, nutmeg, salt and butter until mixture resembles crumbs. Add the water; pulse until mixture just forms a dough. Shape into a disc, wrap in plastic wrap; refrigerate for 1 hour.

prep + cook time 30 minutes makes 18

Cacao & hazelnut COOKIES

- » ½ cup (80g) firmly packed fresh dates, pitted
- » 2 cups (200g) hazelnut meal
- » 1½ cups (225g) wholemeal spelt flour
- » ¼ cup (50g) chia seeds
- » 1 teaspoon ground cinnamon
- » pinch sea salt flakes
- » ¼ cup (50g) coconut oil, at room temperature
- » ½ cup (170g) rice malt syrup
- » 1 egg
- » 2 teaspoons pure vanilla extract
- » ½ cup (50g) cacao nibs (see tips)

1 Preheat oven to 160°C/325°F. Line two oven trays with baking paper.

2 Place dates in a small heatproof bowl, cover with boiling water; stand for 5 minutes. Drain.

3 Process dates, hazelnut meal, flour, chia seeds, cinnamon, salt, coconut oil, maple syrup, egg and vanilla until well combined. Stir in cacao nibs.

4 Using damp hands, roll 2-tablespoonfuls of mixture into balls, place on tray; flatten with the palm of your hand into 4cm (1½-inch) rounds. Using the back of a damp fork, mark each cookie with an indent.

5 Bake cookies for 15 minutes or until a cookie can gently be pushed without breaking. Cool on trays.

tips Cacao nibs are created in the early stages of chocolate production; cocoa beans are dried then roasted, after which they are crushed into what is termed 'nibs'. The nibs are then ground to separate the cocoa butter and cocoa solids. Nibs are both textural and chocolatey with no sweetness. Buy from health food stores and specialist food stores.

prep + cook time 1 hour 45 minutes (+ standing) serves 12

Carrot cakes with DATE CREAM CHEESE FROSTING

- ⅓ cup (35g) sultanas
- ¼ cup (60ml) boiling water
- 2 free-range eggs
- ¾ cup (185g) powdered stevia
- ¼ cup (85g) rice malt syrup
- ⅔ cup (140g) coconut oil, melted
- 2 teaspoons pure vanilla extract
- 2 cups (340g) firmly packed coarsely grated carrot
- ½ cup (60g) chopped pecans, roasted
- 1⅔ cups (250g) self-raising flour
- ½ teaspoon bicarbonate of soda (baking soda)
- 1 teaspoon ground allspice
- 3 teaspoons ground cinnamon
- 1 teaspoon ground ginger

DATE CREAM CHEESE FROSTING

- 125g (4 ounces) dried pitted dates, chopped finely
- 2 tablespoons boiling water
- 250g (8 ounces) cream cheese, softened
- 125g (4 ounces) butter, softened

1 Preheat oven to 180°C/350°F. Grease a 6-hole (¾-cup/180ml) texas muffin pan.

2 Place sultanas in a small heatproof bowl, pour over the boiling water; stand for 10 minutes.

3 Meanwhile, whisk eggs, stevia, syrup, coconut oil and vanilla in a small bowl with an electric mixer for 5 minutes. Transfer mixture to a large bowl; stir in carrot, sultanas and soaking liquid, then pecans and sifted remaining dry ingredients. Spoon mixture evenly into muffin pan holes.

4 Bake cakes for 35 minutes or until a skewer inserted into the centre of a cake comes out clean. Leave in pan for 5 minutes before turning, top-side up, onto a wire rack to cool.

5 Make date cream cheese frosting; spread on cakes. Top with extra finely chopped pecans, if you like.

date cream cheese frosting Process dates and the boiling water until almost smooth, scraping down the side of the bowl. Add cream cheese and butter; process, scraping down the side of the bowl, until frosting is light and fluffy.

tips You need about 2½ medium carrots to make 2 cups grated carrot. You could also cook the cake recipe as a slice using a 20cm x 30cm x 3cm (8-inch x 12-inch x 1¼-inch) slice pan. Line the base with baking paper, extending the paper 5cm (2 inches) over the long sides; bake for 25 minutes.

prep + cook time 1 hour 45 minutes serves 6

Flourless almond, plum & ORANGE BLOSSOM LOAF

- 2 medium green apples (300g), grated coarsely
- 2 eggs, beaten lightly
- ¼ cup (60ml) unsweetened almond milk
- 2 tablespoons raw honey or pure maple syrup
- 2 teaspoons pure vanilla extract
- 1 teaspoon orange blossom water
- 2 cups (240g) almond meal (ground almonds)
- 2 teaspoons gluten-free baking powder
- 5 small plums (375g), halved
- 2 teaspoons raw honey or pure maple syrup, extra
- 2 tablespoons flaked coconut, toasted

1 Preheat oven to 160°C/325°F. Lightly grease a 10.5cm x 21cm x 6cm (4-inch x 8½-inch x 2½-inch) (base measure) loaf pan; line base and long sides with baking paper.

2 Combine apple, egg, almond milk, honey, vanilla and orange blossom water in a large bowl. Add almond meal and baking powder; stir until just combined.

3 Spread mixture into pan, level surface; top with plums, cut-side up, pressing them slightly into the batter. Drizzle with extra honey.

4 Bake for 1½ hours or until a skewer inserted into the centre comes out clean. Top loaf with flaked coconut and serve warm.

tips You can also make this loaf with other stone fruit such as small peaches or apricots. You may need to cover the loaf loosely with baking paper during the last 10 minutes of baking to prevent overbrowning.

prep + cook time 40 minutes serves 6

Cinnamon & fig BAKED APPLES

- ¼ cup (35g) roasted hazelnuts, skins removed
- 3 dried figs
- 6 pitted prunes
- ½ teaspoon ground cinnamon
- 1 teaspoon pure vanilla extract
- 6 large red apples (1.2kg), cored (see tip)

RICOTTA CREAM

- 1 cup (240g) fresh firm ricotta
- ½ cup (125ml) milk
- 1 teaspoon pure vanilla extract
- ½ teaspoon finely grated mandarin rind

MAPLE SAUCE

- 2 large mandarins (500g)
- ¼ cup (60ml) pure maple syrup
- 30g (1 ounce) cold butter, chopped finely

1 Preheat oven to 160°C/325°F. Line an oven tray with baking paper.

2 Process hazelnuts, figs, prunes, cinnamon and vanilla until coarsely chopped.

3 Using a small, sharp knife, score around the centre of each apple. Press hazelnut mixture into the cavities of each apple; place apples upright on tray. Bake for 30 minutes or until apples are tender.

4 Meanwhile, make ricotta cream. Make maple sauce.

5 Serve apples with ricotta cream and maple sauce.

ricotta cream Process ricotta, milk and vanilla until smooth; stir in rind.

maple sauce Squeeze juice from mandarins; you will need ⅔ cup. Place juice and maple syrup in a small saucepan over medium heat; simmer until reduced by half and mixture is syrupy. Remove pan from heat; whisk in butter a few pieces at a time, until melted and combined.

tip We used royal gala apples in this recipe.

Muffins

prep + cook time 40 minutes makes 12

COCONUT & VANILLA MUFFINS

Preheat oven to 180°C/350°F. Line a 12-hole (⅓ cup/80ml) muffin pan with paper cases. Sift 2 cups spelt flour and 2 teaspoons baking powder into a medium bowl. Whisk 1 teaspoon pure vanilla extract (see tip), 1 cup yoghurt, ½ cup melted cooled coconut oil, ½ cup pure maple syrup and 2 eggs in a medium jug. Pour over dry ingredients; stir with a fork to just combine. Spoon mixture into cases; top with 1 cup coconut flakes. Bake for 30 minutes or until a skewer inserted into the centre of one of the muffins comes out clean.

tip Vanilla extract contains a tiny amount of refined sugar; if you prefer, either use the scraped seeds of a vanilla bean or vanilla bean powder available from health food stores.

prep + cook time 40 minutes makes 12

PEACH & GINGER CRUMBLE MUFFINS

Preheat oven to 180°C/350°F. Line a 12-hole (⅓ cup/80ml) muffin pan with paper cases. Sift 2 cups spelt flour, 2 teaspoons baking powder, 1½ teaspoons ground ginger and 1 teaspoon ground cinnamon into a medium bowl; stir in 2 coarsely chopped small (250g) peaches. Whisk 1 teaspoon pure vanilla extract (see tip left), 1 cup yoghurt, ½ cup melted cooled coconut oil, ½ cup pure maple syrup and 2 eggs in a medium jug. Pour over dry ingredients; stir with a fork to just combine. Spoon mixture into cases. Place ⅓ cup coconut sugar, ½ cup spelt flour and 1 teaspoon ground cinnamon in a small bowl; rub in 60g (2oz) chopped cold unsalted butter until mixture resembles coarse crumbs. Sprinkle crumble on muffins. Bake for 30 minutes or until a skewer inserted into the centre comes out clean.

prep + cook time 40 minutes makes 12

LEMON, THYME & FETTA CHEESE

Preheat oven to 180°C/350°F. Line a 12-hole (⅓ cup/80ml) muffin pan with paper cases. Sift 2 cups spelt flour and 2 teaspoons baking powder into a medium bowl; stir in 2 teaspoons finely grated lemon rind and 1 tablespoon finely chopped fresh thyme. Whisk 1¼ cups yoghurt, ½ cup melted cooled coconut oil, ¼ cup pure maple syrup and 2 eggs in a medium jug. Pour over dry ingredients; stir with a fork until almost combined. Fold through ½ cup crumbled goat's fetta. Spoon mixture into cases; top with combined ⅔ cup crumbled goat's fetta, ⅓ cup pepitas and 2 tablespoons fresh thyme leaves. Bake for 30 minutes or until a skewer inserted into the centre comes out clean.

prep + cook time 40 minutes makes 12

CHOC, BEETROOT & WALNUT MUFFINS

Preheat oven to 180°C/350°F. Line a 12-hole (⅓ cup/80ml) muffin pan with paper cases. Sift 2 cups spelt flour, ⅓ cup cacao powder and 2½ teaspoons baking powder into a medium bowl. Coarsely grate 1 medium (130g) washed, unpeeled beetroot, place in a large jug. Add 1½ cups yoghurt, ½ cup melted cooled coconut oil, ½ cup pure maple syrup and 2 eggs to the jug; whisk with a fork to combine. Pour over dry ingredients; stir with the fork until almost combined. Fold in 8 pitted and coarsely chopped fresh medjool dates and ½ cup chopped roasted walnuts. Spoon mixture into cases. Bake for 30 minutes or until a skewer inserted into the centre comes out clean.

prep + cook time 1 hour 30 minutes (+ refrigeration & cooling) serves 8

Rosemary, labneh & ORANGE TART

You need to start the recipe the day before.

- 800g (1½ pounds) Greek-style yoghurt
- 3 eggs
- 2 tablespoons raw honey
- 1 teaspoon pure vanilla extract
- 2 teaspoons finely chopped fresh rosemary leaves
- 2 cups (500ml) clear pure apple juice
- 1 sprig fresh rosemary, extra
- 3 small oranges (540g), sliced thinly

AMARANTH PASTRY

- 1½ cups (225g) fine amaranth flour
- 2 tablespoons arrowroot starch
- pinch salt
- ⅓ cup (70g) coconut oil
- ½ cup (125ml) ice-cold water

1 To make labneh, line a medium sieve with a piece of muslin (or a clean loosely-woven cotton cloth); place sieve over a large bowl. Spoon yoghurt into muslin, cover bowl and sieve with plastic wrap; refrigerate overnight.
2 Make amaranth pastry.
3 Grease an 11cm x 34cm (4½-inch x 14-inch) rectangular loose-based fluted tart pan. Roll pastry between sheets of baking paper until 3mm (⅛-inch) thick. Lift pastry into pan, press into base and sides; trim excess pastry. Prick base all over with a fork. Cover, refrigerate for 30 minutes.
4 Preheat oven to 200°C/400°F.
5 Place tart pan on an oven tray; line with baking paper, fill with dried beans or rice. Bake for 15 minutes. Remove paper and beans; bake for a further 5 minutes or until browned lightly. Cool.
6 Reduce oven temperature to 140°C/285°F.
7 Drain labneh; whisk in a large bowl with eggs, honey, vanilla and chopped rosemary. Spoon into cooled pastry case. Bake for 25 minutes or until just set. Cool to room temperature. Refrigerate until cold.
8 Meanwhile, place apple juice and extra rosemary in a medium saucepan; bring to the boil over medium heat. Add orange slices to pan, reduce heat to low; simmer for 15 minutes or until tender; cool.
9 Just before serving, drain orange slices and arrange over the cooled tart.
amaranth pastry Process flour, starch, salt and coconut oil until combined. With the motor operating, gradually add the iced water in a thin steady stream until a dough forms. Flatten pastry into a disc, wrap in plastic wrap; refrigerate for 30 minutes.

keeps If you like, make the whole tart a day ahead and store in the fridge. Top tart with the orange slices just before serving.

prep + cook time 1 hour (+ refrigeration) makes 12

Maple gingerbread muffins WITH SWEET POTATO BUTTER

- » ⅓ cup (75g) Natvia
- » 1¾ cups (265g) wholemeal spelt flour
- » ⅓ cup (40g) almond meal (ground almonds)
- » 2 tablespoons ground ginger
- » 1 teaspoon ground cinnamon
- » 1 teaspoon mixed spice
- » 1½ teaspoons baking powder
- » 1 teaspoon bicarbonate of soda (baking soda)
- » 3 eggs
- » ⅓ cup (80ml) olive oil
- » ¾ cup (180ml) unsweetened almond milk
- » 1 teaspoon vanilla extract

SWEET POTATO BUTTER

- » 400g (12½ ounces) orange sweet potato, chopped coarsely
- » ¼ cup (50g) coconut oil
- » 1 teaspoon vanilla extract
- » pinch sea salt

1 Make sweet potato butter.

2 Preheat oven to 160°C/325°F. Grease a 12-hole (⅓-cup/80ml) muffin pan. Cut 12 x 12cm (4¾-inch) squares of baking paper, fold into quarters, then open out again.

3 Blend Natvia in a high-speed blender until consistency of icing sugar.

4 Sift flour, almond meal, powdered Natvia, ginger, cinnamon, mixed spice, baking powder and soda in a large bowl. Whisk eggs, oil, almond milk and vanilla in a medium bowl until combined. Add to the dry ingredients; mix until just combined.

5 Working with one square of baking paper at a time, place in a muffin hole; pour in one-twelfth of the batter. Repeat with the remaining baking paper squares and batter.

6 Bake muffins for 15 minutes or until a skewer inserted into the centre comes out clean. Serve muffins warm with sweet potato butter.

sweet potato butter Place sweet potato in a small saucepan with just enough water to cover. Bring to the boil; boil for 12 minutes or until sweet potato is tender. Drain; return to pan, mash until smooth. Stir in coconut oil, vanilla and salt. Spoon into a small bowl, cover with plastic wrap; refrigerate until firm.

tip You could line the muffin pan with standard paper cases.

keeps These muffins are best made on the day of serving. Store muffins in an airtight container at room temperature for up to 3 days. Sweet potato butter keeps for up to 3 days in an airtight container in fridge.

prep + cook time 1 hour serves 4

Apricot & hazelnut CRUMBLE

- 4 medium apricots (325g)
- 2 medium pears (460g)
- 80g (2½ ounces) dried figs
- 10g (½ ounce) butter
- ¾ cup (180ml) water
- ½ cup (125ml) pure maple syrup
- ¾ cup (60g) quinoa flakes
- ¼ cup (30g) hazelnut meal
- ½ cup (70g) coarsely chopped skinless hazelnuts, roasted
- ½ teaspoon sea salt flakes
- 1 cup (280g) Greek-style yoghurt
- 2 teaspoons long thin strips orange rind

1 Preheat oven to 180°C/350°F.
2 Cut apricots in half; remove and discard stones. Cut unpeeled pears in half; remove core and cut each half into three wedges. Remove stem end from figs and quarter.
3 Combine apricot, pear, fig, butter and the water in a medium saucepan over medium heat; cook, stirring occasionally, for 6 minutes or until pears have softened slightly. Transfer fruit mixture to a 1.5 litre (6-cup) ovenproof dish.
4 Combine maple syrup, quinoa flakes, hazelnut meal, chopped hazelnuts and salt in a medium bowl; sprinkle over fruit.
5 Bake for 45 minutes or until top is lightly golden. Serve crumble warm topped with yoghurt and rind.

swap out 3 peaches for the pears and almond meal for hazelnut meal, and coarsely chopped almonds for hazelnuts and raw honey for maple syrup.

prep + cook time 1 hour 15 minutes (+ standing) serves 12

Olive oil MARMALADE CAKE

- ⅔ cup (160ml) extra virgin olive oil
- 1 cup (285g) cane-sugar-free marmalade
- 3 eggs
- 1 cup (120g) almond meal (ground almonds)
- ⅔ cup (100g) plain (all-purpose) flour
- 3 teaspoons baking powder
- ¼ cup (60ml) orange juice

ORANGE SYRUP

- 1 medium orange (240g)
- ⅔ cup (160ml) orange juice
- ¼ cup (60ml) water
- ¼ cup (85g) rice malt syrup
- 1 cinnamon stick
- 3 whole cloves

1 Preheat oven to 170°C/340°F. Grease and line a deep 20cm (8-inch) round cake pan with baking paper.

2 Beat oil and marmalade in a medium bowl with an electric mixer until pale and fluffy. Beat in eggs, one at a time.

3 Sift almond meal, flour and baking powder into a large bowl. Add almond mixture and juice to marmalade mixture; beat on low speed until just combined. Spread mixture into pan.

4 Bake cake for 55 minutes or until a skewer inserted into the centre comes out clean. Leave cake in pan for 30 minutes before turning, top-side up, onto a wire rack.

5 Meanwhile, make orange syrup.

6 Pierce the top of the cake randomly with a cake skewer. Slowly pour the warm syrup and spices over the cake, allowing the syrup to be absorbed into cake. Serve warm or at room temperature.

orange syrup Using a vegetable peeler, thinly peel rind from orange, with as little white pith as possible. Place rind and remaining ingredients in a small saucepan; bring to the boil. Reduce heat; simmer for 15 minutes or until syrup thickens slightly. Remove from heat; cool syrup for 10 minutes. Remove cinnamon stick and cloves, if you prefer.

prep + cook time 3 hours 20 minutes (+ standing) makes 12

Glazed fig & WHOLE ORANGE CAKES

- 6 dried figs (135g), halved
- 1½ cups (375ml) fresh pure apple juice
- 2 medium oranges (480g), washed
- 1⅔ cups (250g) coconut sugar
- 5 eggs
- 2¾ cups (280g) almond meal (ground almonds)
- 1 teaspoon baking powder
- ¼ cup (20g) flaked almonds

1 Place figs and juice in a medium saucepan; soak for 2 hours. Remove figs with a slotted spoon; reserve apple juice in pan.
2 Meanwhile, fill another medium saucepan two-thirds with water, add whole oranges; bring to the boil. Reduce heat to a simmer. Cover oranges with the lid from a smaller saucepan to keep submerged; simmer for 2 hours, topping up with water if necessary to keep oranges submerged. Drain; cool oranges to room temperature.
3 Preheat oven to 180°C/350°F. Line a 12-hole (⅓ cup/80ml) muffin pan with paper cases.
4 Cut oranges in half, discard any seeds. Process whole oranges (rind and flesh) until smooth. Add coconut sugar, eggs, almond meal and baking powder to the food processor, pulse until well combined. Spoon mixture into paper cases; place a fig, cut-side up, on top; sprinkle with almonds.
5 Bake cakes for 1 hour or until a skewer inserted in the centre comes out clean.
6 Meanwhile, simmer saucepan with apple juice over medium heat for 8 minutes or until syrupy.
7 Brush syrup over warm cakes. Serve with Greek-style yoghurt drizzled with remaining syrup, if you like.

tips You can use mandarins instead of oranges, if prefered. If you find the cakes are getting too brown, cover with foil during cooking.

prep + cook time 40 minutes makes 18

Apricot & cardamom MUESLI SLICE

- 1 cup (150g) dried apricots
- 2 cups (185g) quinoa flakes
- ½ cup (70g) quinoa flour
- ½ cup (75g) sunflower seeds
- ½ cup (80g) coarsely chopped raw almonds
- 1 teaspoon ground cardamom
- 1 teaspoon gluten-free baking powder
- 1 tablespoon finely grated orange rind
- ⅓ cup (70g) coconut oil
- ⅓ cup (115g) raw honey
- 3 eggs, beaten lightly
- 2 teaspoons pure vanilla extract
- 2 tablespoons sugar-free apricot jam, melted, strained

1 Preheat oven to 160°C/325°F. Grease a 16cm x 26cm x 4cm (6½-inch x 10½-inch x 1½-inch) slice pan; line base and long sides with baking paper.

2 Roughly chop half the apricots; place in a large bowl. Cut remaining apricots in half lengthways; set aside.

3 Combine quinoa flakes and flour, sunflower seeds, almonds, cardamom, baking powder and rind with chopped apricots in bowl.

4 Place coconut oil and honey in a small saucepan over medium heat; bring to the boil, stirring until melted and well combined. Pour hot mixture over dry ingredients, add eggs and vanilla; mix well to combine.

5 Spread mixture into pan; level the mixture with the back of a spoon. Top with apricot halves, pressing down lightly into the mixture.

6 Bake slice for 20 minutes or until golden and a skewer inserted into the centre comes out clean. Brush hot slice with apricot jam; cool in the pan. Cut into pieces to serve.

swap out You can use walnuts, pecans, macadamias or cashews instead of almonds.

prep + cook time 1 hour 45 minutes serves 12

Banana & coffee cake WITH CARAMEL SAUCE

- ¾ cup (165g) Natvia
- 185g (6oz) butter, softened, chopped
- 3 eggs
- 2¼ cups (335g) self-raising flour
- ¼ teaspoon salt
- ¾ teaspoon bicarbonate of soda (baking soda)
- 1½ teaspoons ground cinnamon
- 2 cups (525g) mashed ripe banana (see tip)
- 2 teaspoons vanilla extract
- ¾ cup (200g) sour cream
- 1 cup (100g) walnut halves, roasted, chopped coarsely
- ¼ cup (60ml) boiling water
- 3 teaspoons espresso coffee granules

COFFEE CARAMEL SAUCE

- 125g (4 ounces) butter, softened, chopped
- ⅓ cup (80ml) thickened cream
- 2 tablespoons Natvia
- 1 teaspoon espresso coffee granules

1 Preheat oven to 180°C/350°F. Grease and line a deep 22cm (9-inch) round cake pan with baking paper.
2 Blend Natvia in a high-speed blender until consistency of icing sugar.
3 Beat butter and powdered Natvia in a small bowl with an electric mixer until pale and fluffy. Beat in eggs, one at a time, until just combined. Transfer mixture to a large bowl. Stir sifted dry ingredients, banana, vanilla, sour cream, walnuts and combined water and coffee into butter mixture. Spread mixture into pan.
4 Bake cake for 1¼ hours or until a skewer inserted into the centre comes out clean. Leave cake in pan for 10 minutes; before transferring to a wire rack to cool.
5 Meanwhile, make coffee caramel sauce.
6 Serve cake with coffee caramel sauce.

coffee caramel sauce Place butter, cream and Natvia in a small saucepan over medium heat, bring to a simmer; reduce heat and simmer until Natvia dissolves. Remove from heat and add coffee; stir until dissolved.

tip You will need about 4½ medium bananas (900g) to make 2 cups mashed banana.

keeps The cake can be made a day ahead; store in an airtight container at room temperature in a cool place or in the fridge for up to 4 days. Sauce will keep, covered, in the fridge for up to 4 days (sauce will thicken in fridge, re-heat before serving).

prep + cook time 30 minutes makes 35

Zucchini, parmesan & ROSEMARY CRACKERS

- » 60g (2 ounces) pepitas (pumpkin seed kernels)
- » ½ cup (55g) coarsely chopped walnuts
- » 1 small zucchini (90g), chopped coarsely
- » ⅓ cup (25g) finely grated parmesan
- » 1 tablespoon linseeds (flaxseeds)
- » 1 tablespoon sesame seeds
- » 1 tablespoon poppy seeds
- » ½ teaspoon cumin seeds
- » ½ teaspoon dried oregano
- » 1 teaspoon finely chopped fresh rosemary
- » 1 tablespoon fresh rosemary leaves, extra
- » ½ teaspoon sea salt flakes

1 Preheat oven to 180°C/350°F.

2 Process pepitas and walnuts until finely ground. Add zucchini; process to combine. Add parmesan, linseeds, sesame seeds, poppy seeds, cumin seeds, oregano and finely chopped rosemary; pulse to combine. Season.

3 Spread mixture onto a piece of baking paper; top with a second sheet of baking paper. Roll into a 25cm x 35cm (10-inch x 14-inch) rectangle, about 2mm (⅛-inch) thick. Transfer cracker on paper to a large oven tray; remove top sheet of baking paper.

4 Using a knife, score dough at 5cm (2-inch) intervals crossways then lengthways to mark out 5cm (2-inch) squares. Sprinkle with extra rosemary leaves and sea salt.

5 Bake crackers for 20 minutes, rotating tray halfway through cooking, or until golden (cover with foil if it starts to overbrown). Cool on tray. Break into pieces along marked lines before serving.

keeps These crackers will keep in an airtight container for up to 5 days.

prep + cook time 45 minutes makes 24

Chocolate hazelnut BROWNIES

- 1 cup (340g) rice malt syrup
- 1 cup (140g) dried pitted dates, chopped coarsely
- ¼ teaspoon sea salt flakes
- ½ cup (125ml) water
- ½ teaspoon bicarbonate of soda (baking soda)
- 200g (6½ ounces) butter, chopped
- 3 eggs
- ¾ cup (75g) cocoa powder
- ¾ cup (75g) hazelnut meal
- ½ cup (75g) buckwheat flour
- ½ cup (120g) sour cream
- ½ cup (70g) whole roasted skinless hazelnuts, halved
- 1½ teaspoons cocoa powder, extra

1 Preheat oven to 180°C/350°F. Grease a 20cm x 30cm (8-inch x 12-inch) slice pan; line base with baking paper, extending the paper 5cm (2-inches) over long sides.

2 Place syrup, dates, salt and the water in a small saucepan over low heat; simmer for 5 minutes or until dates are soft.

3 Stir soda into date mixture; transfer to a food processor, process until smooth. Return date mixture to pan; add butter, stir over medium heat until butter melts. Transfer mixture to a large bowl; cool for 5 minutes.

4 Whisk in eggs, one at a time. Stir in sifted cocoa, hazelnut meal, flour, sour cream and chopped hazelnuts. Spread mixture into pan; level surface.

5 Bake brownie for 30 minutes or until a skewer inserted into the centre comes out with moist crumbs attached. Cool in pan before dusting with extra cocoa and cutting into pieces.

tip Despite its name, buckwheat is unrelated to wheat and is known as a seed or pseudo-cereal, making it gluten free. It is also high in fibre and protein.

Crumble & topping variations

prep + cook time 40 minutes serves 6

BERRY CRUMBLE

Preheat oven to 180°C/350°F. Grease six 10cm (4in) diameter, 1¼ cup ovenproof dishes. Combine 4 cups fresh pitted cherries, 500g (1lb) fresh or frozen raspberries, scraped seeds from 1 vanilla bean, 2 tablespoons orange juice and 1 tablespoon Natvia in a large bowl. Using your hands, squeeze ingredients together between your fingers until just combined; divide among dishes. Make your choice of topping opposite; sprinkle over fruit. Bake for 20 minutes or until topping is golden and fruit bubbling. Serve berry crumble with cream, sugar-free yoghurt or ice-cream.

keeps Store in an airtight container in the freezer for up to 1 month.

prep + cook time 10 minutes makes 2½ cups

CACAO NIBS & COCONUT TOPPING

Place 1 cup hazelnut meal, ½ cup rolled oats, ¼ cup cacao nibs, ½ cup coconut flakes, 1 tablespoon Natvia and 100g (3oz) chilled coconut oil in a medium bowl. Using fingertips, rub mixture together until it resembles coarse breadcrumbs.

prep + cook time 10 minutes makes 2¾ cups

SEEDS OF LIFE TOPPING

Place 1 cup almond meal, ½ cup quinoa flakes, ¼ cup pepitas, 2 tablespoons each chia and sesame seeds, 1 tablespoon Natvia, 1 tablespoon almond spread and 125g (4oz) finely chopped cold butter in a medium bowl. Using fingertips, rub mixture together until it resembles coarse breadcrumbs.

prep + cook time 10 minutes makes 2 cups

GINGER & SPICE CRUMBLE TOPPING

Place ½ cup almond meal, 1 cup rolled oats, 2 teaspoons ground ginger, 1 teaspoon mixed spice, ⅓ cup flaked almonds, 1 tablespoon Natvia and 125g (4oz) finely chopped cold butter in a medium bowl. Using fingertips, rub mixture together until it resembles coarse breadcrumbs.

prep + cook time 10 minutes makes 2½ cups

ORANGE & POPPYSEED TOPPING

Place 1 cup almond meal, ½ cup rolled oats, 2 tablespoons coarsely chopped natural almonds, 2 tablespoons poppy seeds, 2 teaspoons finely grated orange rind, 125g (4oz) finely chopped cold butter and 1 tablespoon Natvia in a medium bowl. Using fingertips, rub mixture together until it resembles coarse breadcrumbs.

prep + cook time 1 hour 10 minutes (+ cooling & standing) serves 8

Citrus, orange blossom & BEAN CAKE

- » ¼ cup (55g) Natvia
- » 400g (12½ ounces) canned cannellini beans, drained, rinsed
- » 1 tablespoon orange blossom water
- » 2 teaspoons finely grated orange rind
- » 2 teaspoons finely grated lemon rind
- » 1 vanilla bean, split lengthways, seeds scraped
- » ½ cup (125ml) extra virgin olive oil
- » 3 eggs, separated
- » 1½ cups (180g) almond meal
- » 2 teaspoons baking powder
- » strips of orange and lemon rind, to decorate (optional)

ORANGE BLOSSOM-WHIPPED CREAM

- » 1 tablespoon Natvia
- » ¾ cup (180ml) thickened cream
- » ¼ cup (70g) Greek-style yoghurt
- » 1 teaspoon orange blossom water

1 Preheat oven to 160°C/325°F. Grease a 20cm (8-inch) round cake pan; line base and side with baking paper.
2 Blend Natvia in a high-speed blender until consistency of icing sugar.
3 Process beans, orange blossom water, grated citrus rind, vanilla seeds, oil and egg yolks until smooth. Transfer to a large bowl.
4 Beat egg whites in a medium bowl with an electric mixer until soft peaks form. With the motor operating, gradually add powdered Natvia; beat until stiff peaks form. Fold egg white mixture, almond meal and baking powder into bean mixture until combined to form a batter. Spoon batter into pan; smooth top.
5 Bake cake for 55 minutes or until a skewer inserted into the centre comes out clean. Cool cake in pan.
6 Make orange blossom-whipped cream.
7 Spread orange blossom-whipped cream over cooled cake. Serve sprinkled with citrus rind strips, if you like.
orange blossom-whipped cream Process Natvia in a spice grinder until consistency of icing sugar. Beat all ingredients in a small bowl with an electric mixer until soft peaks form.

swap out To make this cake dairy-free, replace the orange blossom-whipped cream with whipped coconut cream. Replace oranges with tangelos or mandarins, if you like.

serving suggestion Serve topped with edible flowers, such as nasturtiums, if you like.

keeps Store iced cake in an airtight container in the fridge for up to 4 days or uniced cake at room temperature for 2 days.

prep + cook time 1 hour (+ standing) makes 26

Lemon, chia & YOGHURT CAKE POPS

You will need a 20-hole (1 tablespoon/20ml) silicone cake pop pan (see tips below) and 26 lollypop sticks or straws for this recipe.

- » 100g (3 ounces) unsalted butter, softened
- » 1 cup (220g) norbu (monk fruit sugar)
- » 2 eggs
- » 2 tablespoons Greek-style yoghurt
- » 1 tablespoon finely grated lemon rind
- » 2 tablespoons lemon juice
- » 1 cup (135g) gluten-free plain (all-purpose) flour
- » 1½ teaspoons baking powder
- » ½ teaspoon xanthan gum
- » 1 tablespoon black chia seeds

YOGHURT GLAZE

- » ½ cup (140g) Greek-style yoghurt
- » 2 teaspoons natural lemon extract
- » 1 vanilla bean, split lengthways, seeds scraped
- » ½ cup (90g) stevia icing mix

1 Preheat oven to 200°C/400°F.
2 Beat butter and norbu in the small bowl of an electric mixer for 4 minutes or until light and fluffy; beat in eggs, one at a time. Add yoghurt, rind and juice; beat until just combined. Sift in flour, baking powder and xanthan gum; stir with a wooden spoon until combined.
3 Lightly grease the base of a 20-hole (1 tablespoon/20ml) silicone cake pop pan (see tips). Fill only the holes around the perimetre of the pan with heaped 2 teaspoons of cake batter; the holes will look over full. Place pop lid on top tightly; bake for 18 minutes or until a toothpick inserted through one of the holes comes out clean. Cool in the pan for 2 minutes; pop cake pops out onto a wire rack. Cool. Repeat with remaining batter. Trim any ragged edges using scissors.
4 Make yoghurt glaze.
5 Put the empty silicone pan together to become the holder. One at a time, insert a stick into the middle of each cake pop, dip into glaze and sprinkle with chia seeds; place in the holder while you finish the rest. To hold the extra cake pops, pierce holes in an egg carton with a wooden skewer. Serve cake pops in jars to keep them upright.
yoghurt glaze Whisk ingredients in a small bowl.

tips Silicon cake pop moulds have two near identical sides to them. One half is filled, while the other with tiny holes at the top forms the lid. To use them the mould is deliberately over filled for the mixture to rise to the other side and form a ball shape. We found even cooking was achieved by only using the perimeter holes. Moulds can be bought from kitchen supply shops and online.

prep + cook time 45 minutes makes 12

Peach & pistachio CAKE POTS

- 4 small peaches (460g), halved
- 1 cup (280g) Greek-style yoghurt
- 2 medium apples (300g), grated coarsely
- 2 eggs, beaten lightly
- ¼ cup (60ml) milk
- 2 tablespoons raw honey
- 2 cups (240g) almond meal (ground almonds)
- 2 teaspoons baking powder
- ⅓ cup (45g) pistachios, chopped coarsely
- 1½ tablespoons raw honey, extra

1 Preheat oven to 180°C/350°F. Cut 12 x 12cm (4-inch) squares from baking paper; line 12 x ⅓ cup (80ml) ovenproof pots with paper squares (see tips).

2 Thinly slice three of the peaches and set aside. Coarsely chop remaining peach; blend or process to a coarse puree. Fold peach puree through yoghurt in a small bowl; cover and refrigerate until required.

3 Place apple, egg, milk, honey, almond meal and baking powder in a large bowl; mix until just combined. Spoon mixture into pots; push peach slices 2cm (¾-inch) into the top of the batter.

4 Bake for 30 minutes or until a skewer inserted in the centre comes out clean.

5 Top cakes with pistachios; drizzle with extra honey. Serve warm or at room temperature with peach yoghurt.

tips We used peat seedling pots available from hardware stores and garden nurseries. You can also cook the cakes in a 12-hole (⅓ cup/80ml) muffin pan, lined with baking paper squares. This recipe is best made on day of serving.

prep + cook time 1 hour (+ standing) serves 6

Caramel coconut BREAD PUDDINGS

TO TOAST THE COCONUT, STIR CONTINUOUSLY IN A HEAVY-BASED FRYING PAN OVER MEDIUM HEAT FOR 3 MINUTES OR UNTIL LIGHTLY BROWNED AND TOASTED.

- ½ cup (80g) coconut sugar
- 1 cup (250ml) coconut cream
- 2 tablespoons pure maple syrup
- 3 teaspoons cornflour (cornstarch)
- 2 teaspoons pure vanilla extract
- 2 cups (500ml) almond milk
- ½ cup (125g) apple sauce
- ½ teaspoon mixed spice
- 620g (1¼-pound) loaf wholemeal sourdough bread, crusts removed, chopped coarsely
- ⅓ cup (55g) sultanas
- ½ cup (60g) pecans
- ½ cup (25g) coconut flakes, toasted

1 Combine ⅓ cup of the coconut sugar, ⅔ cup of the coconut cream, maple syrup, cornflour and half the vanilla in a small saucepan; stir until smooth. Cook, stirring, over medium heat, until mixture boils and thickens. Remove from heat.
2 Transfer half the coconut mixture to a large heatproof jug. Gradually stir in almond milk, sauce, spice and remaining vanilla.
3 Preheat oven to 180°C/350°F. Grease an 8-cup, 22cm x 30cm (8½-inch x 12-inch) baking dish. Layer bread, sultanas and pecans in dish. Pour milk mixture over bread, making sure all the bread is soaked. Stand for 15 minutes.
4 Sprinkle bread with remaining coconut sugar. Bake pudding for 40 minutes or until set.
5 Serve pudding warm or cooled, drizzled with reserved caramel sauce and remaining coconut cream and sprinkled coconut flakes.

tip If reserved caramel sauce becomes a little thick on standing, stir in some extra coconut cream or almond milk and reheat gently over low heat to return to a sauce consistency.

prep + cook time 25 minutes makes 12

Secret ingredient chocolate CHERRY FUDGE COOKIES

THE UNLIKELY SECRET INGREDIENT IN THESE GLUTEN-FREE BISCUITS IS BLACK BEANS. IT MAKES THESE COOKIES EXTRA MOIST AND FUDGE-LIKE AND MEANS YOU ARE GETTING A REALLY NUTRITIOUS TREAT.

- 400g (1½ ounces) canned black beans, drained, rinsed
- 4 fresh pitted dates (80g)
- 2 tablespoons coconut oil, at room temperature
- ½ cup (50g) cacao powder
- 2 eggs
- ¼ cup (60ml) pure maple syrup
- 1 teaspoon pure vanilla extract
- ¼ cup (50g) dried cherries, chopped coarsely
- 100g (3½ ounces) sugar-free dark chocolate, chopped coarsely
- ¼ teaspoon sea salt flakes

1 Preheat oven to 200°C/400°F. Line two oven trays with baking paper.
2 Process beans, dates, coconut oil and cacao until smooth. Add eggs, maple syrup, vanilla and cherries; pulse until just combined. Stir through chocolate.
3 Spoon approximately 2 tablespoonfuls at a time onto trays, leaving 4cm (1½ inches) between cookies to allow for spreading. Sprinkle evenly with salt.
4 Bake for 12 minutes or until cookie edges are firm. Cool on trays.

tips Some dried fruit, such as Craisins and often dried blueberries, contain added sugar, so avoid these if you don't want to use dried cherries. Instead, use sultanas and chopped dried figs as a substitute.

keeps Store cookies in an airtight container for up to 2 days.

Glossary

AGAVE SYRUP from the agave plant; has a low GI, but that is due to the high percentage of fructose present, which may be harmful in large quantities.

ALLSPICE also known as pimento or jamaican pepper; so-named because it tastes like a combination of nutmeg, cumin, clove and cinnamon. Available whole or ground.

ALMONDS

blanched brown skins removed from the kernel.

flaked paper-thin slices.

meal also called ground; almonds are powdered to a coarse flour-like texture.

slivered small pieces cut lengthways.

ANCHOVIES small oily fish. Anchovy fillets are preserved and packed in oil or salt in small cans or jars, and are strong in flavour. Fresh anchovies are much milder in flavour.

ARROWROOT a starch made from the rhizome of a Central American plant, used mostly as a thickening agent.

BAKING PAPER also called parchment paper or baking parchment – is a silicone-coated paper that is used for lining baking pans and oven trays so cooked food doesn't stick, making removal easy.

BAKING POWDER a raising agent consisting mainly of two parts cream of tartar to one part bicarbonate of soda (baking soda).

BASIL

sweet the most common type of basil; used extensively in Italian dishes and one of the main ingredients in pesto.

thai also known as horapa; different from sweet basil in both look and taste, with smaller leaves and purplish stems. It has a slight aniseed taste and is one of the identifying flavours of Thai food.

BAY LEAVES aromatic leaves from the bay tree available fresh or dried; adds a strong, slightly peppery flavour.

BEANS

broad (fava) available dried, fresh, canned and frozen. Fresh should be peeled twice (discarding both the outer long green pod and the beige-green tough inner shell); the frozen beans have had their pods removed but the beige shell still needs removal.

cannellini a small white bean similar in appearance and flavour to other white beans, all of which can be substituted for the other. Available dried or canned.

green also known as french or string beans (although the tough string they once had has generally been bred out of them), this long thin fresh bean is consumed in its entirety once cooked.

sprouts tender new growths of assorted beans and seeds germinated for consumption as sprouts.

white a generic term we use for canned or dried cannellini, haricot, navy or great northern beans belonging to the same family, phaseolus vulgaris.

BEETROOT (BEETS) firm, round root vegetable.

BICARBONATE OF SODA (BAKING SODA) a raising agent.

BROCCOLINI a cross between broccoli and chinese kale; it has long asparagus-like stems with a long loose floret, both are edible. Resembles broccoli but is milder and sweeter in taste.

BRUISING a cooking term to describe the slight crushing given to aromatic ingredients, particularly garlic and herbs, with the flat side of a heavy knife or cleaver to release flavour and aroma.

BUCKWHEAT a herb in the same plant family as rhubarb; not a cereal so it is gluten-free. Available as flour; ground (cracked) into coarse, medium or fine granules (kasha) and used similarly to polenta; or groats, the whole kernel sold roasted as a cereal product.

BUTTER use salted or unsalted (sweet) butter; 125g (4 ounces) is equal to one stick of butter.

BUTTERMILK originally the term given to the slightly sour liquid left after butter was churned from cream, today it is made from no-fat or low-fat milk to which specific bacterial cultures have been added. Despite its name, it is actually low in fat.

CACAO POWDER is made by removing the cocoa butter using a process known as cold-pressing. It retains more of its nutrients than heat-processed cacao powder; it also has a stronger, slightly bitter, taste.

CAPERS grey-green buds of a warm climate shrub (usually Mediterranean), sold either dried and salted or pickled in a vinegar brine. Capers must be rinsed well before using.

CAPSICUM (BELL PEPPER) also called pepper. Comes in many colours: red, green, yellow, orange and purplish-black. Be sure to discard seeds and membranes before use.

CARAWAY SEEDS the small, half-moon-shaped dried seed from a member of the parsley family; adds a sharp anise flavour when used in both sweet and savoury dishes. Used widely, in foods such as rye bread, harissa and the classic Hungarian fresh cheese, liptauer.

CARDAMOM a spice native to India and used extensively in its cuisine; can be purchased in pod, seed or ground form. Has a distinctive aromatic, sweetly rich flavour and is one of the world's most expensive spices.

CASHEWS plump, kidney-shaped, golden-brown nuts having a distinctive sweet, buttery flavour and containing about 48% fat. Because of this high fat content, they should be kept, sealed tightly, under refrigeration to avoid becoming rancid. We use roasted unsalted cashews in this book, unless otherwise stated.

CELERIAC (CELERY ROOT) tuberous root with knobbly brown skin, white flesh and a celery-like flavour. Keep peeled celeriac in acidulated water to stop it discolouring.

CHEESE

cheddar the most common cow-milk 'tasty' cheese; should be aged, hard and have a pronounced bite.

fetta Greek in origin; a crumbly textured goat- or sheep-milk cheese having a sharp, salty taste. Ripened and stored in salted whey.

goat's made from goat's milk, has an earthy, strong taste; available in both soft and firm textures, in various shapes and sizes, and sometimes rolled in ash or herbs.

mascarpone an Italian fresh cultured-cream product made in much the same way as yoghurt. Whiteish to creamy yellow in colour, with a buttery-rich, luscious texture. Soft, creamy and spreadable, it is used in Italian desserts and as an accompaniment to fresh fruit.

parmesan also called parmigiano; is a hard, grainy cow-milk cheese originating in Italy.

pecorino the Italian generic name for cheeses made from sheep-milk; hard, white to pale-yellow in colour. If you can't find it, use parmesan instead.

ricotta a soft, sweet, moist, white cow-milk cheese with a low fat content and a slightly grainy texture. The name roughly translates as 'cooked again' and refers to ricotta's manufacture from a whey that is itself a by-product of other cheese making.

CHIA SEEDS contain protein and all the essential amino acids and a wealth of vitamins, minerals and antioxidants, as well as being fibre-rich.

CHICKPEAS (GARBANZO BEANS) an irregularly round, sandy-coloured legume. Has a firm texture even after cooking, a floury mouth-feel and robust nutty flavour; available canned or dried (soak for several hours in cold water before use).

CHILLI use rubber gloves when seeding and chopping fresh chillies as they can burn your skin. We use unseeded chillies because the seeds contain the heat; use fewer chillies rather than seeding the lot, if you prefer it less spicy.

cayenne pepper a long, thin-fleshed, extremely hot red chilli usually sold dried and ground.

flakes also sold as crushed chilli; dehydrated deep-red extremely fine slices and whole seeds.

green any unripened chilli; also some particular varieties that are ripe when green, such as jalapeño, habanero, poblano or serrano.

jalapeño pronounced hah-lah-pain-yo. Fairly hot, medium-sized, plump, dark green chilli; available pickled, sold canned or bottled, and fresh, from greengrocers.

long available both fresh and dried; a generic term used for any moderately hot, thin, long (6-8cm/2¼-3¼ inch) chilli.

CHINESE COOKING WINE also called shao hsing or chinese rice wine; made from fermented rice, wheat, sugar and salt with a 13.5% alcohol content. Inexpensive and found in Asian food shops; if you can't find it, replace with mirin or sherry.

CHINESE FIVE-SPICE POWDER although the ingredients vary from country to country, five-spice is usually a fragrant mixture of ground cinnamon, cloves, star anise, sichuan pepper and fennel seeds.

CHIVES related to the onion and leek; has a subtle onion flavour. Used more for flavour than as an ingredient; chopped finely, they're good in sauces, dressings, omelettes or as a garnish.
CHOCOLATE, DARK (SEMI-SWEET) also called luxury chocolate; made of a high percentage of cocoa liquor and cocoa butter, and little added sugar. It is ideal for use in desserts and cakes.
CINNAMON available both in the piece (called sticks or quills) and ground into powder; one of the world's most common spices, used universally as a sweet, fragrant flavouring for both sweet and savoury foods. The dried inner bark of the shoots of the Sri Lankan native cinnamon tree; much of what is sold as the real thing is in fact cassia, Chinese cinnamon, from the bark of the cassia tree. Less expensive to process than true cinnamon, it is often blended with Sri Lankan cinnamon to produce the type of "cinnamon" most commonly found in supermarkets.
CLOVES dried flower buds of a tropical tree; can be used whole or in ground form. They have a strong scent and taste so should be used sparingly.
COCONUT
cream comes from the first pressing of the coconut flesh, without the addition of water; the second pressing (less rich) is sold as coconut milk. Look for coconut cream labelled as 100% coconut, without added emulsifiers.
desiccated concentrated, dried, unsweetened and finely shredded coconut flesh.
flaked dried flaked coconut flesh.
milk not the liquid found inside the fruit (coconut water), but the diluted liquid from the second pressing of the white flesh of a mature coconut (the first pressing produces coconut cream).
nectar produced from coconut palm blossoms; it has a low GI and is a good sugar alternative for those with fructose sensitivities.
oil is extracted from the coconut flesh so you don't get any of the fibre, protein or carbohydrates present in the whole coconut. The best quality is virgin coconut oil, which is the oil pressed from the dried coconut flesh, and doesn't include the use of solvents or other refining processes.
shredded thin strips of dried coconut.
sugar is not made from coconuts, but from the sap of the blossoms of the coconut palm tree. The refined sap looks a little like raw or light brown sugar, and has a similar caramel flavour. It also has the same amount of kilojoules as regular table (white) sugar.
water is the liquid from the centre of a young green coconut. It has fewer kilojoules than fruit juice, with no fat or protein. There are sugars present, but these are slowly absorbed giving coconut water a low GI.
CORIANDER (CILANTRO) also known as pak chee or chinese parsley; a bright-green leafy herb with a pungent flavour. Both stems and roots of coriander are also used in cooking; wash well before using. Also available ground or as seeds; these should not be substituted for fresh as the tastes are completely different.
CORNFLOUR (CORNSTARCH) thickening agent available in two forms: 100% corn (maize), which is gluten free, and a wheaten cornflour (made from wheat) which is not.
CRANBERRIES, DRIED they have the same slightly sour, succulent flavour as fresh cranberries.
CREAM
pouring also known as pure or fresh cream. It has no additives and contains a minimum fat content of 35%.
sour a thick, commercially-cultured sour cream with a minimum fat content of 35%.
thickened (heavy) a whipping cream that contains a thickener. It has a minimum fat content of 35%.
CRÈME FRAÎCHE a mature, naturally fermented cream (minimum fat content 35%) having a velvety texture and slightly tangy, nutty flavour.
CUMIN also known as zeera or comino; resembling caraway in size, cumin is the dried seed of a plant related to the parsley family. Its spicy, almost curry-like flavour is essential to the traditional foods of Mexico, India, North Africa and the Middle East. Black cumin seeds are smaller than standard cumin, and dark brown rather than true black.
CURRANTS, DRIED tiny, almost black raisins so-named after a grape variety that originated in Corinth, Greece.

DAIKON also called white radish; this long, white horseradish has a wonderful, sweet flavour. The flesh is white but the skin can be either white or black; buy firm and unwrinkled from Asian food shops.
DILL also known as dill weed; used fresh or dried, in seed form or ground. Its anise/celery sweetness flavours the food of the Scandinavian countries, and Germany and Greece. Its feathery, frond-like fresh leaves are grassier and more subtle than the dried version or the seeds.
EGGPLANT also called aubergine. Ranging in size from tiny to very large and in colour from pale green to deep purple.
EGGS some recipes in this book may call for raw or barely cooked eggs; exercise caution if there is a salmonella problem in your area. The risk is greater for those who are pregnant, elderly or very young, and those with impaired immune systems.
ESSENCE/EXTRACT an essence is either a distilled concentration of a food quality or an artificial creation of it. Coconut and almond essences are synthetically produced substances used in small amounts to impart their respective flavours to foods. An extract is made by actually extracting the flavour from a food product. In the case of vanilla, pods are soaked, usually in alcohol, to capture the authentic flavour. Essences and extracts keep indefinitely if stored in a cool dark place.
FENNEL a white to very pale green-white, firm, crisp, roundish vegetable about 8-12cm (3¼-4¾ inches) in diameter. The bulb has a slightly sweet, anise flavour but the leaves have a much stronger taste. Also the name of dried seeds having a licorice flavour.
FISH SAUCE called nuoc nam (Vietnamese) or nam pla (Thai); made from pulverised salted fermented fish, most often anchovies. Has a pungent smell and strong taste, so use sparingly.
FLOUR
chickpea (besan) creamy yellow flour made from chickpeas and is very nutritious.
gluten-free plain (all-purpose) a blend of gluten-free flours and starches (may include corn, potato, tapioca, chickpea and rice).
plain (all-purpose) a general all-purpose wheat flour.
rice very fine, almost powdery, gluten-free flour; made from ground white rice.
self-raising all-purpose plain or wholemeal flour with baking powder and salt added; make at home in the proportion of 1 cup plain or wholemeal flour to 2 teaspoons baking powder.
wholemeal also known as wholewheat flour; milled with the wheat germ so is higher in fibre and more nutritional than plain flour.
GARAM MASALA a blend of spices that includes cardamom, cinnamon, coriander, cloves, fennel and cumin. Black pepper and chilli can be added for heat.
GELATINE we use powdered gelatine in this book; it's also available in sheet form known as leaf gelatine. A thickening agent made from either collagen or certain algae (agar-agar). Three teaspoons of dried gelatine (8g or one sachet) is about the same as four gelatine leaves. The two types are interchangable but leaf gelatine gives a much clearer mixture than dried gelatine.
GHEE a type of clarified butter used in Indian cooking; milk solids are cooked until golden brown, which imparts a nutty flavour and sweet aroma; it can be heated to a high temperature without burning.
GINGER
fresh also called green or root ginger; thick gnarled root of a tropical plant.
ground used as a flavouring in baking but cannot be substituted for fresh ginger.
pickled pink or red in colour, paper-thin shavings of ginger pickled in a mixture of vinegar, sugar and natural colouring. Available from Asian food shops.
GLUTEN is a combination of two proteins found in wheat (including spelt), rye, barley and oats. When liquid is added to the flour, these two proteins bind to become gluten. Gluten gives elasticity to dough, helping it rise and keep its shape; it also gives the final product a chewy texture.
GOJI BERRIES (dried) small, very juicy, sweet red berries that grow on a type of shrub in Tibet. Believed to be high in nutrients and antioxidants.

GOLDEN SYRUP a by-product of refined sugarcane; pure maple syrup or honey can be substituted.

HAZELNUTS also known as filberts; plump, grape-sized, rich, sweet nut having a brown skin that is removed by rubbing heated nuts together vigorously in a tea-towel.

meal is made by grounding the hazelnuts to a coarse flour texture for use in baking or as a thickening agent.

HONEY the variety sold in a squeezable container is not suitable for the recipes in this book.

HORSERADISH a vegetable with edible green leaves but mainly grown for its long, pungent white root. Commonly purchased in bottles at the supermarket in two forms: prepared horseradish and horseradish cream. These cannot be substituted one for the other in cooking but both can be used as table condiments.

KAFFIR LIME LEAVES also known as bai magrood and looks like two glossy dark green leaves joined end to end, forming a rounded hourglass shape. Sold fresh, dried or frozen, the dried leaves are less potent so double the number if using them as a substitute for fresh; a strip of fresh lime peel may be substituted for each kaffir lime leaf.

LEEKS a member of the onion family, the leek resembles a green onion but is much larger and more subtle in flavour. Tender baby or pencil leeks can be eaten whole with minimal cooking but adult leeks are usually trimmed of most of the green tops then sliced.

LEMON GRASS a tall, clumping, lemon-smelling and -tasting, sharp-edged grass; the white part of the stem is used, finely chopped, in cooking.

LENTILS (RED, BROWN, YELLOW) dried pulses often identified by and named after their colour; also known as dhal.

French-style green lentils related to the famous french lentils du puy; these green-blue lentils have a nutty, earthy flavour and a hardy nature that allows them to be rapidly cooked without disintegrating.

LINSEEDS also known as flaxseeds, they are the richest plant source of omega 3 fats, which are essential for a healthy brain, heart, joints and immune system.

LSA A ground mixture of linseeds (L), sunflower seeds (S) and almonds (A); available from supermarkets and health food stores.

MAPLE SYRUP, PURE distilled from the sap of sugar maple trees found only in Canada and the USA. Maple-flavoured syrup or pancake syrup is not an adequate substitute for the real thing.

MIRIN a Japanese champagne-coloured cooking wine; made of glutinous rice and alcohol and used expressly for cooking. Should not be confused with sake.

MISO fermented soybean paste. There are many types of miso, each with its own aroma, flavour, colour and texture; it can be kept, airtight, for up to a year in the fridge. Generally, the darker the miso, the saltier the taste and denser the texture. Salt-reduced miso is available. Buy in tubs or plastic packs.

MIXED SPICE a blend of ground spices usually consisting of cinnamon, allspice and nutmeg.

MORTAR AND PESTLE a cooking tool whose design has remained the same over the centuries: the mortar is a bowl-shaped container and the pestle a rounded, bat-shaped tool. Together, they grind and pulverise spices, herbs and other foods. The pestle is pressed against the mortar and rotated, grinding the ingredient between the two surfaces. Essential for curry pastes and crushing spices.

MUSHROOMS

button small, cultivated white mushrooms with a mild flavour. When a recipe in this book calls for an unspecified type of mushroom, use button.

enoki tiny long-stemmed, pale mushrooms that grow and are sold in clusters, and can be used that way or separated by slicing off the base. They have a mild fruity flavour and are slightly crisp in texture.

portobello mature, fully opened swiss browns; large, dark brown mushrooms with full-bodied flavour; ideal for filling or barbecuing.

shiitake fresh, are also known as Chinese black, forest or golden oak mushrooms. Although cultivated, they have the earthiness and taste of wild mushrooms. Large and meaty, they can be used as a substitute for meat in some Asian vegetarian dishes.

swiss brown also known as roman or cremini. Light to dark brown mushrooms with full-bodied flavour; suited for use in casseroles or being stuffed and baked.

MUSLIN inexpensive, undyed, finely woven cotton fabric called for in cooking to strain stocks and sauces; if unavailable, use disposable coffee filter papers.

NORI a type of dried seaweed used as a flavouring, garnish or for sushi. Sold in thin sheets, plain or toasted (yaki-nori).

NUTMEG a strong and pungent spice ground from the dried nut of an evergreen tree native to Indonesia. Usually found ground but the flavour is more intense from a whole nut, available from spice shops, so it's best to grate your own.

OIL

coconut *see coconut*

cooking spray we use a cholesterol-free cooking spray made from canola oil.

olive made from ripened olives. Extra virgin and virgin are the first and second press, respectively, of the olives; "light" refers to taste not fat levels.

sesame used as a flavouring rather than a cooking medium.

vegetable oils sourced from plant rather than animal fats.

ONIONS

green (scallions) also called, incorrectly, shallot; an immature onion picked before the bulb has formed, has a long, bright-green stalk.

red also known as spanish, red spanish or bermuda onion; a sweet-flavoured, large, purple-red onion.

shallots also called french or golden shallots or eschalots; small and brown-skinned.

PAPRIKA a ground, dried, sweet red capsicum (bell pepper); there are many grades and types available, including sweet, hot, mild and smoked.

PECANS native to the US and now grown locally; pecans are golden brown, buttery and rich. Good in savoury as well as sweet dishes; walnuts are a good substitute.

PEPITAS (PUMPKIN SEED KERNELS) are the pale green kernels of dried pumpkin seeds; they can be bought plain or salted.

PINE NUTS not a nut but a small, cream-coloured kernel from pine cones. Toast before use to bring out their flavour.

POLENTA also known as cornmeal; a flour-like cereal made of ground corn (maize). Also the name of the dish made from it.

POMEGRANATE dark-red, leathery-skinned fruit about the size of an orange filled with hundreds of seeds, each wrapped in an edible lucent-crimson pulp with a unique tangy sweet-sour flavour.

QUINOA pronounced keen-wa; is the seed of a leafy plant similar to spinach. It has a delicate, slightly nutty taste and chewy texture.

flakes the grains have been rolled and flattened.

puffed has been steamed until it puffs up.

SAFFRON available ground or in strands; imparts a yellow-orange colour to food once infused. The quality can vary greatly; the best is the most expensive spice in the world.

SESAME SEEDS black and white are the most common of this small oval seed, however there are also red and brown varieties. The seeds are used as an ingredient and as a condiment.

SOY SAUCE made from fermented soya beans. Several variations are available in most supermarkets and Asian food stores. We use japanese soy sauce unless stated otherwise.

STAR ANISE dried star-shaped pod with an astringent aniseed flavour; used to flavour stocks and marinades. Available whole and ground, it is an essential ingredient in five-spice powder.

STERLISING JARS

it's important the jars be as clean as possible; make sure your hands, the preparation area, tea towels and cloths etc, are clean, too. The aim is to finish sterilising the jars and lids at the same time the preserve is ready to be bottled; the hot preserve should be bottled into hot, dry clean jars. Jars that aren't sterilised properly can cause deterioration of the preserves during storage. Always start with cleaned washed jars and lids, then follow one of these methods:

(1) Put jars and lids through the hottest cycle of a dishwasher without using any detergent.

(2) Lie jars down in a boiler with the lids, cover them with cold water then cover the boiler with a lid. Bring the water to the boil over a high heat and boil the jars for 20 minutes.
(3) Stand jars upright, without touching each other, on a wooden board on the lowest shelf in the oven. Turn the oven to the lowest possible temperature; leave jars to heat for 30 minutes.
Remove the jars from the oven or dishwasher with a towel, or from the boiling water with tongs and rubber-gloved hands; the water will evaporate from hot wet jars quite quickly. Stand jars upright and not touching on a wooden board, or a bench covered with a towel to protect and insulate the bench. Fill the jars as directed in the recipe; secure the lids tightly, holding jars firmly with a towel or an oven mitt. Leave at room temperature to cool before storing.

SUMAC a purple-red, astringent spice ground from berries growing on shrubs flourishing wild around the Mediterranean; adds a tart, lemony flavour to food. Available from major supermarkets.

TAHINI a rich, sesame-seed paste, used in most Middle-Eastern cuisines, especially Lebanese, in dips and sauces.

TAMARI a thick, dark soy sauce made mainly from soya beans, but without the wheat used in most standard soy sauces.

TAMARIND the tamarind tree produces clusters of hairy brown pods, each of which is filled with seeds and a viscous pulp, that are dried and pressed into the blocks of tamarind found in Asian food shops. Gives a sweet-sour, slightly astringent taste to marinades, pastes, sauces and dressings.

TOFU also called bean curd; an off-white, custard-like product made from the "milk" of crushed soybeans.
firm made by compressing bean curd to remove most of the water. Good used in stir-fries as it can be tossed without disintegrating. Can also be flavoured, preserved in rice wine or brine.
silken not a type of tofu but reference to the manufacturing process of straining soybean liquid through silk; this denotes best quality.
soft delicate texture; does not hold its shape when overhandled.

TURMERIC also called kamin; is a rhizome related to galangal and ginger. Must be grated or pounded to release its acrid aroma and pungent flavour. Known for the golden colour it imparts, fresh turmeric can be substituted with the more commonly found dried powder. When fresh turmeric is called for in a recipe, the dried powder can be substituted (proportions are 1 teaspoon of ground turmeric for every 20g of fresh turmeric). Be aware that fresh turmeric stains your hands and plastic utensils.

VANILLA
bean dried, long, thin pod from a tropical golden orchid; the minuscule black seeds inside the bean impart a luscious flavour in baking and desserts.
extract obtained from vanilla beans infused in water; a non-alcoholic version of essence.
paste made from vanilla beans and contains real seeds. Is highly concentrated: 1 teaspoon replaces a whole vanilla bean.

VINEGAR
balsamic originally from Modena, Italy, there are now many balsamic vinegars on the market ranging in pungency and quality depending on how, and for how long, they have been aged.
cider (apple cider) made from crushed fermented apples.
rice a colourless vinegar made from fermented rice and flavoured with sugar and salt.
white made from the spirit of cane sugar.
wine made from a blend of white or red wine.

XANTHAN GUM is a thickening agent produced by fermentation of, usually, corn sugar. When buying xanthan gum, ensure the packet states 'made from fermented corn sugar'. Found in the health-food section in larger supermarkets.

YEAST (dried and fresh), a raising agent used in dough making. Granular (7g sachets) and fresh compressed (20g blocks) yeast can almost always be substituted for the other.

YOGHURT, GREEK-STYLE plain yoghurt strained in a cloth (muslin) to remove the whey and to give it a creamy consistency.

ZUCCHINI also called courgette; small, pale- or dark-green or yellow vegetable of the squash family.

Conversion chart

MEASURES

One Australian metric measuring cup holds approximately 250ml; one Australian metric tablespoon holds 20ml; one Australian metric teaspoon holds 5ml.

The difference between one country's measuring cups and another's is within a two- or three-teaspoon variance, and will not affect your cooking results. North America, New Zealand and the United Kingdom use a 15ml tablespoon.

All cup and spoon measurements are level. The most accurate way of measuring dry ingredients is to weigh them. When measuring liquids, use a clear glass or plastic jug with the metric markings.

The imperial measurements used in these recipes are approximate only. Measurements for cake pans are approximate only. Using same-shaped cake pans of a similar size should not affect your baking. We measure the inside top of the cake pan to determine sizes.

We use large eggs with an average weight of 60g.

DRY MEASURES

METRIC	IMPERIAL
15G	½OZ
30G	1OZ
60G	2OZ
90G	3OZ
125G	4OZ (¼LB)
155G	5OZ
185G	6OZ
220G	7OZ
250G	8OZ (½LB)
280G	9OZ
315G	10OZ
345G	11OZ
375G	12OZ (¾LB)
410G	13OZ
440G	14OZ
470G	15OZ
500G	16OZ (1LB)
750G	24OZ (1½LB)
1KG	32OZ (2LB)

LIQUID MEASURES

METRIC	IMPERIAL
30ML	1 FLUID OZ
60ML	2 FLUID OZ
100ML	3 FLUID OZ
125ML	4 FLUID OZ
150ML	5 FLUID OZ
190ML	6 FLUID OZ
250ML	8 FLUID OZ
300ML	10 FLUID OZ
500ML	16 FLUID OZ
600ML	20 FLUID OZ
1000ML (1 LITRE)	1¾ PINTS

LENGTH MEASURES

METRIC	IMPERIAL
3MM	⅛IN
6MM	¼IN
1CM	½IN
2CM	¾IN
2.5CM	1IN
5CM	2IN
6CM	2½IN
8CM	3IN
10CM	4IN
13CM	5IN
15CM	6IN
18CM	7IN
20CM	8IN
22CM	9IN
25CM	10IN
28CM	11IN
30CM	12IN (1FT)

OVEN TEMPERATURES

The oven temperatures in this book are for conventional ovens; if you have a fan-forced oven, decrease the temperature by 10-20 degrees.

	°C (CELSIUS)	°F (FAHRENHEIT)
VERY SLOW	120	250
SLOW	150	300
MODERATELY SLOW	160	325
MODERATE	180	350
MODERATELY HOT	200	400
HOT	220	425
VERY HOT	240	475

Index

A

B

C

D

E

F

G

H

I

J

K

L

Q

R

S

T

V

W

Z

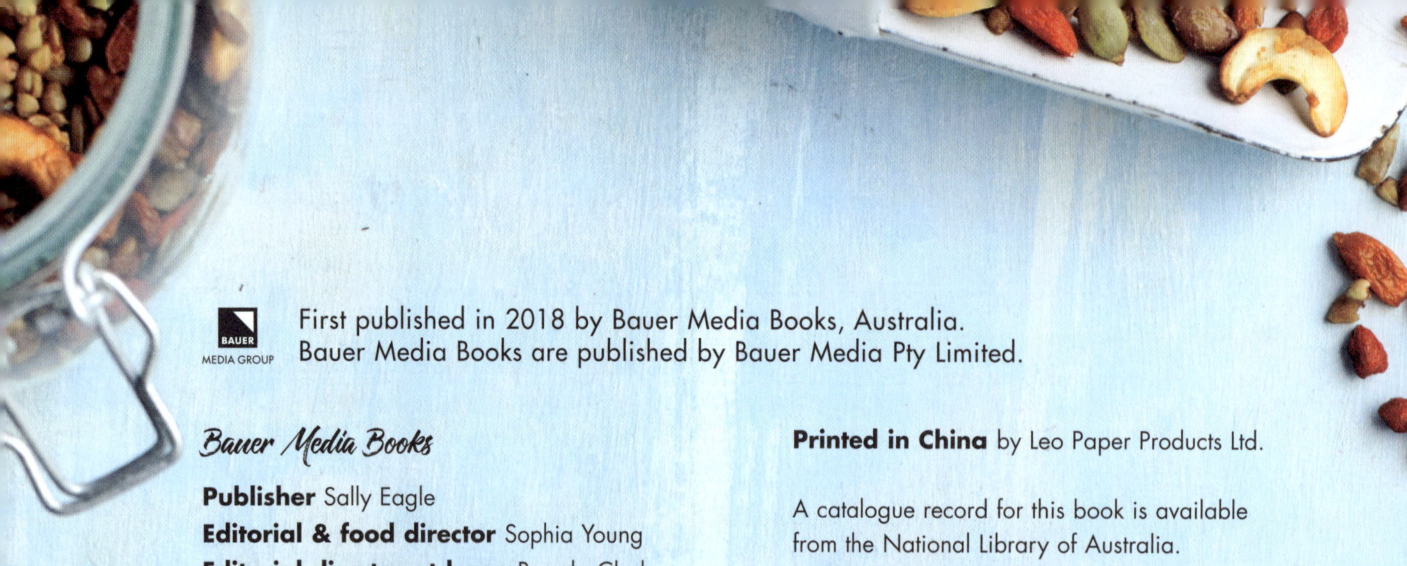

First published in 2018 by Bauer Media Books, Australia.
Bauer Media Books are published by Bauer Media Pty Limited.

Bauer Media Books

Publisher Sally Eagle
Editorial & food director Sophia Young
Editorial director-at-large Pamela Clark
Creative director Hannah Blackmore
Managing editor Stephanie Kistner
Senior designer Jeannel Cunanan
Junior editor Amanda Lees
Food editor Domenica Reddie
Operations manager David Scotto

Photographers James Moffatt, Louise Lister, Cath Muscatt
Stylists Olivia Blackmore, Annette Forrest, Vivian Walsh
Photochefs Cynthia Black, Rebecca Clancy, Sarah-Jane Hallet, Sarah Hobbs, Bree Hutchins, Tessa Immens, Tina Mcleish, Sarah Murphy, Carly Sophia Taylor, Amal Webster
Additional recipe development Bree HutchIns

Published by Bauer Media Books, a division of Bauer Media Pty Limited, 54 Park St, Sydney; GPO Box 4088, Sydney, NSW 2001. Australia
phone +61 2 9282 8618;
fax +61 2 9126 3702
www.awwcookbooks.com.au

Printed in China by Leo Paper Products Ltd.

A catalogue record for this book is available from the National Library of Australia.
ISBN: 9781925694512 (hardback)

International rights manager
Simone Aquilina
saquilina@bauer-media.com.au
Ph +61 2 8268 6278

To order books
phone 136 116 (within Australia) or order online at www.awwcookbooks.com.au
Send recipe enquiries to:
recipeenquiries@bauer-media.com.au

For further recipes and information on our company and range of products, please visit us at https://natvia.com/